CUDA Programming with C++

From Basics to Expert Proficiency

Contents

Introduction

In the landscape of modern computing, the demand for high-performance computation is on a steep rise. Traditional Central Processing Units (CPUs) are inherently limited by their design, which optimizes for sequential task execution. To circumvent these limitations, parallel computing has emerged as a significant paradigm, and among the forefront of this evolution is CUDA (Compute Unified Device Architecture) programming. Developed by NVIDIA, CUDA provides a powerful platform for harnessing the massive parallelism offered by Graphics Processing Units (GPUs).

The objective of this book, "CUDA Programming with C++: From Basics to Expert Proficiency," is to elucidate the principles, practices, and nuances of CUDA programming. This book serves as an extensive guide, starting from the elementary concepts and progressing to advanced techniques, tailored for both novices and seasoned developers aiming to deepen their expertise in GPU computing with CUDA and C++.

CUDA programming leverages the parallel architecture of GPUs, enabling developers to execute thousands of threads simultaneously. This capability is pivotal for applications requiring intensive computational power, such as scientific simulations, rendering, data analysis, and machine learning. By offloading compute-intensive tasks to the GPU, developers can achieve significant performance gains which are unattainable with CPU-only processing.

Understanding the architecture of CUDA and its interaction with the underlying hardware is paramount. This book delves into the specifics of GPU architecture, thread hierarchies, memory management, and the CUDA execution model. Each concept is meticulously presented to build a robust foundation, ensuring that readers are well-equipped to tackle complex computational problems effectively.

Setting up the development environment correctly is the cornerstone of successful CUDA programming. We provide a detailed guide on installing the CUDA Toolkit, configuring integrated development environments (IDEs), and verifying the setup across different operating systems, including Windows, Linux, and macOS. Practical insights and troubleshooting tips are also included to enhance the learning experience.

The book also explores the intricacies of CUDA kernels and threads, which form the core of parallel programming. Readers will gain a deep understanding of writing and optimizing CUDA kernels, effectively managing threads, and utilizing block and grid dimensions for optimized performance.

Memory management is another critical aspect that can significantly impact the performance of CUDA applications. This book covers various types of memory available in CUDA, such as global, shared, constant, and texture memory, along with strategies for efficient memory allocation, transfer, and access patterns.

Parallel programming models in CUDA, including SIMT (Single Instruction Multiple Threads), hybrid models, and domain decomposition, are thoroughly discussed. These models are essential for designing scalable and efficient parallel algorithms. Advanced topics such as dynamic parallelism, CUDA graphs, and multi-GPU programming are also included to provide readers with cutting-edge knowledge and skills.

Debugging and profiling are integral to developing high-performance CUDA applications. Dedicated sections on using tools such as NVIDIA Nsight, CUDA-GDB, and visual profilers are provided to assist developers in identifying bottlenecks, optimizing performance, and ensuring the correctness of their code.

Finally, this book presents insightful case studies and real-world applications of CUDA programming. These examples span across various industries, illustrating the practical applications and transformative impact of GPU computing. From image processing and scientific simulations to deep learning and autonomous vehicles, these case studies highlight the versatility and potential of CUDA programming.

By the end of this book, readers will possess a comprehensive understanding of CUDA programming with C++. They will be adept at designing, optimizing, and deploying high-performance applications leveraging the full potential of GPU computing. Whether you are a student, researcher, or professional developer, this book is an invaluable resource in your journey to mastering CUDA programming.

Chapter 1

Introduction to CUDA Programming and C++

This chapter provides an overview of the evolution of parallel computing and introduces CUDA and GPU computing. It explains the advantages of using CUDA with C++ and covers basic concepts and terminology essential for understanding CUDA programming. Additionally, it guides readers through installing and setting up the CUDA Toolkit, running a simple CUDA program, and introduces essential C++ concepts relevant to CUDA development. The chapter concludes by explaining the CUDA development workflow and highlighting common tools and resources available for developers.

1.1 The Evolution of Parallel Computing

Parallel computing has evolved significantly over the past few decades, driven by the increasing demand for computational power. This evolution can be traced through various stages, each marked by advancements in hardware, software, and algorithms.

Historically, computing began with sequential processing, where tasks were executed one after another on a single processor. This model, though straightforward, was limited by the processor's clock speed and its capacity to handle complex, time-consuming tasks. As scientific problems and data volumes grew, the necessity for more powerful computational methods became apparent.

The initial phase of parallel computing involved vector processors and early multiprocessing systems. Vector processors operated by performing the same operation on multiple data points simultaneously, leveraging data parallelism. On the other hand, multiprocessing systems used multiple processors to execute independent tasks concurrently, exemplifying task parallelism. These early systems laid the groundwork for more sophisticated forms of parallelism.

The rise of supercomputers in the 1980s and 1990s represented a significant leap in parallel computing. Supercomputers integrated numerous processors working in tandem, achieving unprecedented levels of performance. Notable examples include the Cray-1 and its successors, which utilized vector processing and pipelining techniques to dramatically accelerate computational tasks. During this period, parallel architectures and programming models such as shared memory and message passing became increasingly refined.

Shared memory systems allow multiple processors to access the same memory space, facilitating communication and synchronization. This model is relatively easy to program but becomes less efficient as the number of processors grows. Contention for memory access can lead to performance bottlenecks. Common shared memory programming models include OpenMP, which provides constructs for parallelizing loops and sections of code.

Message passing, on the other hand, involves processors communicating by explicitly sending and receiving messages. This model, exemplified by the Message Passing Interface (MPI), is more scalable and suitable for distributed computing environments. However, it introduces additional complexity in managing communication and synchronization between processors.

The turn of the century brought the mainstream adoption of cluster computing. Clusters comprised multiple computers connected via high-speed networks, effectively functioning as a single system. This approach provided a cost-effective means to build powerful parallel computing systems. Middleware such as MPI and software frameworks like Apache Hadoop for processing large-scale data became essential tools for leveraging cluster computing.

The advent of multicore processors in the mid-2000s marked another milestone in parallel computing. Processors with multiple cores could execute numerous threads within a single chip, efficiently increasing performance. This development necessitated changes in software design to exploit the potential of multicore architectures. Programming techniques like thread-level parallelism and tools like pthreads (POSIX threads) became prevalent.

Simultaneously, general-purpose computing on graphics processing units (GPGPU) emerged as a transformative force in parallel computing. Originally designed for rendering graphics, GPUs possess a highly parallel architecture, making them suitable for computational tasks amenable to parallel processing. NVIDIA's Compute Unified Device Architecture (CUDA), introduced in 2007, enabled developers to harness the power of GPUs for general-purpose computing. CUDA significantly simplified GPU programming by extending the C++ language with constructs for parallel execution on GPUs.

The utilization of GPUs for scientific computation catalyzed various fields, including physics simulations, molecular dynamics, and artificial intelligence. GPUs' massive parallelism and high throughput made them ideal for tasks involving large-scale numerical calculations and data processing.

Modern parallel computing encompasses diverse architectures and paradigms, each suited to specific types of problems. These include shared memory systems, distributed systems, and accelerators like GPUs and FPGAs (Field-Programmable Gate Arrays). Programming models such as OpenMP, MPI, and CUDA provide the necessary abstractions for developing parallel applications across these architectures.

The heterogeneous computing model, which combines CPUs, GPUs, and other accelerators, is increasingly prevalent. This model leverages the strengths of different processing units to optimize performance and efficiency for a wide range of applications. Languages and frameworks like OpenCL (Open Computing Language) facilitate the development of portable code that can run on various types of processors.

The relentless pursuit of higher performance and efficiency continues to drive innovations in parallel computing. Research in areas such as quantum computing, neuromorphic computing, and advanced parallel algorithms holds the promise of further revolutionizing how we solve complex computational problems.

```
#include <iostream>
#include <omp.h>
```

```
int main() {
    #pragma omp parallel
    {
        int thread_id = omp_get_thread_num();
        std::cout << "Hello, World from thread " << thread_id << std::endl;
    }
    return 0;
}
```

```
Output:
Hello, World from thread 0
Hello, World from thread 1
Hello, World from thread 2
Hello, World from thread 3
```

Integrating these historical milestones and technological advancements, parallel computing has transcended from a niche area to a critical component of modern computational science and engineering. Understanding its evolution provides a foundation for comprehending the current state and future potential of parallel computing technologies.

1.2 Overview of CUDA and GPU Computing

CUDA (Compute Unified Device Architecture) is a parallel computing platform and application programming interface (API) model created by NVIDIA. It allows developers to use GPUs (Graphics Processing Units) for general-purpose processing (an approach termed GPGPU, or General-Purpose computing on Graphics Processing Units). This section elucidates the foundational concepts of CUDA and GPU computing, the architecture of CUDA-enabled GPUs, and how CUDA enables high-performance parallel computing.

The main components of the CUDA programming model include a host (the CPU) and a device (the GPU). The host is responsible for executing sequential parts of the code and managing overall application logic, while the device executes parallel parts of the application, harnessing its massive computational power.

Let us illustrate the basic program structure with CUDA. Here's a simple example:

```
#include <iostream>
__global__ void kernel(void) {
    printf("Hello, World from GPU!\n");
}

int main(void) {
    // Launch the kernel function
```

```
    kernel<<<1, 1>>>();
    // Wait for the GPU to finish
    cudaDeviceSynchronize();
    return 0;
}
```

In the code above, the kernel function is defined with the __global__ declaration specifier, marking it as a function that runs on the GPU but can be called from the host and executed in parallel. The «<1, 1»> syntax specifies the execution configuration: one block with one thread. The cudaDeviceSynchronize() ensures the CPU waits for the GPU to complete execution before terminating the program.

Key to leveraging the full power of CUDA is understanding the GPU architecture. NVIDIA GPUs are comprised of Streaming Multiprocessors (SMs). Each SM can manage multiple threads concurrently, making GPUs exceptionally suitable for data-parallel computations where the same operation is applied to multiple data items. For instance, matrix multiplication, image processing, and physical simulations often benefit from GPU acceleration.

A typical CUDA-enabled GPU contains many SMs, each of which can execute thousands of threads. These threads are organized into blocks, which themselves are organized into grids. Each block runs on a single SM, allowing threads within the block to share data through fast shared memory and synchronize their execution.

Memory hierarchy in CUDA consists of several layers:

- **Global Memory:** Accessible by all the threads which have high latency and is uncached.
- **Shared Memory:** On-chip memory shared among threads of the same block, much faster than global memory.
- **Registers:** Each thread has its private registers, providing the fastest but limited memory.
- **Constant and Texture Memory:** Cached memories optimized for different access patterns.

Consider the following example that demonstrates vector addition:

```
#include <iostream>
#include <cuda_runtime.h>

#define N 512
```

```
__global__ void add(int *a, int *b, int *c) {
    int index = threadIdx.x;
    c[index] = a[index] + b[index];
}

int main(void) {
    int a[N], b[N], c[N];
    int *d_a, *d_b, *d_c;

    cudaMalloc((void **) &d_a, N * sizeof(int));
    cudaMalloc((void **) &d_b, N * sizeof(int));
    cudaMalloc((void **) &d_c, N * sizeof(int));

    for (int i = 0; i < N; i++) {
        a[i] = i;
        b[i] = i * i;
    }

    cudaMemcpy(d_a, a, N * sizeof(int), cudaMemcpyHostToDevice);
    cudaMemcpy(d_b, b, N * sizeof(int), cudaMemcpyHostToDevice);

    add<<<1, N>>>(d_a, d_b, d_c);

    cudaMemcpy(c, d_c, N * sizeof(int), cudaMemcpyDeviceToHost);

    for (int i = 0; i < N; i++) {
        printf("%d + %d = %d\n", a[i], b[i], c[i]);
    }

    cudaFree(d_a); cudaFree(d_b); cudaFree(d_c);

    return 0;
}
```

In this code:

- cudaMalloc allocates memory on the GPU.
- cudaMemcpy transfers data between host and device.
- add«<1, N»> launches the kernel with one block of N threads.
- After kernel execution, results are copied back to host memory.

CUDA provides tools for handling errors and inspecting the GPU's state. Functions like cudaGetErrorString(cudaGetLastError()) return readable error messages if something goes wrong.

When discussing GPU computing's benefits, three key aspects often come to the forefront:

- **Massive Parallelism:** GPUs consist of hundreds or thousands of smaller, more efficient cores designed for handling multiple tasks simultaneously.

- **High Throughput:** Due to their architecture, GPUs can process vast amounts of data per time unit.
- **Energy Efficiency:** Modern GPUs deliver high computational power with lower energy consumption compared to traditional CPUs.

Overall, CUDA and GPU computing empower developers to achieve substantial performance gains for various applications involving data-level parallelism and demanding computational tasks. The combination of hardware advancements and a robust programming model makes CUDA an indispensable tool for high-performance computing solutions.

1.3 Why Use CUDA with C++?

CUDA (Compute Unified Device Architecture) is a parallel computing platform and application programming interface (API) model created by NVIDIA. It allows developers to use NVIDIA GPUs for general purpose processing, an approach known as GPGPU (General-Purpose computing on Graphics Processing Units). Leveraging C++ in conjunction with CUDA offers several compelling advantages, from performance gains to robust software engineering capabilities.

Performance and Parallelism: CUDA is specifically designed to exploit the parallel processing capabilities of NVIDIA GPUs. GPUs consist of a large number of cores that can run thousands of threads simultaneously. By using CUDA with C++, developers can break down complex computational problems into smaller tasks that can be executed in parallel, significantly reducing computation time. For example, matrix multiplication, a task that is computationally expensive on a CPU due to its sequential nature, becomes highly efficient on a GPU using CUDA.

```
__global__ void matrixMulKernel(float* A, float* B, float* C, int N) {
    int row = blockIdx.y * blockDim.y + threadIdx.y;
    int col = blockIdx.x * blockDim.x + threadIdx.x;
    float sum = 0.0f;
    if(row < N && col < N) {
        for(int k = 0; k < N; k++) {
            sum += A[row * N + k] * B[k * N + col];
        }
        C[row * N + col] = sum;
    }
}
```

The above code leverages CUDA to perform matrix multiplication in parallel, where each thread computes an element of the resulting matrix. The __global__ qualifier indicates that this function runs on the device (GPU) and can be called from the host (CPU).

Advanced C++ Features: C++ is a powerful language that offers advanced features such as object-oriented programming (OOP), templates, and the Standard Template Library (STL). Using CUDA with C++ allows developers to write reusable, maintainable, and scalable code. OOP principles enable encapsulation, inheritance, and polymorphism, which are essential for managing complex software projects.

```
class Matrix {
private:
    float* data;
    int N;
public:
    Matrix(int size): N(size) {
        cudaMallocManaged(&data, N * N * sizeof(float));
    }
    ~Matrix() {
        cudaFree(data);
    }
    float* getData() {
        return data;
    }
    int getSize() {
        return N;
    }
    // Additional member functions to manipulate matrix data
};
```

In the provided class Matrix, dynamic memory allocation is performed using 'cudaMallocManaged', which allocates unified memory that is accessible by both the CPU and the GPU. The class encapsulates the matrix data and provides methods to manage it.

Interoperability: C++ is widely used across various domains such as game development, scientific computing, and financial modeling. CUDA's interoperability with existing C++ codebases allows for seamless integration of GPU acceleration into existing applications, without rewriting the entire code. Developers can incrementally optimize performance-critical sections by offloading them to the GPU.

```
void cpuFunction(float* A, float* B, float* C, int N) {
    // Perform some CPU-specific operations
    for(int i = 0; i < N; i++) {
        //...
    }

    // Launch CUDA kernel for GPU-specific operations
    dim3 threadsPerBlock(16, 16);
    dim3 numBlocks((N + threadsPerBlock.x - 1) / threadsPerBlock.x, (N +
```

```
        threadsPerBlock.y - 1) / threadsPerBlock.y);
    matrixMulKernel<<<numBlocks, threadsPerBlock>>>(A, B, C, N);
    cudaDeviceSynchronize();
}
```

This function demonstrates how one could mix CPU and GPU operations within a single workflow. It performs initial data manipulation on the CPU and then launches a CUDA kernel to execute operations on the GPU.

Hardware Abstraction: CUDA provides a high level of abstraction over the GPU hardware. While CUDA still requires an understanding of GPU architecture to optimize performance fully, it abstracts away the lower-level details, making it easier for developers to write efficient code. C++ programming constructs such as classes, inheritance, and polymorphism integrate well with CUDA, leading to a more intuitive and organized codebase.

Extensive Ecosystem and Support: NVIDIA has developed a robust ecosystem around CUDA that includes a wealth of development tools, libraries, and resources. The CUDA Toolkit provides various utilities such as nvcc (NVIDIA CUDA Compiler), cuda-gdb (CUDA Debugger), and profiling tools like nvprof and Nsight Systems. Additionally, numerous libraries like cuBLAS (CUDA Basic Linear Algebra Subprograms) and cuDNN (CUDA Deep Neural Network library) offer optimized routines that significantly speed up development.

```
#include <cublas_v2.h>

void cublasExample() {
    cublasHandle_t handle;
    cublasCreate(&handle);

    float alpha = 1.0f;
    float beta = 0.0f;
    int N = 1024;

    float* d_A;
    float* d_B;
    float* d_C;
    cudaMalloc((void**)&d_A, N * N * sizeof(float));
    cudaMalloc((void**)&d_B, N * N * sizeof(float));
    cudaMalloc((void**)&d_C, N * N * sizeof(float));

    cublasSgemm(handle, CUBLAS_OP_N, CUBLAS_OP_N, N, N, N, &alpha, d_A,
        N, d_B, N, &beta, d_C, N);

    cublasDestroy(handle);
    cudaFree(d_A);
    cudaFree(d_B);
    cudaFree(d_C);
}
```

In the use of cuBLAS for matrix multiplication, 'cublasSgemm' performs the operation $C = \alpha \cdot A \cdot B + \beta \cdot C$, leveraging the highly optimized BLAS routines provided by the library.

By combining C++ with CUDA, developers harness both the computational power of GPUs and the advanced programming constructs of C++, paving the way for creating high-performance, efficient, and maintainable applications.

1.4 Basic Concepts and Terminology

To proficiently leverage CUDA for parallel computing in C++, it is vital to understand fundamental concepts and terminology that are specific to GPU programming. We will examine key terms and principles that form the foundation of CUDA programming, encompassing the architecture of CUDA, the execution model, memory hierarchy, and the programming model.

CUDA Architecture: CUDA (Compute Unified Device Architecture) is NVIDIA's parallel computing platform and application programming interface (API). CUDA allows developers to use NVIDIA GPUs for general purpose processing. A GPU consists of an array of Streaming Multiprocessors (SMs), each containing hundreds to thousands of CUDA cores. A SM is a multiply-threaded processor that executes instructions for multiple threads concurrently, and CUDA cores are the individual processors that execute the thread instructions.

Kernel: A kernel is a function written in CUDA C++ that runs on the GPU. Unlike standard C++ functions that execute on the CPU, CUDA kernels are executed N times in parallel by N different CUDA threads, as opposed to only once. Each thread that executes the kernel has a unique ID, enabling them to handle different data.

```
__global__ void simpleKernel(int* d_array) {
    int idx = threadIdx.x;
    d_array[idx] *= 2;
}
```

In this example, the kernel simpleKernel operates on an integer array. Each thread, identified by its threadIdx, processes a distinct element of the array.

Thread Hierarchy: CUDA uses a hierarchy of threads to manage the execution of parallel tasks:

- **Thread**: The smallest unit of execution in CUDA.
- **Block**: A group of threads that execute the same kernel and can cooperate through shared memory. Threads within a block can synchronize using __syncthreads.
- **Grid**: A collection of blocks that execute the same kernel. An entire grid of blocks can be launched from the host (CPU) side.

Each thread and block have unique IDs, making it possible for threads to determine which data to process. Blocks are arranged in a grid, and these blocks can be either one-dimensional (1D), two-dimensional (2D), or three-dimensional (3D).

Memory Hierarchy: The memory hierarchy in CUDA is vitally important to understanding performance optimization. CUDA provides several types of memory, each with different performance characteristics and use cases:

- **Global Memory**: The largest memory space available, accessible by all threads. It is off-chip and has high latency.
- **Shared Memory**: On-chip memory accessible by all threads within the same block. It has much lower latency compared to global memory.
- **Local Memory**: Memory used for variables that are private to each thread. It is stored off-chip and has similar latency to global memory.
- **Constant Memory**: Read-only memory for storing constant data that does not change over the duration of kernel execution. It has cached access, which provides faster access than global memory if the data access patterns exhibit spatial locality.
- **Texture Memory**: Cached read-only memory, particularly beneficial for spatially localized memory access patterns. It provides advantages for specific operations like texture mapping in graphics and certain computational patterns.

Warp: A warp is a group of 32 threads that are executed simultaneously on an SM. Each SM schedules and executes instructions at the level of warps. It's crucial for performance to consider the behavior of warps, ensuring that threads within a warp follow similar execution paths (i.e., avoiding warp divergence).

Thread Divergence: Thread divergence occurs when threads within a single warp take different execution paths (e.g., due to branches in code such as if statements). Divergence can lead to reduced performance, as the warp serially executes each branch path taken by threads within the warp.

```
// Example of potential warp divergence
__global__ void divergenceExample(int* d_data) {
    int idx = threadIdx.x;
    if (idx % 2 == 0) {
        d_data[idx] *= 2;
    } else {
        d_data[idx] += 1;
    }
}
```

Synchronization: Synchronization is crucial in CUDA when threads within a block need to coordinate or ensure that certain operations have completed before progressing. CUDA provides the __syncthreads() function to synchronize threads within a block.

```
__global__ void syncExample(int* d_data) {
    __shared__ int sharedData[256];
    int idx = threadIdx.x;
    sharedData[idx] = d_data[idx];
    __syncthreads(); // Ensure all threads have written to sharedData
    d_data[idx] = sharedData[(idx + 1) % 256];
}
```

Execution Configuration: When launching a kernel, the developer specifies the execution configuration, defining the grid and block dimensions. This is done using the triple angle bracket syntax.

```
int numBlocks = 16;
int threadsPerBlock = 256;
simpleKernel<<<numBlocks, threadsPerBlock>>>(d_array);
```

Streams: CUDA streams are sequences of operations that execute in order on the GPU. Streams enable overlapping computation and data transfer between the host and device or multiple kernel executions. The default stream is stream 0, which serializes operations.

Event: Events are used to measure the time taken by CUDA operations. They can be recorded at specific points in the workflow to mark the start and end of execution segments.

```
cudaEvent_t start, stop;
cudaEventCreate(&start);
cudaEventCreate(&stop);
cudaEventRecord(start, 0);

// Kernel call
simpleKernel<<<numBlocks, threadsPerBlock>>>(d_array);
```

```
cudaEventRecord(stop, 0);
cudaEventSynchronize(stop);

float elapsedTime;
cudaEventElapsedTime(&elapsedTime, start, stop);
```

Understanding these basic concepts and terminologies is essential for advancing in CUDA programming with C++. Embracing these principles will enable efficient utilization of GPU resources and the development of high-performing parallel applications.

1.5 Installing and Setting Up CUDA Toolkit

To leverage CUDA for parallel programming in C++, it is imperative to ensure the proper installation and setup of the CUDA Toolkit. This section outlines the detailed steps required to install the CUDA Toolkit on various operating systems, configure the environment, and verify the setup.

Step 1: Check System Requirements

Before proceeding with the installation, verify that your system meets the minimum requirements for the CUDA Toolkit. These requirements typically include specific hardware and software prerequisites:

- **Operating System:** Windows 10, Linux (various distributions), or macOS.
- **GPU:** NVIDIA GPU with CUDA Compute Capability 3.5 or higher. A list of supported GPUs can be found on the NVIDIA website.
- **Driver:** NVIDIA driver compatible with the CUDA version you intend to install.
- **Compiler:** A suitable C++ compiler, e.g., Visual Studio for Windows or GCC for Linux.

Step 2: Download the CUDA Toolkit

Navigate to the CUDA Toolkit download page on the NVIDIA website (https://developer.nvidia.com/cuda-downloads). Choose the appropriate version for your operating system and follow the download instructions. The page provides detailed information about specific installers for Windows, Linux, and macOS.

Step 3: Install the CUDA Toolkit

- **Windows:** Double-click the downloaded executable file and follow the installation wizard's instructions. Ensure that you select the options to install the CUDA Toolkit, samples, and appropriate NVIDIA drivers.

- **Linux:** Execute the downloaded .run file or use a package manager like apt or yum. For instance, on Ubuntu, you can install CUDA using the following command:

```
sudo dpkg -i cuda-repo-<distro>_<version>_amd64.deb
sudo apt-key adv --fetch-keys http://developer.download.nvidia.com/
    compute/cuda/repos/<distro>/x86_64/7fa2af80.pub
sudo apt-get update
sudo apt-get install cuda
```

- **macOS:** Follow the instructions in the .dmg installer. Note that CUDA support on macOS is often limited to specific macOS versions and compatible Mac hardware.

Step 4: Set Up Environment Variables

After installation, configure the system environment to include paths to CUDA binaries and libraries.

- **Windows:** Add the following paths to the system's environment variables:

  - CUDA Toolkit: C:\Program Files\NVIDIA GPU Computing Toolkit\CUDA\v<version>\bin
  - NVCC Compiler: C:\Program Files\NVIDIA GPU Computing Toolkit\CUDA\v<version>\libnvvp

- **Linux:** Add the following lines to your ~/.bashrc or ~/.zshrc file:

```
export PATH=/usr/local/cuda-<version>/bin${PATH:+:${PATH}}
export LD_LIBRARY_PATH=/usr/local/cuda-<version>/lib64\
                    ${LD_LIBRARY_PATH:+:${LD_LIBRARY_PATH}}
```

  Apply the changes by reloading the configuration file:

```
source ~/.bashrc
```

Step 5: Validate the Installation

To verify that the CUDA Toolkit is correctly installed and configured, compile and run a sample program provided with the toolkit.

- Navigate to the CUDA Samples directory (usually located in C:\ProgramData\NVIDIA Corporation\CUDA Samples on Windows or /usr/local/cuda/samples on Linux).
- Compile the samples using the provided makefile or Visual Studio project.
- Run the deviceQuery sample to verify that your system recognizes the NVIDIA GPU and that it meets the CUDA requirements.

```
cd /usr/local/cuda/samples/1_Utilities/deviceQuery
make
./deviceQuery
```

```
...
Device 0: "GeForce GTX 1080"
  CUDA Driver Version / Runtime Version          11.0 / 11.0
  CUDA Capability Major/Minor version number:    6.1
  Total amount of global memory:                 8119 MBytes (8507990016 bytes)
  ...
Result = PASS
```

Step 6: Install CUDA Development Tools

Depending on your development platform, additional tools such as NVIDIA Nsight, CUDA Profiler, and Visual Studio Code can enhance your development experience with CUDA. Follow the respective installation instructions for these tools to complete your setup.

Troubleshooting Tips

If you encounter issues during installation, consult the following resources:

- CUDA Installation Guide: https://docs.nvidia.com/cuda/cuda-installation-guide
- NVIDIA Developer Forums: https://forums.developer.nvidia.com
- OS-specific troubleshooting sections in the official documentation.

Properly installing and configuring the CUDA Toolkit is essential for developing efficient parallel programs in C++. This involves ensuring your system meets the requirements, downloading and installing the appropriate CUDA Toolkit version, configuring environment variables, and validating the installation by running sample programs.

1.6 First CUDA Program: Hello World

We now turn our attention to writing and running our first CUDA program, traditionally a "Hello World" program. This is an essential step that demonstrates the fundamental process of writing, compiling, and executing a basic CUDA application. Understanding this process will lay the groundwork for more complex CUDA applications later in the book.

A basic "Hello World" program in CUDA will demonstrate the following key components: 1. The structure of a CUDA program. 2. How to write a simple kernel function. 3. How to launch a kernel function from the host (CPU) to be executed on the device (GPU). 4. Compilation and execution of the program.

We start by examining the structure of a basic CUDA program and the code segments needed to execute a simple kernel.

Begin by including the necessary headers and defining the kernel function.

```
#include <iostream>
#include <cuda_runtime.h>

// Kernel function to print "Hello World" from GPU
__global__ void helloCUDA() {
    printf("Hello World from GPU!\n");
}
```

The first line includes the essential header for CUDA runtime APIs, enabling the use of CUDA-specific functions and macros. Additionally, `#include <iostream>` allows for standard input-output operations, which, although not typical for CUDA kernels, is conventional for completeness in C++ code.

The kernel function `helloCUDA()` is annotated with the `__global__` keyword, indicating that it will be executed on the device (GPU) and can be called from the host (CPU). The `printf` function, when used within the kernel, facilitates printing directly from the GPU.

Next, implement the *main* function that initiates the program's execution.

```
int main() {
    // Launch the kernel function
    helloCUDA<<<1, 1>>>();

    // Synchronize the device
    cudaDeviceSynchronize();

    // Successfully end the program
    return 0;
}
```

In the *main* function, the kernel helloCUDA is launched with a specific execution configuration. <<<1, 1>>> specifies the «<number of blocks, number of threads per block»>. In this simple case, we use a single block and a single thread. Following the kernel launch, cudaDeviceSynchronize() is called to synchronize the host and device, ensuring that the GPU has completed its tasks before the CPU proceeds or exits. The program concludes by returning 0, indicating successful execution.

The entire program is as follows:

```
#include <iostream>
#include <cuda_runtime.h>

// Kernel function to print "Hello World" from GPU
__global__ void helloCUDA() {
    printf("Hello World from GPU!\n");
}

int main() {
    // Launch the kernel function
    helloCUDA<<<1, 1>>>();

    // Synchronize the device
    cudaDeviceSynchronize();

    // Successfully end the program
    return 0;
}
```

Upon successful compilation and execution of this program, the expected output is:

```
Hello World from GPU!
```

The next step is to compile the CUDA program. This process involves using the NVIDIA CUDA Compiler, **nvcc**, to convert the CUDA code into an executable. Assuming the code is saved in a file named hello_cuda.cu, open a terminal and execute the following command:

```
nvcc hello_cuda.cu -o hello_cuda
```

The nvcc command will compile hello_cuda.cu and produce an executable named hello_cuda. To run the program, type:

```
./hello_cuda
```

Running this command should display the message "Hello World from GPU!" in the terminal.

We observe core features of CUDA programming such as defining kernel functions, launching them from the host, and utilizing device synchronization. These foundational concepts enable the creation of more advanced programs and are integral to effective CUDA programming.

1.7 Understanding CUDA Development Workflow

The CUDA development workflow is a structured process that allows developers to leverage the computational power of GPUs effectively. By understanding each step, one can develop, optimize, and debug CUDA applications more efficiently. This section elucidates the critical aspects of the CUDA development workflow and the corresponding tools and practices.

The workflow can be broken down into the following main stages:

- **Code Design and Structuring**
- **Host and Device Code Separation**
- **Kernel Configuration**
- **Memory Management**
- **Kernel Launch**
- **Debugging and Profiling**

Code Design and Structuring: The first step involves designing your application such that it identifies which parts of the code will benefit from parallel execution on the GPU. This step typically includes identifying computationally intensive sections of code that can be parallelized. The design phase should consider data dependencies and possible data races to ensure correctness when executing in parallel.

Host and Device Code Separation: CUDA applications consist of host (CPU) code and device (GPU) code. The host code runs on the CPU and manages the overall application flow, while the device code (kernels) runs on the GPU. The __global__ declaration specifier is used to define a kernel function that will run on the device but be called from the host. The separation of host and device code is crucial for understanding and managing the application's execution flow.

Kernel Configuration: Before launching a kernel, you need to configure it. Kernel configuration involves defining the number of threads per block and the number of blocks per grid. The syntax for launching a kernel takes these configurations as arguments. For example:

```
// Kernel declaration
__global__ void myKernel(int *data) {
    int idx = threadIdx.x + blockIdx.x * blockDim.x;
    data[idx] = data[idx] + 1;
}

// Kernel launch configuration
int blockSize = 256;
int numBlocks = (N + blockSize - 1) / blockSize;
myKernel<<<numBlocks, blockSize>>>(data);
```

In this code, blockSize defines the number of threads per block, and numBlocks computes the appropriate number of blocks to launch based on the size of data array, ensuring all elements are processed.

Memory Management: Efficient memory management is crucial in CUDA programming. You must allocate memory on both the host and the device, and transfer data between them as needed. CUDA provides API functions such as cudaMalloc, cudaFree, cudaMemcpy, etc., to manage memory. For instance:

```
int size = N * sizeof(int);
int *hostData = (int *)malloc(size);
int *deviceData;

cudaMalloc((void **)&deviceData, size);
cudaMemcpy(deviceData, hostData, size, cudaMemcpyHostToDevice);

// Kernel execution
myKernel<<<numBlocks, blockSize>>>(deviceData);

// Copy results back to host
cudaMemcpy(hostData, deviceData, size, cudaMemcpyDeviceToHost);

// Free device memory
cudaFree(deviceData);
```

This code allocates memory for a data array on both the host and device, transfers data to the device, runs a kernel, and then copies the results back to the host.

Kernel Launch: After configuring the kernel and managing memory, the actual kernel launch is a straightforward process. The kernel execution is asynchronous, meaning the control returns to the CPU immediately while the GPU continues processing. Synchronization mechanisms, such as cudaDeviceSynchronize, may be used to ensure that kernel execution is complete before proceeding.

```
myKernel<<<numBlocks, blockSize>>>(deviceData);
cudaDeviceSynchronize();
```

Debugging and Profiling: Debugging and profiling are essential for developing efficient CUDA applications. CUDA provides tools like cuda-gdb for debugging and nvprof and NVIDIA Visual Profiler (nvvp) for profiling. These tools help identify bottlenecks, memory access issues, and other performance-related problems.

cuda-gdb allows stepping through the device code, setting breakpoints, and examining variable values, similar to standard GDB debugging:

```
cuda-gdb ./myCudaApplication
(gdb) break myKernel
(gdb) run
```

For profiling, nvprof provides detailed reports on kernel execution times, memory transfers, and other performance metrics:

```
nvprof ./myCudaApplication
```

These profiling results can be used to optimize kernel performance through strategies such as minimizing memory transfers, optimizing memory access patterns, and maximizing occupancy.

Understanding the CUDA development workflow and the tools available allows developers to build efficient and high-performance CUDA applications. By meticulously following the structured workflow, developers can debug, optimize, and ensure the correctness of their CUDA code effectively.

1.8 Brief Introduction to C++ Concepts for CUDA

A thorough grasp of C++ is essential for effective CUDA programming, as CUDA extends C++ with parallel computing capabilities. This section delves into critical C++ concepts pivotal for developing CUDA applications, placing emphasis on identifying and using them appropriately within the CUDA framework.

C++ is a statically typed, compiled language offering a blend of low-level memory manipulation capabilities and high-level abstraction mechanisms. Its support for object-oriented, procedural, and generic programming paradigms makes it highly versatile. Understanding these paradigms and their implementations will facilitate leveraging CUDA's parallelism.

Pointers and Memory Management

In CUDA, pointers are fundamental for managing memory on both the host (CPU) and the device (GPU). Pointers store memory addresses, allowing variables and arrays to be dynamically allocated, accessed, and manipulated. Consider the following basic pointer manipulation in C++:

```
int main() {
    int a = 10;
    int *p = &a; // p now holds the address of a
    *p = 20; // dereferencing p to modify value at address of a
    printf("Value of a: %d\n", a);
    return 0;
}
```

In CUDA, device memory allocation requires 'cudaMalloc' and memory transfers between host and device are managed by 'cudaMemcpy'. Below is an example demonstrating memory management in CUDA:

```
#include <cuda_runtime.h>
#include <iostream>

__global__ void kernel() {
    // Kernel code here
}

int main() {
    int *d_a;
    cudaMalloc((void**)&d_a, sizeof(int) * 10); // Allocate device memory

    kernel<<<1, 10>>>();

    cudaMemcpy(d_a, h_a, sizeof(int) * 10, cudaMemcpyHostToDevice); // Transfer
          data from host to device
    cudaMemcpy(h_a, d_a, sizeof(int) * 10, cudaMemcpyDeviceToHost); // Transfer
          data from device to host

    cudaFree(d_a); // Free device memory

    return 0;
}
```

Arrays and Multidimensional Arrays

Cuda programming extensively employs arrays and multidimensional arrays, facilitating storage and manipulation of large datasets parallelly. In C++, arrays are contiguous memory blocks.

```
int main() {
    int arr[5] = {1, 2, 3, 4, 5};
    for(int i = 0; i < 5; i++) {
        printf(”%d ”, arr[i]);
    }
    return 0;
}
```

CUDA handles arrays similarly, but for large datasets processed in parallel, optimizing memory access patterns is crucial. Consider a 2D matrix transposition example:

```
#include <cuda_runtime.h>
#include <iostream>

__global__ void transpose(int *in, int *out, int width, int height) {
    int x = blockIdx.x * blockDim.x + threadIdx.x;
    int y = blockIdx.y * blockDim.y + threadIdx.y;
    if (x < width && y < height) {
        out[y * width + x] = in[x * height + y];
    }
}

int main() {
    int width = 16, height = 16;
    int size = width * height;
    int *h_in = (int*)malloc(size * sizeof(int));
    int *h_out = (int*)malloc(size * sizeof(int));
    int *d_in, *d_out;

    cudaMalloc((void**)&d_in, size * sizeof(int));
    cudaMalloc((void**)&d_out, size * sizeof(int));

    cudaMemcpy(d_in, h_in, size * sizeof(int), cudaMemcpyHostToDevice);

    dim3 threadsPerBlock(16, 16);
    dim3 blocksPerGrid((width + threadsPerBlock.x - 1) / threadsPerBlock.x,
                       (height + threadsPerBlock.y - 1) / threadsPerBlock.y);

    transpose<<<blocksPerGrid, threadsPerBlock>>>(d_in, d_out, width, height);

    cudaMemcpy(h_out, d_out, size * sizeof(int), cudaMemcpyDeviceToHost);

    cudaFree(d_in);
    cudaFree(d_out);
    free(h_in);
    free(h_out);

    return 0;
}
```

Templates and Generic Programming

Templates in C++ enable writing flexible and reusable code. CUDA also supports templates, facilitating generic kernel functions and device code.

```
template <typename T>
__global__ void add(T *a, T *b, T *c, int N) {
    int i = blockIdx.x * blockDim.x + threadIdx.x;
    if (i < N) c[i] = a[i] + b[i];
}

int main() {
    int N = 1024;
    float *d_a, *d_b, *d_c;

    // Memory allocations, initializations, and copies omitted for brevity

    dim3 threadsPerBlock(256);
    dim3 blocksPerGrid((N + threadsPerBlock.x - 1) / threadsPerBlock.x);

    add<<<blocksPerGrid, threadsPerBlock>>>(d_a, d_b, d_c, N);

    // Memory copies and cleanup omitted for brevity

    return 0;
}
```

Object-Oriented Programming

CUDA supports object-oriented programming (OOP) features of C++. Using classes, inheritance, and polymorphism within CUDA kernels can make complex codes more manageable and modular.

```
class Vector {
private:
    float *data;
    int size;
public:
    Vector(int n) : size(n) {
        cudaMalloc((void**)&data, n * sizeof(float));
    }
    ~Vector() {
        cudaFree(data);
    }

    __device__ float get(int i) const {
        return data[i];
    }

    __host__ __device__ void set(int i, float val) {
        data[i] = val;
    }
};

__global__ void vectorAdd(Vector *a, Vector *b, Vector *c, int N) {
    int i = blockIdx.x * blockDim.x + threadIdx.x;
    if (i < N) {
        c->set(i, a->get(i) + b->get(i));
    }
}
```

```
int main() {
    int N = 1024;
    Vector *d_a, *d_b, *d_c;

    cudaMalloc((void**)&d_a, sizeof(Vector));
    cudaMalloc((void**)&d_b, sizeof(Vector));
    cudaMalloc((void**)&d_c, sizeof(Vector));

    vectorAdd<<<(N + 255) / 256, 256>>>(d_a, d_b, d_c, N);

    cudaFree(d_a);
    cudaFree(d_b);
    cudaFree(d_c);

    return 0;
}
```

Incorporating these C++ concepts into CUDA programming can significantly enhance the development of efficient and scalable parallel applications. By intertwining the power of C++ with CUDA's parallel computing capabilities, developers can exploit GPU resources to handle computationally intensive tasks elegantly.

1.9 Compiling and Running CUDA Programs

The process of compiling and running CUDA programs involves several steps, from writing the source code to executing it on a GPU. Understanding these steps is essential for developers to effectively utilize CUDA for parallel programming. This section discusses the nuances of compiling CUDA programs using nvcc, the NVIDIA CUDA Compiler, and executing the compiled binaries.

To begin, let's discuss the role of the nvcc compiler. nvcc is a command-line compiler that is responsible for compiling CUDA code. It separates host code (run on the CPU) from device code (run on the GPU) and compiles them appropriately. This duality necessitates certain specifics during the compilation process.

A simple CUDA program consists of code that runs on the host (usually C++) and kernels that run on the device. Consider the following example of a basic CUDA program:

```
#include <iostream>
__global__ void helloFromGPU() {
    printf("Hello World from GPU!\n");
}

int main() {
    // Launch the kernel with a single thread
    helloFromGPU<<<1, 1>>>();
```

```
    // Wait for the device to finish all preceding tasks
    cudaDeviceSynchronize();

    std::cout << "Hello World from CPU!" << std::endl;
    return 0;
}
```

This code defines a kernel function helloFromGPU that prints a message from the GPU and then calls this kernel from the host code within the main function. The kernel is invoked using the triple angle bracket syntax («<...»>). The cudaDeviceSynchronize() function ensures that the GPU completes its tasks before the program proceeds to the next instruction.

To compile this program, we use the nvcc compiler as follows:

```
nvcc -o hello_world hello_world.cu
```

The -o flag specifies the output filename, which in this case is hello_-world. After executing this command, an executable named hello_-world is created.

Running the compiled program is straightforward:

```
./hello_world
```

The expected output will be:

```
Hello World from GPU!
Hello World from CPU!
```

This output demonstrates that the message from the GPU (Hello World from GPU!) is printed before the message from the CPU (Hello World from CPU!), consistent with the program's synchronization mechanism.

Advanced Compilation Options

The nvcc compiler provides several options that can be used to control the compilation process. For instance, to specify the CUDA architecture for which the code should be compiled, we use the -arch flag. This is important for ensuring that the binaries are optimized for specific GPU architectures. For example:

```
nvcc -arch=sm_50 -o hello_world hello_world.cu
```

Here, sm_50 corresponds to the compute capability 5.0 of the GPU. Compute capabilities are detailed in the CUDA documentation and indicate the specific features supported by a GPU.

Debugging and Profiling

For developers, debugging and profiling are crucial aspects of the development process. nvcc supports the generation of debug information with the -G flag:

```
nvcc -G -o hello_world_debug hello_world.cu
```

This flag embeds debug symbols in the compiled binary, facilitating the debugging process using tools such as cuda-gdb, NVIDIA's CUDA-enabled debugger, or Nsight, an integrated development environment provided by NVIDIA for CUDA.

Using Makefiles

For larger projects, managing compilation through nvcc command lines can become cumbersome. Makefiles offer a more organized approach to handle builds. A simple Makefile for the earlier example might look like this:

```
# Name of the executable
TARGET = hello_world

# Compiler
NVCC = nvcc

all: $(TARGET)

$(TARGET): hello_world.cu
  $(NVCC) -o $(TARGET) hello_world.cu

clean:
  rm -f $(TARGET)
```

To compile the program using this Makefile, we run the make command in the terminal:

```
make
```

The *clean* target can be invoked to remove the compiled binary:

```
make clean
```

This approach centralizes the build commands and simplifies recompilation and cleanup processes.

Error Handling and Verification

It is important to capture and handle errors during kernel execution. CUDA provides a suite of error handling functions for this purpose. The function cudaGetLastError() returns the code for the last error that occurred during the execution of a kernel. Integrating error checks can be done as follows:

```
#include <iostream>
__global__ void helloFromGPU() {
    printf("Hello World from GPU!\n");
}

int main() {
    helloFromGPU<<<1, 1>>>();
    cudaError_t err = cudaGetLastError();
    if (err != cudaSuccess) {
        std::cerr << "CUDA Error: " << cudaGetErrorString(err) << std::endl;
        return -1;
    }
    cudaDeviceSynchronize();
    err = cudaGetLastError();
    if (err != cudaSuccess) {
        std::cerr << "CUDA Error: " << cudaGetErrorString(err) << std::endl;
        return -1;
    }
    std::cout << "Hello World from CPU!" << std::endl;
    return 0;
}
```

If a kernel launch fails, cudaGetLastError() will capture the error, and cudaGetErrorString() will convert the error code into a readable string. Similarly, post-synchronization checks ensure all GPU operations have completed successfully before proceeding. This approach helps developers identify and debug issues that may arise during kernel execution.

1.10 Common Tools and Resources for CUDA Development

Integrated Development Environments (IDEs):
One of the primary tools utilized in CUDA development is an Integrated Development Environment (IDE). IDEs provide a cohesive environment for writing, debugging, and optimizing code. Notably, *NVIDIA Nsight* is an IDE tailored for CUDA development. Nsight integrates seamlessly with popular environments like Microsoft Visual Studio and Eclipse, offering advanced features such as debugging, profiling, and code analysis specifically for GPU-accelerated applications.

Compilers:
The NVIDIA CUDA Compiler (nvcc) is crucial for translating CUDA code written in C++ into executable binaries that can run on NVIDIA GPUs. nvcc is a component of the CUDA Toolkit and is designed to handle the intricacies of compiling parallel code. It allows developers to compile both the host (CPU) and device (GPU) code, managing the complex-

ities behind code segmentation and optimization for different architectures. The usage of nvcc may typically resemble:

```
nvcc -o my_cudaprogram my_cudaprogram.cu
```

Libraries:
CUDA development benefits from a comprehensive suite of libraries that accelerate numerous computational tasks. Some notable libraries include:

- **cuBLAS**: An optimized library for dense linear algebra, implementing many standard Basic Linear Algebra Subprograms (BLAS).
- **cuFFT**: Provides functionalities for performing Fast Fourier Transforms, useful in signal processing and related fields.
- **cuRAND**: A library for generating high-quality random numbers, aiding in simulations and Monte Carlo methods.
- **Thrust**: A parallel algorithm library resembling the C++ Standard Template Library (STL), making it easier to develop high-performance CUDA code.

Debugging Tools:
Efficient debugging is vital for effective CUDA development. Traditional CPU debugging tools are inadequate for handling the complexities of GPU debugging. CUDA developers rely on tools like *cuda-gdb*, a widely-used debugger tailored for CUDA applications, providing features like setting breakpoints, stepping through code, and inspecting memory state specific to the GPU. A simple usage scenario includes:

```
cuda-gdb ./my_cudaprogram
```

Profiling Tools:
To optimize GPU performance, profiles of application behavior are essential. *NVIDIA Visual Profiler* and *Nsight Systems* are capable tools in this regard. These profilers enable monitoring of GPU workload, memory transfer times, kernel performance, and more. Such insights facilitate the identification of bottlenecks and inefficiencies, empowering developers to refine their code iteratively.

Documentation and Guides:
Comprehensive documentation and well-structured guides are indispensable resources for CUDA developers at all levels. The official

CUDA Toolkit Documentation provides extensive details about API functions, compiler options, hardware compatibility, and performance optimization techniques. NVIDIA also maintains various *CUDA Programming Guides* and *Best Practices Guidelines*, which serve as valuable references.

Online Communities and Forums:
Engagement with the community is a powerful aspect of any development ecosystem. Platforms like *NVIDIA Developer Forums*, *Stack Overflow*, and GitHub repositories facilitate interaction with fellow developers, allowing the exchange of knowledge, troubleshooting support, and collaboration on open-source projects. Community-driven content, such as tutorials and sample projects, further enriches the developer experience.

Package Managers:
The utilization of package managers can simplify the installation and management of dependencies in CUDA development. Tools like *Conda* and *Spack* automate the process of setting up development environments, ensuring that the correct versions of required libraries and tools are utilized. An example command for setting up a CUDA environment using Conda might be:

```
conda create --name my_cuda_env cudatoolkit=11.2
```

Code Repositories:
Version control systems and code repositories are crucial for managing and collaborating on CUDA projects. Platforms like *GitHub*, *GitLab*, and *Bitbucket* offer extensive functionalities for code versioning, issue tracking, and collaborative development. Leveraging these tools ensures a streamlined workflow and efficient management of code bases.

The synergy of these tools and resources forms a robust foundation for CUDA development. The careful selection and proficient usage of these components significantly enhance the productivity and efficiency of developers, ultimately contributing to the successful implementation of high-performance GPU-accelerated applications.

Chapter 2

CUDA Architecture and GPU Computing

This chapter elucidates the fundamentals of GPU architecture and the CUDA programming model, contrasting it with traditional CPU programming. It delves into the intricacies of CUDA cores, thread hierarchy, and warp and block scheduling. The discussion extends to the memory architecture in GPUs, including global, shared, and constant memory. Additionally, it covers the CUDA execution model, streaming multiprocessors (SMs), and introduces the concept of CUDA compute capability, providing an overview of various NVIDIA GPU hardware models.

2.1 Understanding GPU Architecture

Modern GPUs are designed to handle highly parallel tasks, making them uniquely suited for workloads that can exploit such parallelism. Unlike CPUs, which are optimized for low latency execution of individual threads, GPUs are optimized for high throughput execution of many threads. This distinction is in part due to the fundamental differences in the architecture of CPUs and GPUs.

A fundamental building block of a GPU is the Streaming Multiprocessor (SM). Each SM contains multiple CUDA cores, also referred to as streaming processors (SPs), which are capable of executing instructions. Typically, an SM can execute a large number of threads concurrently. The architecture of an SM also includes other critical components such as warp schedulers, special-function units (SFUs), and load/store units.

- **CUDA Cores (Streaming Processors):** These cores are responsible for executing the arithmetic and logical instructions of the threads. Each CUDA core can perform integer and floating-point calculations. The efficiency and speed of these calculations are largely influenced by the number and architecture of the CUDA cores within an SM.
- **Special-Function Units (SFUs):** These units handle more complex mathematical functions such as sine, cosine, reciprocal, and square root calculations. By offloading these specialized operations to SFUs, the CUDA cores are free to manage other tasks, thereby improving overall efficiency.
- **Warp Schedulers:** Warp schedulers manage the execution of warps. A warp is a group of 32 threads that execute the same instruction at the same time in a SIMD fashion. The warp scheduler is responsible for maximizing the utilization of the CUDA cores by ensuring that the warps are issued efficiently.
- **Load/Store Units:** These units manage memory operations, including loading data from global memory into registers or shared memory and storing data back to global memory. Efficient handling of these memory operations is critical for overall performance, as memory latency can significantly impact thread execution.

Each GPU consists of multiple SMs, which collectively form the entire GPU. The exact number of SMs and their internal configurations vary across different GPU models, directly influencing the computing power and suitability for various tasks.

GPU Model	Number of SMs	CUDA Cores per SM
NVIDIA Tesla V100	80	64
NVIDIA RTX 3090	82	128
NVIDIA A100	108	64

A fundamental concept in GPU architecture is the way it handles parallelism. GPUs are designed to execute thousands of threads concur-

rently, leveraging the hardware resources efficiently. This is managed through the use of warps, blocks, and grids.

Warps: As mentioned earlier, a warp is a basic unit of execution in an SM consisting of 32 threads. In a given time unit, all threads of a warp execute the same instruction but can operate on different data, a programming model known as Single Instruction, Multiple Threads (SIMT).

Blocks and Grids: Threads are organized into blocks, and blocks into grids. A block is a group of threads that can share data through shared memory and can synchronize their execution. Each block is scheduled on an SM and can be divided into multiple warps. A grid represents the total number of threads required for a task and is composed of many blocks.

$$\text{GridDim} = \lceil \frac{\text{TotalThreads}}{\text{ThreadsPerBlock}} \rceil$$

The architecture accommodates massive parallelism by dividing tasks among many threads and warps, disseminating workload across SMs, and leveraging shared resources such as shared memory and L1 cache efficiently.

Consider a sample CUDA code to illustrate the execution of a kernel in this architecture:

```
// Sample CUDA Kernel illustrating execution with blocks and grids
__global__ void vectorAdd(const float *A, const float *B, float *C, int N) {
    int i = blockDim.x * blockIdx.x + threadIdx.x;
    if (i < N) {
        C[i] = A[i] + B[i];
    }
}
```

```
Vector addition executed on a GPU:
A = (1.0, 2.0, 3.0)
B = (4.0, 5.0, 6.0)
C = (5.0, 7.0, 9.0)
```

This code demonstrates the division of the task of adding two vectors into blocks and threads, managed by the GPU's hardware scheduler. Each thread computes one element of the resulting vector C.

The SM's ability to handle many threads concurrently, combined with its internal memory hierarchy (including register files, shared memory, and cache), allows GPUs to excel at problems that can be parallelized effectively. This makes them particularly valuable in domains such as scientific computing, image processing, and deep learning. Understanding the architecture is critical to harnessing the full potential of GPU computing.

2.2 CUDA Programming Model vs CPU Programming

The CUDA programming model offers a paradigm shift from traditional CPU-centric programming. The contrast between these two models is pivotal for understanding how to effectively leverage the computational power of GPU architectures. At the core of this distinction lies the differences in hardware and the resulting programming strategies tailored to maximize performance.

In the conventional CPU programming model, the CPU executes tasks sequentially using a limited number of cores, typically ranging from 2 to 64 in modern systems. Each core is designed for extensive control logic and high individual thread performance, excelling in tasks that benefit from complex branching and out-of-order execution. This model prioritizes low-latency operations due to the diverse array of tasks a general-purpose CPU might handle.

Conversely, the CUDA programming model capitalizes on the massive parallelism of GPUs. An NVIDIA GPU might possess thousands of simpler cores, each capable of executing threads in parallel. These CUDA cores are grouped into Streaming Multiprocessors (SMs), and the architecture is specifically optimized for throughput rather than individual thread latency. CUDA programming involves organizing computations into a grid of thread blocks, which can scale to handle extensive parallel tasks efficiently.

In CUDA, computations are expressed as **kernels**, which are functions executed on the GPU, where each thread runs an instance of the kernel. Threads are organized into blocks and grids:

- A **block** is a group of threads that execute on the same SM. They can cooperate through shared memory and synchronize their execution using barrier synchronization.
- A **grid** is a collection of blocks that execute the same kernel function.

Each thread and block is identified by unique indices, enabling them

to process distinct portions of data. Here's an example to illustrate the indexing mechanism:

```
__global__ void vectorAdd(const float *A, const float *B, float *C, int N) {
    int i = blockIdx.x * blockDim.x + threadIdx.x;
    if (i < N) C[i] = A[i] + B[i];
}

int main() {
    // Memory allocation and initialization omitted for brevity
    int threadsPerBlock = 256;
    int blocksPerGrid = (N + threadsPerBlock - 1) / threadsPerBlock;
    vectorAdd<<<blocksPerGrid, threadsPerBlock>>>(A, B, C, N);
    // Further code omitted for brevity
}
```

In this snippet, kernel vectorAdd performs vector addition. Each thread computes one element of the result vector $C[i]$, and the thread index calculation ensures proper data division among the threads.

The memory hierarchy also differs significantly between CPU and CUDA programming models. CPUs typically manage a hierarchy with levels of cache and main memory. CUDA, however, introduces a more complex structure:

- **Global Memory**: Accessible by all threads, but with higher latency.
- **Shared Memory**: A low-latency memory region shared among threads within the same block. This facilitates efficient cooperation and data sharing.
- **Constant and Texture Memory**: Optimized for specific access patterns, offering cached read-only access.

Effective usage of these memory types is crucial for performance optimization. Here's an example utilizing shared memory:

```
__global__ void matrixMulShared(float *A, float *B, float *C, int N) {
    __shared__ float As[BLOCK_SIZE][BLOCK_SIZE];
    __shared__ float Bs[BLOCK_SIZE][BLOCK_SIZE];

    int tx = threadIdx.x, ty = threadIdx.y;
    int row = blockIdx.y * BLOCK_SIZE + ty;
    int col = blockIdx.x * BLOCK_SIZE + tx;

    float Pvalue = 0;
    for (int ph = 0; ph < N / BLOCK_SIZE; ++ph) {
        As[ty][tx] = A[row * N + (ph * BLOCK_SIZE + tx)];
        Bs[ty][tx] = B[(ph * BLOCK_SIZE + ty) * N + col];
        __syncthreads();

        for (int k = 0; k < BLOCK_SIZE; ++k)
```

```
            Pvalue += As[ty][k] * Bs[k][tx];
        __syncthreads();
    }
    C[row * N + col] = Pvalue;
}
```

This kernel performs matrix multiplication utilizing shared memory to reduce redundant global memory accesses, thereby enhancing performance.

While the CPU's programming model typically does not necessitate intricate memory and thread management, CUDA involves explicit handling of numerous threads and memory hierarchies to exploit the hardware's full potential. This distinction demands a mental shift for developers transitioning from CPU-centric to GPU-centric programming practices.

In essence, optimizing CUDA programs requires a deep understanding of both thread hierarchies and the diverse memory types available on modern GPUs. Developers must learn to partition tasks efficiently, avoid memory contention, and utilize the memory hierarchy to their advantage, contrasting significantly with traditional CPU programming paradigms.

2.3 CUDA Cores and Thread Hierarchy

CUDA (Compute Unified Device Architecture) cores are the fundamental processing units within the GPU, designed for high-performance parallel computation. Each CUDA core performs integer and floating-point calculations, forming the foundation of GPU's capability to handle a large number of concurrent threads efficiently. Understanding the thread hierarchy in CUDA is crucial for leveraging the full computational power of a GPU.

CUDA employs a grid, block, and thread hierarchy to organize computation. At the highest level, the grid contains one or more blocks, each of which contains one or more threads. This three-level hierarchy (grid, block, thread) allows for a flexible and scalable parallel programming model.

Threads are the smallest units of execution in the CUDA programming model. Each thread executes the same code but operates on different data, a model known as Single Instruction, Multiple Threads (SIMT). Threads are organized into blocks, typically ranging from tens to hundreds of threads per block. Each thread within a block has a unique identifier, accessible via the built-in threadIdx variable, which enables threads to access different data elements.

```
__global__ void myKernel(float *data) {
    int idx = threadIdx.x;
    data[idx] = data[idx] * 2.0f;
}
```

In this kernel function, each thread squares the element of the array data corresponding to its thread index. The threadIdx.x variable provides the thread's unique index within its block, enabling access to distinct array elements.

Blocks are groups of threads that execute concurrently. Each block can contain up to 1024 threads, with this limit varying based on the compute capability of the GPU. Blocks are indexed within a grid through the blockIdx variable, allowing computation to be organized in a multi-dimensional grid. This enables fine-grained parallelism at the block level.

```
__global__ void myKernel(float *data) {
    int tid = threadIdx.x + blockIdx.x * blockDim.x;
    data[tid] = data[tid] * 2.0f;
}
```

Here, blockIdx.x and blockDim.x are used to compute a global thread index tid, accounting for both the block and thread indices. This way, every thread across all blocks operates on a unique data element.

Grids are composed of multiple blocks and provide an additional layer of parallelism. Grids can be one-dimensional, two-dimensional, or three-dimensional, enabling extensive data parallelism suited for large-scale computations. By launching a kernel with a grid of blocks, a developer can orchestrate thousands to millions of threads executing concurrently.

```
dim3 blockDim(256);
dim3 gridDim((N + blockDim.x - 1) / blockDim.x);
myKernel<<<gridDim, blockDim>>>(data);
```

The blockDim variable specifies the dimensions of each block, while gridDim defines the grid's size. This configuration launches a kernel where each block contains 256 threads, and the grid size is determined by the total number of elements N. The flexibility of the grid-block-thread hierarchy allows CUDA to scale from small to large problem sizes, fully utilizing GPU resources.

Synchronization and Memory Sharing Among Threads Threads within a block can synchronize their execution using __syncthreads() to coordinate shared memory accesses or avoid race conditions. Shared memory is a fast, limited region of memory accessible by all threads within a block, offering reduced access latency compared to global memory.

```
__global__ void sharedMemoryKernel(float *data) {
    __shared__ float sharedData[256];
    int idx = threadIdx.x;
    sharedData[idx] = data[idx];
    __syncthreads();
    // Perform operations on sharedData
    sharedData[idx] = sharedData[idx] * 2.0f;
    __syncthreads();
    data[idx] = sharedData[idx];
}
```

In this kernel, sharedData is a shared memory array accessible by all threads in the block. Threads read from global memory into shared memory, synchronize with __syncthreads(), perform operations on the shared data, and finally write back to global memory.

Warp Execution A warp is a group of 32 threads that execute instructions in lockstep on a streaming multiprocessor (SM). Warps form the basic execution units for scheduling and executing instructions on the GPU. Ensuring that threads within a warp follow similar execution paths avoids divergence, maintaining high performance.

Understanding the CUDA cores and thread hierarchy provides a fundamental building block for developing efficient parallel programs on GPUs. This knowledge enables effective utilization of the GPU's computational resources, achieving significant performance improvements for a wide range of applications.

2.4 Warp and Block Scheduling

Warp and block scheduling is a critical aspect of achieving optimal performance in CUDA programming. It affects how threads execute on the GPU and determines the efficiency of resource utilization. Understanding the fundamentals of warps and blocks, along with their scheduling, is essential for writing code that fully leverages the capabilities of GPU hardware.

A **warp** is a group of 32 threads that execute the same instruction at the same time. This is the basic unit of execution and scheduling in

CUDA's Single Instruction, Multiple Threads (SIMT) architecture. All threads in a warp start their execution together and follow the same control flow, although they may diverge based on conditional branches. If threads within a warp diverge, execution will be serialized, which can reduce performance.

Threads are organized into blocks, referred to as **thread blocks**. Each thread block comprises one or more warps. The size of a thread block can be specified by the programmer, but it cannot exceed the maximum block size defined by the compute capability of the GPU. Each thread block is assigned to a **Streaming Multiprocessor (SM)** for execution. The SM schedules warps within each block for execution in a round-robin or similar fashion.

Given that thread execution is managed at the warp level, optimal performance is often achieved when threads in a warp follow the same execution path. **Thread divergence** occurs when different threads inside a warp take different execution paths. CUDA handles divergence by serializing the execution of the different paths and then converging the threads back at a common execution point. This serialization can reduce the effective parallelism and thus degrade performance.

To see the impact of warp and block scheduling in practice, consider the following CUDA kernel:

```
__global__ void SimpleKernel(int *data) {
    int idx = blockIdx.x * blockDim.x + threadIdx.x;
    if (idx % 2 == 0)
        data[idx] *= 2;
    else
        data[idx] *= 3;
}
```

In this kernel, each thread processes an element of the array data. The threads within a warp perform different operations based on the value of idx modulo 2, potentially causing divergence.

```
Output (after kernel execution):
data = {0, 3, 4, 9, 8, 15, 12, 21, 16, 27, ...}
```

To minimize thread divergence, it is beneficial to structure the code to ensure that threads within a warp follow the same execution path. For example, modifying the previous kernel to reduce divergence might look as follows:

```
__global__ void OptimizedKernel(int *data) {
    int idx = blockIdx.x * blockDim.x + threadIdx.x;
    int value = (idx % 2 == 0) ? 2 : 3;
    data[idx] *= value;
}
```

Here, all threads perform multiplication, and conditional logic is simplified, thus minimizing the chance of divergent execution paths within a warp.

Execution scheduling at the block level involves mapping thread blocks to SMs. Each SM can execute multiple blocks concurrently, depending on hardware resources such as registers, shared memory, and the number of warps. The CUDA runtime and driver are responsible for distributing thread blocks among available SMs to balance the workload and improve overall GPU utilization.

Considerations of block scheduling include:

- **Occupancy**: This refers to the ratio of active warps to the maximum number of warps supported per SM. Higher occupancy can hide memory latency and improve throughput.
- **Resource Usage**: Each block consumes resources such as registers and shared memory. The total available resources on an SM limit the number of concurrently active blocks. Optimizing resource usage can increase concurrency.
- **Synchronization**: Global memory accesses are typically slower than shared memory accesses. Using shared memory within a block can reduce latency, but it requires careful synchronization to avoid race conditions.
- **Granularity**: Choosing the right block size is a balance between resource usage and performance. Fine-grained execution (smaller blocks) can achieve better load balancing but may have higher scheduling overhead.

For instance, examining the compute capability of a GPU can help determine optimal block configurations. The following code demonstrates querying the device properties:

```
cudaDeviceProp prop;
cudaGetDeviceProperties(&prop, 0);
printf("Max Threads Per Block: %d\n", prop.maxThreadsPerBlock);
printf("Max Threads Per SM: %d\n", prop.maxThreadsPerMultiProcessor);
printf("Number of SMs: %d\n", prop.multiProcessorCount);
```

```
Output:
Max Threads Per Block: 1024
Max Threads Per SM: 2048
Number of SMs: 16
```

Understanding these parameters helps in configuring thread blocks and grid dimensions to maximize GPU utilization effectively.

Warp and block scheduling are central to the performance of CUDA applications. Efficiently managing thread divergence, optimizing resource usage, and understanding device capabilities are crucial for achieving high performance in CUDA programming. Effective scheduling strategies ensure that GPUs operate at their maximum potential, leveraging parallelism inherent in GPU architecture.

2.5 Memory Architecture in GPUs

Memory architecture in GPUs plays a crucial role in determining the performance and efficiency of CUDA applications. To fully exploit the computational power of GPUs, it is essential to understand the different types of memory available and how to utilize them effectively. This section explores the various memory types within the GPU, discussing their characteristics, access patterns, and best use cases. The memory types typically include global memory, shared memory, constant memory, texture memory, and register memory.

Global memory is the largest memory space available on a GPU and can be accessed by all threads. It is off-chip, which makes it the slowest type of memory due to high latency and low bandwidth compared to other memory types. Access to global memory therefore needs to be optimized. Strategies such as coalesced memory access, where threads in a warp access contiguous memory locations, can significantly improve global memory performance.

Shared memory is an on-chip memory space that is shared among threads within the same block. Its low latency and high bandwidth make it ideal for scenarios where threads need to cooperate and share data efficiently. Shared memory is organized into banks, and bank conflicts can occur if multiple threads access the same bank concurrently, leading to serialization. Kernel code needs to be carefully designed to avoid such conflicts by ensuring that memory accesses are evenly distributed across the banks.

Constant memory is a read-only memory space optimized for situations where all threads in a grid read the same value. Since constant memory is cached, broadcasting the same value to multiple threads is extremely efficient. However, this memory type has limited size, typically 64 KB, and should be used judiciously.

Texture memory is another specialized read-only memory that is cached and optimized for 2D spatial locality patterns. While initially designed for graphics applications, texture memory can be beneficial in general-purpose computing scenarios. It can handle non-coalesced access patterns efficiently and provides additional functionality such as automatic interpolation and addressing modes.

Register memory is the fastest type of memory but is severely limited in size. Each thread has its own set of registers, and excessive usage can lead to register spilling, where data is moved to slower local memory. This can degrade performance, making it essential to carefully manage register usage in kernel code.

To illustrate these concepts, consider the following example code snippet where global memory usage is optimized through coalesced access patterns:

```
__global__ void matrixMul(const float* A, const float* B, float* C, int N) {
    int row = blockIdx.y * blockDim.y + threadIdx.y;
    int col = blockIdx.x * blockDim.x + threadIdx.x;

    float value = 0.0f;
    for (int k = 0; k < N; ++k) {
        value += A[row * N + k] * B[k * N + col];
    }
    C[row * N + col] = value;
}
```

In the above code, matrices A and B are accessed in a coalesced fashion, ensuring that memory transactions are minimized and efficiency is maximized. This pattern exemplifies the importance of organizing memory accesses to exploit the capabilities of global memory.

Shared memory usage can be demonstrated through a kernel for matrix multiplication that loads tile sub-matrices into shared memory:

```
__global__ void tiledMatMul(const float* A, const float* B, float* C, int N) {
    __shared__ float tileA[TILE_SIZE][TILE_SIZE];
    __shared__ float tileB[TILE_SIZE][TILE_SIZE];

    int row = blockIdx.y * TILE_SIZE + threadIdx.y;
    int col = blockIdx.x * TILE_SIZE + threadIdx.x;
    float value = 0.0f;

    for (int m = 0; m < N / TILE_SIZE; ++m) {
        tileA[threadIdx.y][threadIdx.x] = A[row * N + (m * TILE_SIZE + threadIdx.x)
            ];
        tileB[threadIdx.y][threadIdx.x] = B[(m * TILE_SIZE + threadIdx.y) * N + col];

        __syncthreads();

        for (int e = 0; e < TILE_SIZE; ++e) {
            value += tileA[threadIdx.y][e] * tileB[e][threadIdx.x];
        }
```

```
        __syncthreads();
    }
    C[row * N + col] = value;
}
```

This kernel uses shared memory to load sub-matrices, reducing the number of global memory accesses and increasing performance. It highlights the efficient use of shared memory to benefit from low latency and high bandwidth.

Considerations such as the type of memory to use, access patterns, and the potential for bank conflicts are critical in designing efficient CUDA kernels. By leveraging the strengths of different memory types, such as the global, shared, constant, texture, and register memory, CUDA programmers can optimize their applications to achieve maximum performance and efficiency on NVIDIA GPUs.

2.6 CUDA Execution Model

The CUDA execution model is a comprehensive framework designed to efficiently run computations on the GPU. It intricately maps the logical structure of programs onto the physical hardware, optimizing performance and resource utilization. The execution model revolves around two primary abstractions: grids and blocks, and their hierarchical relation is crucial for leveraging the GPU's parallel processing capabilities.

A CUDA program, or kernel, is executed by an array of parallel threads organized into a grid of thread blocks. Each thread is assigned a unique identifier that it uses to execute code and access memory. The grid structure allows for a scalable design, where a program can run on various GPU configurations with different numbers of cores.

Thread Hierarchy: Each kernel launch involves a grid of thread blocks. The grid is structured into a two-level hierarchy:

- **Thread Blocks:** These are the basic units of a grid. A block contains a set of threads that can cooperate among themselves via shared memory. Threads within a block can synchronize their execution and communicate through shared memory.
- **Threads:** They are the smallest execution units, capable of being processed concurrently. Each thread within a block has a unique thread index, which can be derived using the built-in variables like threadIdx, blockIdx, and blockDim.

The following code snippet demonstrates a simple kernel with a grid and block setup:

```
__global__ void kernelFunction() {
    int idx = blockIdx.x * blockDim.x + threadIdx.x; // Calculate global index
    // Kernel code to execute
}
```

Here, blockIdx.x represents the block index, while blockDim.x and threadIdx.x represent the dimensions of the block and the thread index within the block, respectively. The calculation of idx yields the global index of each thread, which is a unique identifier.

Grids: Grids can be uni-dimensional, bi-dimensional, or tri-dimensional, providing flexibility in mapping complex data structures to CUDA threads. The dimension and size of the grids and blocks are specified during the kernel launch:

```
dim3 gridSize(16, 16); // 16x16 grid
dim3 blockSize(8, 8); // 8x8 threads per block
kernelFunction<<<gridSize, blockSize>>>();
```

Warp Execution: Threads within a block are executed in groups of 32, known as warps. Warp scheduling is managed by the GPU hardware's scheduler, allowing for efficient parallel execution. All threads in a warp execute the same instruction simultaneously on different data. Divergence, which occurs when threads within a warp take different execution paths, can adversely affect performance.

Synchronization: Threads within a block can synchronize their execution using explicit synchronization primitives such as __syncthreads(). This function ensures that all threads within the block have reached the same execution point before proceeding. This is particularly useful for operations that require collective computation or sharing intermediate results via shared memory.

```
__global__ void reductionKernel(int *data) {
    __shared__ int sdata[BLOCK_SIZE];
    int tid = threadIdx.x;
    sdata[tid] = data[tid];
    __syncthreads();

    // Perform reduction within a block
    for (int s = blockDim.x / 2; s > 0; s >>= 1) {
        if (tid < s) {
            sdata[tid] += sdata[tid + s];
        }
        __syncthreads();
    }
    // Write result for this block to global memory
    if (tid == 0) data[blockIdx.x] = sdata[0];
}
```

Grid Synchronization: CUDA does not natively support synchronization across the entire grid. However, grid-level synchronization can be achieved using techniques such as launching separate kernels in sequence and relying on the CUDA runtime for implicit synchronization. Nonetheless, finer control at the block level provides adequate flexibility for many parallel algorithms.

Resource Constraints: The execution of a kernel is subject to hardware constraints like the number of registers per thread, shared memory per block, and the maximum number of threads per block. Efficient utilization of these resources is critical for achieving optimal performance. Developers can query the device properties using CUDA runtime API functions to tailor their kernel configurations.

```
cudaDeviceProp prop;
cudaGetDeviceProperties(&prop, 0);
printf("Max threads per block: %d\n", prop.maxThreadsPerBlock);
printf("Max shared memory per block: %lu\n", prop.sharedMemPerBlock);
printf("Max registers per block: %d\n", prop.regsPerBlock);
```

```
Max threads per block: 1024
Max shared memory per block: 49152
Max registers per block: 65536
```

By thoroughly understanding and leveraging the CUDA execution model, developers can optimize their programs to fully exploit the parallel processing capabilities of modern GPUs, leading to substantial performance gains for a wide range of computationally intensive applications.

2.7 Global, Shared, and Constant Memory

In CUDA programming, understanding the various types of memory available on the GPU is crucial for optimizing performance. The three primary types of memory are global, shared, and constant memory. Each of these has distinct characteristics, advantages, and use cases.

Global memory is the largest memory space available on the GPU, accessible by all threads of a kernel. It is not cached, leading to higher latency and lower bandwidth compared to shared memory. Data stored in global memory persists across kernel launches, making it suitable for storing large datasets. However, due to its lower performance characteristics, careful considerations are necessary when accessing global memory. Coalescing memory accesses, where threads in a warp access contiguous memory locations, can significantly improve global memory throughput.

```
__global__ void kernel(float *data) {
    int idx = threadIdx.x + blockIdx.x * blockDim.x;
    data[idx] = some_computation(idx);
}

int main() {
    float *d_data;
    int size = 1024 * sizeof(float);
    cudaMalloc((void**)&d_data, size);
    kernel<<<gridSize, blockSize>>>(d_data);
    cudaFree(d_data);
    return 0;
}
```

Shared memory is an on-chip memory accessible by threads within the same block, offering much lower latency compared to global memory. Each Streaming Multiprocessor (SM) has its own shared memory, divided among the blocks running on it. Shared memory's low latency and high throughput make it ideal for data shared among threads of a block and for achieving high performance in algorithms that require significant inter-thread communication.

```
__global__ void kernel(float *data) {
    __shared__ float s_data[BLOCK_SIZE];
    int idx = threadIdx.x;
    s_data[idx] = data[idx];
    __syncthreads();
    // Perform computations using shared memory
    data[idx] = some_computation(s_data[idx]);
}

int main() {
    float *d_data;
    float h_data[BLOCK_SIZE] = {0}; // initialize data
    int size = BLOCK_SIZE * sizeof(float);
    cudaMalloc((void**)&d_data, size);
    cudaMemcpy(d_data, h_data, size, cudaMemcpyHostToDevice);
    kernel<<<1, BLOCK_SIZE>>>(d_data);
    cudaMemcpy(h_data, d_data, size, cudaMemcpyDeviceToHost);
    cudaFree(d_data);
    return 0;
}
```

Constant memory is a read-only memory space that is cached on-chip, providing low-latency access for constant values that do not change over the course of kernel execution. This is advantageous for kernel parameters and constants used across all threads. The use of constant memory can significantly speed up the access time compared to global memory, assuming the constants are accessed frequently and beneficially fit in the cache.

```
__constant__ float const_data[64];
```

```
__global__ void kernel(float *data) {
    int idx = threadIdx.x;
    data[idx] = data[idx] + const_data[idx];
}

int main() {
    float *d_data;
    float h_data[64] = {1.0f}; // initialize data
    float h_const_data[64] = {2.0f}; // initialize constant data
    int size = 64 * sizeof(float);

    cudaMalloc((void**)&d_data, size);
    cudaMemcpy(d_data, h_data, size, cudaMemcpyHostToDevice);
    cudaMemcpyToSymbol(const_data, h_const_data, size);

    kernel<<<1, 64>>>(d_data);

    cudaMemcpy(h_data, d_data, size, cudaMemcpyDeviceToHost);
    cudaFree(d_data);
    return 0;
}
```

Efficient use of these memory types is pivotal for optimizing GPU performance. Global memory should be accessed in a coalesced manner to exploit maximum bandwidth. Shared memory should be used to minimize global memory accesses, particularly in scenarios requiring high inter-thread communication within blocks. Constant memory should be employed for read-only data that is accessed by all threads, benefiting from the low-latency offered by on-chip caching.

The understanding and strategic application of global, shared, and constant memory in CUDA programming enable leveraging the full computational capabilities of the GPU. This foundation is pivotal as we proceed to more advanced topics in optimizing and fine-tuning CUDA applications.

2.8 Streaming Multiprocessors (SMs)

Streaming Multiprocessors (SMs) are the core computational units within NVIDIA GPUs, which execute the CUDA program kernels. Each SM contains an array of CUDA cores, responsible for executing individual instructions from multiple threads in a massively parallel fashion. The architecture of SMs is fundamental to understanding CUDA programming, as it directly influences the efficiency and performance of GPU applications.

Every SM incorporates several critical components: CUDA cores, Special Function Units (SFUs), Load/Store Units (LSUs), and scheduling units. The CUDA cores perform the standard arithmetic and logic operations. The SFUs handle more specialized instructions such as trigonometric calculations, exponentials, and reciprocals. The LSUs manage memory operations by loading data from and storing data to the various memory regions in the GPU. These components work together harmoniously under the control of the scheduling units, which orchestrate the execution of threads.

The number of CUDA cores per SM and the corresponding architectural features can vary depending on the specific GPU model and its compute capability. For example, GPUs with compute capability 7.x (Volta and Turing architectures) have more CUDA cores per SM compared to earlier architectures. This increase translates to greater computational power and potential for higher thread parallelism within each SM.

The SM employs a Single Instruction, Multiple Threads (SIMT) architecture, which means it executes the same instruction across multiple threads concurrently. Threads are organized into warps of 32 threads each. A warp is the unit of execution in an SM, meaning all threads within a warp execute the same instruction at any given time. This uniform execution facilitates efficient hardware and software design, but it also introduces challenges such as warp divergence. Warp divergence occurs when threads in the same warp follow different execution paths, causing the SM to serialize the divergent paths and potentially degrade performance.

Each SM has several registers and a specific amount of shared memory that threads within a block can use for fast, on-chip data storage. Shared memory access times are significantly shorter than global memory access times, making it crucial to optimize the use of shared memory for performance-critical parts of the application. Here is an example of how to declare and use shared memory in a CUDA kernel:

```
__global__ void matrixMulKernel(float* C, float* A, float* B, int width) {
    __shared__ float tileA[TILE_WIDTH][TILE_WIDTH];
    __shared__ float tileB[TILE_WIDTH][TILE_WIDTH];

    int row = blockIdx.y * TILE_WIDTH + threadIdx.y;
    int col = blockIdx.x * TILE_WIDTH + threadIdx.x;
    float value = 0.0;

    for (int i = 0; i < width/TILE_WIDTH; ++i) {
        tileA[threadIdx.y][threadIdx.x] = A[row * width + (i * TILE_WIDTH +
              threadIdx.x)];
        tileB[threadIdx.y][threadIdx.x] = B[(i * TILE_WIDTH + threadIdx.y) * width
              + col];
        __syncthreads();

        for (int j = 0; j < TILE_WIDTH; ++j) {
            value += tileA[threadIdx.y][j] * tileB[j][threadIdx.x];
```

```
        }
        __syncthreads();
    }
    C[row * width + col] = value;
}
```

In the above kernel, tileA and tileB are shared memory arrays storing sub-matrices (or tiles) of matrix A and B, respectively. The __syncthreads() function call ensures all threads within the block have completed their memory writes before any thread reads from tileA or tileB. This synchronization is critical to avoid data hazards.

The execution capacity of an SM is also defined by the number of active warps it can handle concurrently, referred to as warp occupancy. High occupancy implies that the SM is utilizing most or all of its execution units, leading to better performance. Achieving high occupancy requires careful consideration of resource allocation, including registers and shared memory, as these resources are divided among all active warps.

The register file and the shared memory size are typically partitioned among the active warps and thread blocks dynamically. This partitioning can be influenced by setting kernel launch parameters and using CUDA API features to dictate the maximum block size and shared memory usage. Consider the following example:

```
int numBlocks = (N + BLOCK_SIZE - 1) / BLOCK_SIZE;
cudaFuncSetAttribute(kernel, cudaFuncAttributeMaxDynamicSharedMemorySize, 2048)
    ;
kernel<<<numBlocks, BLOCK_SIZE>>>(d_A, d_B, d_C, N);
```

The cudaFuncSetAttribute function sets the maximum dynamic shared memory size for the kernel, which can be critical for ensuring the SM efficiently manages its resources and achieves optimal performance.

Advanced GPUs incorporate multiple SMs, allowing for incredible parallelism by executing thousands of threads simultaneously. Each generation introduces enhancements to the SM architecture, increasing computational resources and improving power efficiency. These developments necessitate continuous learning and adaptation for CUDA programmers to exploit the full potential of new hardware capabilities.

2.9 Understanding the CUDA Compute Capability

CUDA compute capability (CC) is a fundamental concept for understanding the capabilities and performance characteristics of NVIDIA GPUs. The compute capability defines the features supported by a CUDA GPU, including available memory sizes, supported instructions, and the maximum number of threads per block. This section elaborates on compute capability, exploring its implications on GPU functionality and how it influences CUDA programming practices.

Compute capability is specified using a major and minor version number (e.g., CC 7.5), where the major version number indicates fundamental architectural features and the minor version number denotes incremental improvements on those architectures. Each compute capability version introduces new features and optimizations, offering enhanced performance and more efficient utilization of hardware resources.

Major Architectural Features: The major version number reflects the architectural generation of the GPU. Significant differences between major versions might encompass the number of CUDA cores per streaming multiprocessor (SM), enhancements to the memory subsystem, and changes to the physical structure of the cores themselves. For instance, the transition from CC 3.x (Kepler architecture) to CC 5.x (Maxwell architecture) included considerable improvements in energy efficiency and instruction throughput.

Incremental Improvements: Within each major version, minor version upgrades represent refinements and additions to the existing architecture. Such improvements might include additional instructions for specialized computations, enhancements for atomic operations, or optimizations in memory bandwidth. For instance, the change from CC 6.0 to CC 6.1 introduced support for half-precision floating-point arithmetic, which is particularly beneficial for applications in machine learning.

CUDA Programming Model Adaptations: Understanding compute capability is critical when developing CUDA applications because code must be designed to align with the capabilities of the target GPU. For example, the maximum number of threads per block and the amount of shared memory per block can vary with different compute capabilities. The following table outlines some critical compute capability parameters:

Compute Capability	Max Threads/Block	Max Grid Size (dim 0)	Max Shared Memory/Block	Max Registers/Block
3.x (Kepler)	1024	$2^{31}-1$	48 KB	64K 32-bit
5.x (Maxwell)	1024	$2^{31}-1$	64 KB	64K 32-bit
6.x (Pascal)	1024	$2^{31}-1$	64 KB	64K 32-bit
7.x (Volta)	1024	$2^{31}-1$	96 KB	64K 32-bit
8.x (Ampere)	1024	$2^{31}-1$	100 KB	64K 32-bit

Feature Support in Different Compute Capabilities: Compute capability also dictates feature availability, affecting how software is developed and optimized. The following list outlines some of the notable features introduced across different compute capability versions:

- **CC 3.0 (Kepler):** Dynamic Parallelism, Hyper-Q
- **CC 5.0 (Maxwell):** Unified Memory, improved atomics
- **CC 6.0 (Pascal):** Enhanced L2 Cache, 16-bit floating-point (FP16) support
- **CC 7.0 (Volta):** Tensor Cores for deep learning, improved warp synchronization
- **CC 8.0 (Ampere):** Sparsity support in Tensor Cores, asynchronous copy instructions

Implications for Performance Optimization: An optimal CUDA program must leverage the functionalities provided by the compute capability of the target GPU. For instance, utilizing the tensor cores available in Volta (CC 7.x) or newer GPUs can significantly accelerate deep learning computations. Similarly, making full use of the enhanced shared memory in CC 8.0 (Ampere) can further optimize memory-bound operations.

Let us consider a simple CUDA kernel and how different compute capabilities might influence its implementation.

```
__global__ void vectorAdd(float *A, float *B, float *C, int N) {
    int i = blockDim.x * blockIdx.x + threadIdx.x;
    if (i < N) C[i] = A[i] + B[i];
```

```
}

int main() {
    // Assume N, device pointers d_A, d_B, d_C have been initialized
    int threadsPerBlock = 256;
    int blocksPerGrid = (N + threadsPerBlock - 1) / threadsPerBlock;
    vectorAdd<<<blocksPerGrid, threadsPerBlock>>>(d_A, d_B, d_C, N);
    cudaDeviceSynchronize();
    return 0;
}
```

This basic vector addition kernel might need to be adapted depending on the compute capability of the GPU. If running on a GPU with CC 7.x, one could use tensor cores if performing matrix multiplications, but these are not utilized in this example. For CC 8.x, one might take advantage of larger shared memory for more complex operations requiring efficient data reuse.

Compute capability plays a pivotal role in determining the available features, the constraints, and the optimal performance strategy for a given CUDA program. When writing CUDA code, it is crucial to query the compute capability of the target GPU and adjust algorithms and data structures accordingly to ensure compatibility and optimal performance.

```
cudaDeviceProp prop;
cudaGetDeviceProperties(&prop, 0);
printf("Compute Capability: %d.%d\n", prop.major, prop.minor);
```

```
$ nvcc -o vectorAdd vectorAdd.cu
$ ./vectorAdd
Compute Capability: 8.0
```

This output confirms the compute capability of the device running the application. Checking this information programmatically ensures that the code can adapt to various GPUs, leveraging the full power of the available hardware.

2.10 Introduction to NVIDIA's GPU Hardware Models

NVIDIA's GPU hardware models are integral to understanding the evolution and capabilities of CUDA-based computing. Over the years, NVIDIA has introduced a series of GPU architectures, each aiming to enhance computing power, efficiency, and versatility. This section delves into the prominent GPU architectures developed by NVIDIA, discussing their features and improvements. Specifically, we will cover the Tesla, Fermi, Kepler, Maxwell, Pascal, Volta, Turing, and Ampere architectures, highlighting their significance in the context of CUDA programming.

Tesla Architecture

The Tesla architecture, introduced in 2006, marks NVIDIA's first unified GPU architecture, designed primarily for high-performance computing (HPC) applications. Tesla GPUs were pivotal in introducing general-purpose computing on GPUs (GPGPU). Key features of the Tesla architecture include:

- **Unified Shader Design**: Combines vertex and pixel shaders, allowing for more efficient use of computational resources.
- **Scalability**: Scalable to support multiple GPUs, facilitating large-scale computational tasks.
- **CUDA Compatibility**: Initial support for CUDA, enabling parallel programming using C, C++, and Fortran.

Fermi Architecture

Launched in 2010, the Fermi architecture brought significant advancements in GPU computing by introducing several new features to enhance programmability, performance, and accuracy. Notable features of the Fermi architecture include:

- **Parallel Data Cache**: Includes L1 and L2 caches to reduce memory latency and improve performance.
- **Improved Double Precision Performance**: Enhanced floating-point performance, critical for scientific computations.
- **Error Correction Codes (ECC)**: ECC memory support for increased reliability in HPC applications.
- **Concurrent Kernel Execution**: Ability to run multiple kernels simultaneously, improving resource utilization.

Kepler Architecture

The Kepler architecture, introduced in 2012, focused on energy efficiency and further improvements in performance. Key features of Kepler GPUs are:

- **SMX (Streaming Multiprocessor eXtension)**: Redesigned SM units that provide better performance per watt.
- **Dynamic Parallelism**: Allows kernels to invoke other kernels, enabling more complex and dynamic execution patterns.
- **Hyper-Q**: Improves GPU utilization by enabling multiple CPU threads to launch work on the GPU simultaneously.

Maxwell Architecture

Unveiled in 2014, the Maxwell architecture emphasized power efficiency and memory optimization. Features include:

- **Second Generation SM (Streaming Multiprocessor)**: Improved performance per watt compared to the Kepler SMX.
- **Unified Memory**: Simplifies the programming model by allowing more straightforward memory management.
- **NVENC (NVIDIA Encoder)**: Dedicated hardware for video encoding, reducing the load on CUDA cores.

Pascal Architecture

Launched in 2016, the Pascal architecture brought several key innovations to enhance compute performance and GPU memory capabilities. Key features include:

- **16nm FinFET Technology**: A more advanced manufacturing process allowing higher clock speeds and energy efficiency.
- **NVLink**: A high-speed interconnect for multi-GPU systems, allowing faster data transfer between GPUs.
- **High Bandwidth Memory (HBM2)**: Increases memory bandwidth, leading to improved performance in memory-intensive applications.

Volta Architecture

Introduced in 2017, the Volta architecture aimed at deep learning and HPC environments. Its notable features are:

- **Tensor Cores**: Specialized cores designed to accelerate deep learning workloads, significantly boosting training performance.

- **Improved NVLink**: Enhanced NVLink interconnect offering even higher bandwidth.
- **Mixed-Precision Computing**: Supports mixed-precision calculations, balancing performance and accuracy efficiently.

Turing Architecture

Released in 2018, the Turing architecture focused on real-time ray tracing, AI, and programmable shading. Key advances include:

- **RT Cores**: Dedicated hardware for real-time ray tracing, accelerating rendering tasks.
- **Tensor Cores (Improved)**: Enhanced Tensor Cores for better AI and deep learning inference.
- **Variable Rate Shading (VRS)**: Allows for more efficient rendering by varying the shading rate across the frame.

Ampere Architecture

The Ampere architecture, launched in 2020, represents NVIDIA's latest major GPU architecture, pushing the boundaries in several domains, including AI, HPC, and gaming. Its fundamental enhancements are:

- **Third Generation Tensor Cores**: Significantly faster Tensor Cores supporting a wide range of precisions with higher efficiency.
- **Second Generation RT Cores**: Improved real-time ray tracing capabilities with higher performance and efficiency.
- **Enhanced Memory Subsystem**: Greater memory bandwidth and capacity, supporting large datasets and models.

The evolution of NVIDIA's GPU architectures underscores the progressive enhancement in computational capabilities, power efficiency, and support for complex applications. Each new generation introduces novel features that cater to the increasing demands of both scientific and consumer applications, making CUDA programming increasingly powerful and efficient. Understanding these hardware models allows developers to optimize their applications fully, leveraging the unique strengths of each architecture.

Chapter 3

Setting Up Your Development Environment

This chapter details the system requirements and provides step-by-step instructions for installing the CUDA Toolkit on Windows, Linux, and macOS, as well as setting up NVIDIA drivers. It covers the configuration of integrated development environments (IDEs) and environment variables necessary for CUDA development. Additionally, it includes guidelines for testing the installation, updating, and uninstalling the CUDA Toolkit, and offers insights into using Docker for a streamlined CUDA development environment.

3.1 System Requirements for CUDA Development

The setup for CUDA development necessitates specific hardware and software configurations to ensure optimal functionality and efficiency. This section outlines these prerequisites, providing a detailed understanding of the system requirements essential for successful CUDA programming.

A CUDA-capable GPU is paramount. NVIDIA's CUDA platform primarily operates with NVIDIA GPUs that support the parallel computing architecture. The minimum requirement for a GPU to support CUDA is Compute Capability 3.0. Nvidia maintains a comprehensive list of GPUs and their respective compute capabilities on the official CUDA website, which should be consulted to verify GPU compatibility.

Memory requirements vary based on application complexity. For a fundamental setup, a minimum of 2 GB of host system RAM is recommended, although 4 GB or more is preferred for handling larger datasets and more complex computations efficiently. It is also advisable to have a GPU with at least 1 GB of graphics memory to support basic CUDA applications, while more demanding applications will benefit from higher GPU memory.

Processor requirements and operating system support are equally critical. CUDA development can be conducted on:

- **Windows:**
  - Windows 7, 8, 10, and newer versions. Both 32-bit and 64-bit systems are supported, but 64-bit versions are preferable due to better performance and larger addressable memory space.
- **Linux:**
  - Distributions such as Ubuntu, Fedora, CentOS, and others supported by NVIDIA's CUDA Toolkit.
- **macOS:**
  - macOS High Sierra (10.13) or newer is required for CUDA development on Apple systems.

Additionally, a multicore CPU, though not a strict requirement, can significantly enhance performance by complementing the parallel processing power of the GPU. This is particularly pertinent when performing operations that can be parallelized between the CPU and GPU.

For software requirements, the following are essential:

- **CUDA Toolkit:** The toolkit provides the compiler (nvcc), libraries, and other essential tools. Ensure you download the version compatible with your operating system and GPU.

- **C++ Compiler:** A compiler compatible with nvcc is required. On Windows, Microsoft Visual Studio is recommended, while on Linux, GNU Compiler Collection (GCC) is widely used. Xcode is used on macOS.

- **CUDA Samples:** Included with the CUDA Toolkit, these samples provide example codes to test and understand CUDA functionalities.

- **NVIDIA Drivers:** The driver version must support the installed CUDA Toolkit version. The NVIDIA installer usually indicates the compatible driver versions.

It is essential to have an integrated development environment (IDE) suited for coding in C++. IDEs such as Microsoft Visual Studio (on Windows), Eclipse (cross-platform), and CLion (cross-platform) are popular choices as these tools simplify coding, debugging, and project management.

Network connectivity is another significant factor; it is necessary for downloading and updating software packages, accessing documentation, and obtaining technical support from NVIDIA and other online communities.

To summarize, ensuring that the hardware and software configuration meets these specified requirements will lead to a seamless and productive CUDA development experience. Properly configured systems confer both stability and performance, allowing developers to fully harness the parallel processing power intrinsic to CUDA-enabled GPUs. The following verification steps will ascertain if your environment is correctly configured:

```
// Sample code to verify CUDA installation
#include <cstdio>
void query_device_info() {
    int device_count = 0;
    cudaGetDeviceCount(&device_count);
    for (int device = 0; device < device_count; ++device) {
        cudaDeviceProp device_properties;
        cudaGetDeviceProperties(&device_properties, device);
        printf("Device %d: %s\n", device, device_properties.name);
    }
}

int main() {
    query_device_info();
    return 0;
}
```

Executing this program should list the details of all CUDA-capable GPUs on your system, confirming that the development environment is ready for CUDA programming. The output will provide information such as the device name, compute capability, and other pertinent characteristics of each GPU.

```
Device 0: NVIDIA GeForce GTX 1080 Ti
Device 1: NVIDIA Tesla K80
```

Such output indicates that the system has recognized the NVIDIA GPUs available for CUDA development, verifying that your setup meets the necessary requirements.

3.2 Installing CUDA Toolkit on Windows

To begin the installation of the CUDA Toolkit on a Windows operating system, ensure your system meets the necessary hardware and software requirements. The installation involves several steps, including downloading the CUDA Toolkit from the official NVIDIA website, installing the toolkit, verifying the installation, and configuring the environment. This section provides a comprehensive guide to each of these steps.

Step 1: Verify System Requirements

Before installing the CUDA Toolkit, it is essential to verify that your system meets the minimum requirements for both hardware and software. The primary requirements include a CUDA-capable GPU, a supported version of Windows, and the appropriate system configurations. As of the latest toolkit version, the following are the key requirements:

- A CUDA-capable GPU with a compute capability of at least 3.0.
- Windows 7, Windows 10, or Windows Server 2016/2019.
- Microsoft Visual Studio 2017, 2019, or later. Ensure you have the Desktop development with C++ workload installed.
- At least 8 GB of system RAM and a few GB of free space on the system drive.

Step 2: Download the CUDA Toolkit

Navigate to the NVIDIA CUDA Toolkit download page: https://developer.nvidia.com/cuda-toolkit. Select the appropriate version for your system and click on the link to download the installer.

Step 3: Installation of CUDA Toolkit

Run the installer that you downloaded. The installer offers two installation modes: Express and Custom. The Express installation is recommended for most users, as it automatically installs the required components. For greater control over the installation process, select the Custom installation.

- **Express Installation**: This mode installs all CUDA Toolkit components, including the CUDA Samples, NVIDIA drivers, and other necessary libraries.
- **Custom Installation**: This mode allows you to select specific components to install. It is useful if you want to exclude certain libraries or have specific preferences for the installation location.

After selecting the installation mode, proceed with the installation by following the on-screen instructions. Accept the license agreement and select the appropriate options based on your preferences and system configuration. The installer will then copy the CUDA Toolkit files to your system.

Step 4: Install NVIDIA Drivers

The CUDA installer also provides an option to install the NVIDIA drivers necessary for your GPU. It is generally recommended to install the latest drivers provided by the installer. If you have a specific requirement for driver versions or wish to manage drivers independently, you can choose to skip this step during the toolkit installation and download the drivers separately from the NVIDIA website.

Step 5: Verify the Installation

To ensure that the CUDA Toolkit has been installed correctly, it is useful to compile and run a sample program. Open a command prompt and navigate to the directory containing the CUDA samples. You can typically find them in C:\ProgramData\NVIDIA Corporation\CUDA Samples\vXX.X (replace XX.X with the appropriate version number).

Compile a sample program using the following command:

```
cd C:\ProgramData\NVIDIA Corporation\CUDA Samples\vXX.X\1_Utilities\
    deviceQuery
nvcc deviceQuery.cu -o deviceQuery
```

After compilation, execute the program to verify that the CUDA Toolkit can correctly interact with your GPU:

```
deviceQuery.exe
```

Upon successful execution, the program should output the specifications of your GPU, similar to the following:

```
cudaGetDeviceCount returned 1
Found 1 CUDA Capable device(s)

Device 0: "GeForce GTX 1080"
  CUDA Driver Version / Runtime Version          11.2 / 11.1
  CUDA Capability Major/Minor version number:    6.1
  Total amount of global memory:                 8192 MBytes (8589934592 bytes)
  (13) Multiprocessors, (128) CUDA Cores/MP:     1664 CUDA Cores
  GPU Max Clock rate:                            1733 MHz (1.73 GHz)
  ...
```

This output confirms the successful installation and functioning of the CUDA Toolkit on your system.

Step 6: Configure Environment Variables

It is essential to configure the necessary environment variables to ensure smooth functioning of the CUDA Toolkit. Add the following paths to your system's PATH environment variable:

- C:\Program Files\NVIDIA GPU Computing Toolkit\CUDA\vXX.X\bin
- C:\Program Files\NVIDIA GPU Computing Toolkit\CUDA\vXX.X\libnvvp

Additionally, set the CUDA_HOME environment variable to the root directory of the CUDA Toolkit installation:

```
CUDA_HOME=C:\Program Files\NVIDIA GPU Computing Toolkit\CUDA\vXX.X
```

To set these on Windows, navigate to Control Panel >System and Security >System >Advanced system settings >Environment Variables. Add a new user variable for CUDA_HOME and edit the system variable Path to include the paths mentioned.

Step 7: Restart and Verify the Environment Variables

After setting the environment variables, restart your system to ensure that all changes take effect. Open a command prompt and type the following commands to verify:

```
echo %CUDA_HOME%
```

This should return the path set in the environment variable. You can also verify the PATH variable configuration by typing:

```
echo %PATH%
```

Check that the CUDA paths appear in the output list. The successful echo of these variables confirms that the environment is correctly set up for CUDA development.

These steps comprehensively cover the installation of the CUDA Toolkit on a Windows operating system, ensuring that your setup is correctly configured for CUDA development.

3.3 Installing CUDA Toolkit on Linux

To install the CUDA Toolkit on Linux, follow these instructions. The process encompasses verifying system compatibility, downloading the necessary files, installing the toolkit and drivers, and finally, configuring your environment to facilitate CUDA development.

Prerequisites:

- Verify that your Linux distribution is supported by the CUDA Toolkit. Refer to the official NVIDIA CUDA documentation for supported distributions.
- Ensure you have a compatible NVIDIA GPU. Verify on the NVIDIA CUDA Supported GPUs page.
- Ensure a supported version of the GCC compiler is installed. The version requirements are specified in the CUDA release notes.

Step-by-Step Installation:

1. Verify System Compatibility: Open a terminal and check your Linux distribution version and kernel version using the following command:

```
$ uname -r && lsb_release -a
```

Ensure the GCC version meets the requirements:

```
$ gcc --version
```

2. Download the CUDA Toolkit: Visit the official NVIDIA Developer website at https://developer.nvidia.com/cuda-downloads. Select your target platform as "Linux", then choose your distribution and version, and click "Download".

Alternatively, you can use 'wget' to download the necessary files directly from the terminal. For example:

```
$ wget https://developer.download.nvidia.com/compute/cuda/12.x/12.x/
    local_installers/cuda_12.xx.xx_linux.run
```

Replace the URL with the actual link to the CUDA version you need.

3. Install the CUDA Toolkit: Navigate to the directory where you downloaded the installer and make it executable:

```
$ chmod +x cuda_12.xx.xx_linux.run
```

Run the installer with root privileges:

```
$ sudo ./cuda_12.xx.xx_linux.run
```

The installer presents a series of prompts. Follow these guidelines:

- Accept the EULA.
- Choose the components to install (typically, you will want to install the driver, the toolkit, and the samples).

The installation process may take several minutes.

4. Install NVIDIA Drivers: If you opted not to install the driver during the CUDA installation process, you can install it separately. Ensure that any pre-existing NVIDIA drivers are removed to avoid conflicts:

```
$ sudo apt-get remove --purge '^nvidia-.*'
```

Install the recommended driver:

```
$ sudo apt install nvidia-driver-460
```

Replace '460' with the appropriate version number recommended for your GPU.

5. Configure Environment Variables: Add the CUDA toolkit and compiler to the system PATH for easy access. Edit the .bashrc file in your home directory:

```
$ gedit ~/.bashrc
```

Append the following lines:

```
# CUDA Toolkit
export PATH=/usr/local/cuda-12.x/bin${PATH:+:${PATH}}
export LD_LIBRARY_PATH=/usr/local/cuda-12.x/lib64\
${LD_LIBRARY_PATH:+:${LD_LIBRARY_PATH}}
```

Save and close the file. Source .bashrc to apply the changes:

```
$ source ~/.bashrc
```

6. Verify the Installation: Compile and run the sample programs provided with the CUDA Toolkit to ensure everything is set up correctly. Navigate to the $CUDA_HOME/samples directory:

```
$ cd /usr/local/cuda-12.x/samples
$ make
```

After compilation, navigate to the bin directory in the samples:

```
$ cd /usr/local/cuda-12.x/samples/bin/x86_64/linux/release
$ ./deviceQuery
```

A successful output is shown below:

```
./deviceQuery Starting...

 CUDA Device Query (Runtime API) version (CUDART static linking)

Detected 1 CUDA Capable device(s)

Device 0: "NVIDIA GeForce GTX 1050 Ti"
  CUDA Driver Version / Runtime Version          12.0 / 12.0
  ...
  Total amount of global memory:                 4096 MBytes
  ...

Result = PASS
```

If any issues are encountered, refer to the CUDA Toolkit installation logs and rectify any discrepancies.

Updating and Maintenance: It is advisable to keep your CUDA Toolkit and drivers up-to-date. Regularly check for updates on the NVIDIA website. To update the CUDA Toolkit, download the latest version and repeat the installation steps. To uninstall the CUDA Toolkit, use the following command:

```
$ sudo /usr/local/cuda-12.x/bin/uninstall_cuda_12.x.pl
```

Replace '12.x' with your installed CUDA version. For NVIDIA drivers:

```
$ sudo apt-get remove --purge '^nvidia-.*'
```

This ensures a clean removal before installing new versions. Properly managing your CUDA installations ensures a stable and efficient development environment.

3.4 Installing CUDA Toolkit on macOS

The installation of the CUDA Toolkit on macOS involves several necessary steps, including downloading the toolkit, installing it, and ensuring the appropriate drivers and supporting software are in place. This section provides a detailed guide for each of these stages.

Firstly, verify that your macOS version and hardware meet the necessary requirements for CUDA development by visiting the official CUDA macOS installation guide found on NVIDIA's website. As of the latest CUDA release, macOS 10.13 and newer are generally supported on systems with an NVIDIA GPU. Assume the previous installation steps in the chapter do not cover macOS-specific scenarios, so we will address them uniquely here.

1. **Download the CUDA Toolkit:** Navigate to the NVIDIA CUDA Toolkit download page provided on the NVIDIA Developer website. Select Mac OS in the operating system dropdown, and then choose the appropriate version of the toolkit. Click on the Download button to obtain the installer.

2. **Install the Toolkit:** Locate the downloaded dmg file, usually found in your Downloads folder. Open this file, then follow these sub-steps:

    - Double-click on the .dmg file to mount the disk image.
    - Open the mounted image, and you should see the cuda-macOS-<version>.pkg file. Double-click this .pkg file to begin the installation process.
    - Follow the on-screen instructions provided by the installer. This typically involves agreeing to the license agreement and selecting the destination for the installation. Unless specific requirements are dictated, the default options are sufficient.

    The installation process may prompt you to authenticate with an administrator username and password. Once authentication is confirmed, the installer will proceed until it completes.

3. **Post-Installation Steps:** To ensure your system recognizes the newly installed CUDA tools, you need to update the system's path

environment variable. This involves editing shell profiles depending on the shell you are using. For instance, if you are using zsh (which is the default on newer macOS versions), open a terminal and execute the following command:

```
echo 'export PATH=/usr/local/cuda/bin:$PATH' >> ~/.zshrc
source ~/.zshrc
```

If you use bash, replace ~/.zshrc with ~/.bash_profile in the above command.

Additionally, add the CUDA libraries to your DYLD_LIBRARY_PATH to ensure that all tools correctly link to the necessary libraries:

```
echo 'export DYLD_LIBRARY_PATH=/usr/local/cuda/lib:
      $DYLD_LIBRARY_PATH' >> ~/.zshrc
source ~/.zshrc
```

4. **Verify Installation:** Validate the successful installation of the CUDA Toolkit with these steps:

    - Open a new Terminal window.
    - Confirm the CUDA compiler (nvcc) is installed by checking its version:

    ```
    nvcc --version
    ```

    You should observe output indicating the installed version of the CUDA compiler. For example:

    ```
    nvcc: NVIDIA (R) Cuda compiler driver
    Copyright (c) 2005-2023 NVIDIA Corporation
    Built on Fri_Apr_01_18:22:06_PDT_2023
    Cuda compilation tools, release 11.4, V11.4.48
    Build cuda_11.4.r11.4/compiler.29440493_0
    ```

    - Additionally, execute a sample program, such as the deviceQuery program provided in the CUDA samples, to confirm the CUDA development and runtime environment:

    ```
    cd /usr/local/cuda/samples/1_Utilities/deviceQuery
    make
    ./deviceQuery
    ```

    If the CUDA Toolkit is correctly installed and functioning, you should see output detailing the GPU present in your system and confirming that CUDA is available.

5. **Install Xcode Command Line Tools:** The CUDA Toolkit requires the Xcode Command Line Tools for compilation. Install these tools by running:

```
xcode-select --install
```

Follow the on-screen instructions to complete this installation.

6. **Keep the System Updated:** Regularly updating the macOS, CUDA Toolkit, and related drivers ensures optimal performance and compatibility. Check NVIDIA's website for updates and read the release notes to understand the changes and enhancements.

Having followed these steps, the CUDA Toolkit should now be operational on your macOS system. Ensure that you routinely check for updates to both macOS and the CUDA Toolkit, allowing you to leverage the latest features and performance improvements.

3.5 Installing NVIDIA Drivers

The installation of NVIDIA drivers is a critical step for ensuring proper functioning and performance of the CUDA Toolkit. These drivers are required for the CUDA-enabled GPU to interact with your operating system and development environment effectively. Incorrect or outdated driver installations can lead to suboptimal performance and compatibility issues. This section covers the detailed steps for installing NVIDIA drivers on Windows, Linux, and macOS.

Windows:

1. **Verify System Specifications**: Ensure that your GPU is compatible with the version of the NVIDIA drivers you intend to install. You can verify system compatibility on the [NVIDIA website](https://www.nvidia.com/Download/index.aspx).

2. **Download the Drivers**: Navigate to the [NVIDIA Drivers Download](https://www.nvidia.com/Download/index.aspx) page. Enter your graphics card information, select your operating system, and click 'Search'. Download the appropriate driver for your hardware.

3. **Execute the Installer**: Locate the downloaded driver executable file and double-click to start the installation process. Follow the on-screen instructions. It is recommended to choose the 'Custom (Advanced)' installation option and check the 'Perform a clean installation' box. This ensures that previous drivers are completely removed.

```
C:\Users\YourUser\Downloads\NVIDIA-Driver-Installation.exe
```

4. **Restart Your System**: After the installation completes, restart your computer to ensure all changes take effect.

Linux:

1. **Identify Your GPU**: Open the terminal and execute the command to identify your GPU model.

```
$ lspci | grep -i nvidia
```

2. **Add the NVIDIA Repository**: Adding the NVIDIA repository simplifies the installation and updating of drivers. The following commands are for Ubuntu-based distributions. Adjust accordingly if using a different distribution.

```
$ sudo add-apt-repository ppa:graphics-drivers/ppa
$ sudo apt update
```

3. **Install the Drivers**: Find the recommended driver version for your GPU using software such as 'ubuntu-drivers'.

```
$ ubuntu-drivers devices
```

After identifying the recommended version, install the driver.

```
$ sudo apt install nvidia-driver-460
```

Replace '460' with the version number identified as appropriate.

4. **Load the NVIDIA Drivers**: Restart your system to enable the drivers.

```
$ sudo reboot
```

To verify the driver installation, execute:

```
$ nvidia-smi
```

```
+-----------------------------------------------------------------------------+
| NVIDIA-SMI 460.32.03    Driver Version: 460.32.03    CUDA Version: 11.2     |
|-------------------------------+----------------------+----------------------+
```

macOS:

1. **Check System Compatibility**: macOS drivers support most NVIDIA GPUs. You can check compatibility on the [NVIDIA macOS drivers page](https://www.nvidia.com/download/driverResults.aspx/112097/en-us).

2. **Download and Install the Drivers**: Navigate to the [NVIDIA Driver

Download](https://www.nvidia.com/Download/index.aspx) page. Input the product type, product series, and select 'macOS' as the operating system. Download the latest driver.

3. **Run the Installer**: Locate the downloaded '.dmg' file, open it, and follow the on-screen instructions to install the driver. You may need to allow the installation in 'System Preferences > Security & Privacy' once prompted.

```
file://path_to_download/NVIDIA-Web-Driver-XYZ-v387.dmg
```

4. **Restart Your System**: Upon completion of the installation, restart your Mac for the changes to take effect.

These steps ensure that the NVIDIA drivers are properly installed on your respective operating system, verifying that your development environment will function efficiently for CUDA programming tasks.

3.6 Setting Up Integrated Development Environments (IDEs)

The choice and configuration of an Integrated Development Environment (IDE) can significantly enhance the productivity and efficiency of your CUDA development workflow. In this section, we will examine the setup procedures for some of the most popular IDEs used in CUDA development: Visual Studio, Eclipse, and Visual Studio Code. Each of these tools offers distinct features and advantages, and the setup process requires some specific steps to ensure compatibility and optimal performance with CUDA.

Visual Studio:

1. **Installation of Visual Studio:** Begin by downloading and installing Visual Studio from the official Microsoft website. Ensure you select the appropriate edition that supports the required features such as debugging and code analysis tools. During installation, include the "Desktop development with C++" workload to ensure all necessary components for CUDA development are installed.

2. **Integration with CUDA:** After Visual Studio is installed, proceed to install the CUDA Toolkit if you have not done so already. The installation of the CUDA Toolkit will automatically integrate CUDA with Visual Studio by setting up the appropriate project templates, code samples,

and debugging support.

3. **Creating a CUDA Project:** To create a new CUDA project, open Visual Studio and select $\text{File} > \text{New} > \text{Project}$. In the project template explorer, navigate to $\text{Installed} > \text{Templates} > \text{Visual C++} > \text{NVIDIA}$ and select CUDA 11.0 Runtime. This template sets up a basic CUDA project with the necessary configurations.

4. **Project Configuration:** Once the project is created, right-click on the project name in the Solution Explorer and select Properties. Under $\text{CUDA C/C++} > \text{Common}$, ensure that the appropriate compute capability for your GPU is set. Additionally, under VC++ Directories, add the paths to CUDA Toolkit headers and libraries.

5. **Building and Running the Project:** To build your CUDA project, select $\text{Build} > \text{Build Solution}$. The output console will display the build process, and any errors or warnings will be shown. To run your project, select $\text{Debug} > \text{Start Without Debugging}$ or press $\text{Ctrl} + \text{F5}$.

Eclipse:

1. **Installation of Eclipse:** Download and install Eclipse CDT (C/C++ Development Tooling) from the official Eclipse website. It is crucial to select the correct version that supports C++ development.

2. **Integration with CUDA:** After installing the Eclipse IDE, install the CUDA Toolkit. During the CUDA Toolkit installation, ensure that you choose the options to install Eclipse plugins if prompted.

3. **Configuring Eclipse for CUDA:** Open Eclipse and go to $\text{Help} > \text{Eclipse Marketplace}$. Search for and install the $\text{PTP (Parallel Tools Platform)}$ if it is not already included. Once installed, configure the preferences by navigating to $\text{Window} > \text{Preferences} > \text{CUDA}$ and specifying the CUDA Toolkit paths.

4. **Creating a CUDA Project:** To create a new CUDA project in Eclipse, go to $\text{File} > \text{New} > \text{C++ Project}$. Choose CUDA C++ Project from the list of available templates. Eclipse will generate the necessary project configuration.

5. **Building and Running the Project:** Right-click the project in the Project Explorer and select Build Project to compile your CUDA code. To execute the project, right-click the built executable and select $\text{Run As} > \text{Local C/C++ Application}$.

Visual Studio Code:

1. **Installation of Visual Studio Code:** Download and install Visual

Studio Code from the official website. Visual Studio Code offers a lightweight and versatile environment for coding, with extensive support for extensions.

2. **Installing Extensions for C++ and CUDA:** Upon opening Visual Studio Code, go to the Extensions view by clicking the Extensions icon in the Activity Bar. Install the C/C++ extension by Microsoft to enable C++ language support. Next, install the CUDA extension for syntax highlighting and other CUDA-specific features.

3. **Configuring Build Tasks:** Create a new folder for your CUDA project and open it in Visual Studio Code. Create a blank tasks.json file in the .vscode directory with the following configuration to set up build tasks:

```
{
    "version": "2.0.0",
    "tasks": [
        {
            "label": "build",
            "type": "shell",
            "command": "/usr/local/cuda/bin/nvcc",
            "args": [
                "-o",
                "outputFile",
                "sourceFile.cu"
            ],
            "group": {
                "kind": "build",
                "isDefault": true
            },
            "problemMatcher": ["$gcc"]
        }
    ]
}
```

Modify the paths and filenames according to your CUDA Toolkit location and the source file names in your project.

4. **Running the Code:** Build your project by executing the task defined. Open the command palette (Ctrl+Shift+P), then type and select Run Task, and choose build. This will compile and link your CUDA application.

5. **Debugging Configurations:** To set up debugging, create or update the launch.json file in the .vscode directory to configure GDB or any other debugger suited to your environment.

```
{
    "version": "0.2.0",
    "configurations": [
        {
            "name": "(gdb) Launch",
            "type": "cppdbg",
```

```
            "request": "launch",
            "program": "${workspaceFolder}/outputFile",
            "args": [],
            "stopAtEntry": false,
            "cwd": "${workspaceFolder}",
            "environment": [],
            "externalConsole": true,
            "MIMode": "gdb",
            "setupCommands": [
                {
                    "description": "Enable pretty-printing for gdb",
                    "text": "-enable-pretty-printing",
                    "ignoreFailures": true
                }
            ],
            "preLaunchTask": "build",
            "miDebuggerPath": "/usr/bin/gdb",
            "setupCommands": [
                {
                    "text": "set breakpoint pending on",
                    "description": "Allow gdb to set breakpoints in any file",
                    "ignoreFailures": true
                }
            ],
            "miDebuggerArgs": "",
            "logging": {
                "trace": true,
                "traceResponse": true
            }
        }
    ]
}
```

Testing the setup through debugging and running the configurations ensures that the environment is correctly set up for CUDA development.

3.7 Configuring Environment Variables

Configuring the environment variables is essential to ensure that the CUDA toolkit and accompanying libraries are correctly recognized by the system and your development tools. Environment variables allow your operating system to dynamically locate application resources like executables, libraries, and include files without requiring absolute paths to be specified in your code.

Environment variables commonly configured for CUDA development include PATH, LD_LIBRARY_PATH, CUDA_HOME, and CUDA_ROOT. In this section, we will explore the configuration of these environment variables on Windows, Linux, and macOS platforms.

Windows:

1. Open the Start Menu and search for *Environment Variables*, then click on *Edit the system environment variables*. 2. In the System Properties window, click on the *Environment Variables* button. 3. In the Environment Variables window, you can add or modify environment variables under *User variables* for user-specific settings or *System variables* for system-wide settings. 4. To add the CUDA paths:

- Select Path in the *System variables* section and click *Edit*.
- Click *New* and add the path to the CUDA bin directory, typically C:\Program Files\NVIDIA GPU Computing Toolkit\CUDA11.0\bin.
- Add another new entry for the CUDA library path, typically C:\Program Files\NVIDIA GPU Computing Toolkit\CUDA11.0\libnvvp.

5. Click *OK* to save changes.

In some cases, you might need to set the CUDA_HOME and CUDA_-ROOT variables as well:

- Click on *New* under the *System variables* section.
- Enter CUDA_HOME as the variable name and C:\Program Files\NVIDIA GPU Computing Toolkit\CUDA11.0 as the value.
- Click *OK* to add it.
- Repeat the process to add CUDA_ROOT with the same value.

Linux:

1. Open a terminal window. 2. Edit the .bashrc file (or .bash_profile, .profile depending on your shell and distribution) located in your home directory using your preferred text editor, e.g., nano or vim:

```
nano ~/.bashrc
```

3. Add the following lines to set up the CUDA environment variables:

```
export PATH=/usr/local/cuda-11.0/bin:$PATH
export LD_LIBRARY_PATH=/usr/local/cuda-11.0/lib64:$LD_LIBRARY_PATH
export CUDA_HOME=/usr/local/cuda-11.0
export CUDA_ROOT=/usr/local/cuda-11.0
```

4. Save and close the file. Apply the changes using:

```
source ~/.bashrc
```

macOS:

1. Open a terminal window. 2. Edit the .bash_profile file (or .zshrc if using zsh shell) located in your home directory using your preferred text editor:

```
nano ~/.bash_profile
```

3. Add the following lines to configure the environment variables for CUDA:

```
export PATH=/usr/local/cuda-11.0/bin:$PATH
export DYLD_LIBRARY_PATH=/usr/local/cuda-11.0/lib:
    $DYLD_LIBRARY_PATH
export CUDA_HOME=/usr/local/cuda-11.0
export CUDA_ROOT=/usr/local/cuda-11.0
```

4. Save and close the file. Apply the changes using:

```
source ~/.bash_profile
```

These steps ensure that your system can locate the CUDA tools and libraries whenever needed. To verify that the environment variables are set correctly:

```
echo $PATH
echo $LD_LIBRARY_PATH
echo $CUDA_HOME
echo $CUDA_ROOT
```

The output should display the paths you have added, confirming the configuration. For Windows, you can check the variables by opening a Command Prompt and using:

```
echo %PATH%
echo %CUDA_HOME%
echo %CUDA_ROOT%
```

Correctly setting these environment variables is crucial for seamless CUDA development, enabling your system to efficiently find and use the necessary CUDA components.

3.8 Testing the Installation

After completing the installation of the CUDA Toolkit and appropriate NVIDIA drivers, testing the installation is crucial to ensure that the environment is correctly configured and ready for development. This section outlines the steps to verify the installation's integrity on your system by compiling and running sample CUDA programs.

Once the CUDA Toolkit is installed, the first task is to verify the installation directory. By default, the CUDA Toolkit installation path is /usr/local/cuda on Unix-based systems or C:\Program Files\NVIDIA GPU Computing Toolkit\CUDA\vX.Y on Windows, where X.Y refers to the version number.

Verify the path by executing the following command in your terminal or command prompt:

```
# For Unix-based systems
ls /usr/local/cuda

# For Windows systems
dir "C:\Program Files\NVIDIA GPU Computing Toolkit\CUDA\vX.Y"
```

```
bin doc extras include lib64 nvvm samples share src
```

Next, confirm that the NVIDIA drivers are installed and compatible with the CUDA Toolkit by using the nvidia-smi command:

```
nvidia-smi
```

The output should display information about your GPU, driver version, and CUDA version, as shown below:

```
+-----------------------------------------------------------------------------+
| NVIDIA-SMI 470.57.02    Driver Version: 470.57.02    CUDA Version: 11.4     |
|-------------------------------+----------------------+----------------------+
| GPU  Name        Persistence-M| Bus-Id        Disp.A | Volatile Uncorr. ECC |
| Fan  Temp  Perf  Pwr:Usage/Cap| Memory-Usage | GPU-Util  Compute M. SM       |
|                               |                      |               MIG M. |
|===============================+======================+======================|
|   0  Tesla V100-PCIE...  On   | 00000000:00:1E.0 Off |                    0 |
| N/A   35C    P0    25W / 250W |      0MiB / 16160MiB |      0%      Default N/A |
+-----------------------------------------------------------------------------+
```

Following the driver verification, navigate to the CUDA samples directory. The samples provide quick and effective means to ascertain whether the toolkit functions correctly. The samples directory can be located within the CUDA installation directory. Execute the following on Unix-based systems:

```
cd /usr/local/cuda/samples/1_Utilities/deviceQuery
```

Or on Windows:

```
cd "C:\Program Files\NVIDIA GPU Computing Toolkit\CUDA\vX.Y\samples\1
    _Utilities\deviceQuery"
```

Compile the deviceQuery sample to verify the device's attributes using the make utility on Unix-based systems:

```
sudo make
```

On Windows, use the Visual Studio Developer Command Prompt:

```
msbuild deviceQuery_vs2019.vcxproj /t:Build /p:Configuration=Release
```

Run the compiled executable:

```
./deviceQuery
```

For Windows:

```
deviceQuery.exe
```

A successful test will print detailed information about the CUDA-capable device, including its compute capability, memory, hierarchy, and more comprehensive details, as shown below:

```
./deviceQuery Starting...

 CUDA Device Query (Runtime API) version (CUDART static linking)

Detected 1 CUDA Capable device(s)

Device 0: "Tesla V100-PCIE-32GB"
  CUDA Driver Version / Runtime Version          11.4 / 11.4
  CUDA Capability Major/Minor version number:    7.0
  Total amount of global memory:                 32510 MBytes (34172432384 bytes)
  (80) Multiprocessors, (64) CUDA Cores/MP:      5120 CUDA Cores
  GPU Max Clock rate:                            1530 MHz (1.53 GHz)
  Memory Clock rate:                             877 Mhz
  Memory Bus Width:                              4096-bit
  L2 Cache Size:                                 6291456 bytes
  ...

deviceQuery, CUDA Driver = CUDART, CUDA Devices found = 1

Result = PASS
```

Additionally, another sample program, bandwidthTest, can be executed to check the memory bandwidth between the device and the host. Navigate to the bandwidthTest directory:

On Unix-based systems:

```
cd /usr/local/cuda/samples/1_Utilities/bandwidthTest
```

On Windows:

```
cd "C:\Program Files\NVIDIA GPU Computing Toolkit\CUDA\vX.Y\samples\1
    _Utilities\bandwidthTest"
```

Compile and run the test:

For Unix-based systems:

```
sudo make && ./bandwidthTest
```

For Windows:

```
msbuild bandwidthTest_vs2019.vcxproj /t:Build /p:Configuration=Release
bandwidthTest.exe
```

The output will show the performance metrics of the memory transfers, aiding in identifying any potential issues:

```
[CUDA Bandwidth Test] - Starting...
Running on...

 Device 0: Tesla V100-PCIE-32GB
 Quick Mode

 Host to Device Bandwidth, 1 Device(s)
 PINNED Memory Transfers
   Transfer Size (Bytes)   Bandwidth(MB/s)
   33554432                12638.4

 Device to Host Bandwidth, 1 Device(s)
 PINNED Memory Transfers
   Transfer Size (Bytes)   Bandwidth(MB/s)
   33554432                12628.2

...

Result = PASS
```

Performing these tests confirms that the CUDA Toolkit and NVIDIA drivers are properly installed and functioning correctly, setting the stage for CUDA-based development and computation tasks. Here is the corrected LaTeX text:

3.9 Updating and Uninstalling CUDA Toolkit

Updating and uninstalling the CUDA Toolkit is crucial for maintaining an up-to-date and efficient development environment. This section provides comprehensive instructions for performing these tasks on Windows, Linux, and macOS. It is assumed the reader has administrative privileges where required and is familiar with basic command line operations.

Updating CUDA Toolkit

To update the CUDA Toolkit, the following steps should be performed:

- **Check for Updates**

  Before updating, check the current version of CUDA Toolkit installed on your system. This can be done via the command line:

  ```
  nvcc --version
  ```

  The output indicates the version of CUDA installed. Compare this with the latest version available on the NVIDIA website.

- **Download the Latest Toolkit**

  Navigate to the CUDA Toolkit download page on the NVIDIA Developer website. Select the appropriate version for your operating system and download the installer.

- **Install the Update**

  Follow the installation instructions for your operating system, as described in earlier sections of this chapter. When prompted, opt to upgrade the existing CUDA Toolkit installation.

Uninstalling CUDA Toolkit

Uninstalling the CUDA Toolkit involves removing any associated files and reverting environment settings to their original state. The process varies across operating systems.

Uninstalling on Windows

- **Open Control Panel**

  Access the Control Panel from the Start menu and navigate to *Programs and Features*.

- **Select NVIDIA CUDA Toolkit**

  In the list of installed programs, find and select *NVIDIA CUDA Toolkit*. Click *Uninstall/Change*.

- **Follow the Uninstallation Wizard**

  The uninstallation wizard will guide you through the process. Ensure all components of the CUDA Toolkit are selected for removal.

Uninstalling on Linux

The process for Linux can vary between distributions. Most commonly, package managers such as apt for Ubuntu or yum for Fedora are used:

```
# For Ubuntu
sudo apt-get --purge remove "cuda*"
sudo apt-get autoremove

# For Fedora
sudo yum remove cuda
```

Additionally, ensure that the CUDA installation path is removed:

```
rm -rf /usr/local/cuda*
```

Finally, remove any environment variable settings added during the installation process. These are typically found in ~/.bashrc, ~/.profile, or ~/.bash_profile.

Uninstalling on macOS

- **Open Terminal**

  Launch the Terminal application.

- **Execute the Uninstaller**

  NVIDIA provides an uninstall script with the installation package. Execute the following command:

  ```
  sudo /Developer/NVIDIA/CUDA-X.Y/bin/uninstall_cuda_X.Y.pl
  ```

  Replace X.Y with the version number of CUDA installed on your system (e.g., 10.1).

Verifying Completion:

To confirm that the CUDA Toolkit has been completely uninstalled, check for the presence of CUDA directories and binaries:

```
nvcc --version
```

If the command is not found, the uninstallation was successful.

3.10 Using Docker for CUDA Development

Docker provides an efficient and reproducible environment for CUDA development. It allows developers to encapsulate code, dependencies, and runtime environments into a standardized unit called a container. This section delves into the setup and usage of Docker for CUDA development.

To utilize Docker with CUDA, one must ensure the installation of Docker, the NVIDIA Docker runtime, and the appropriate NVIDIA drivers.

Prerequisites:

- A system with an NVIDIA GPU.
- NVIDIA drivers appropriate for your GPU.
- Docker CE (Community Edition).
- NVIDIA Docker runtime.

Step 1: Installing Docker CE

First, Docker must be installed on your system. The following instructions are for Ubuntu-based systems:

```
sudo apt-get update
sudo apt-get install \
    apt-transport-https \
    ca-certificates \
    curl \
    software-properties-common
curl -fsSL https://download.docker.com/linux/ubuntu/gpg | sudo apt-key add -
sudo add-apt-repository \
   "deb [arch=amd64] https://download.docker.com/linux/ubuntu \
   $(lsb_release -cs) \
   stable"
sudo apt-get update
sudo apt-get install docker-ce
```

To verify Docker installation, run:

```
sudo docker run hello-world
```

```
Output:
Hello from Docker!
This message shows that your installation appears to be working correctly.
```

Step 2: Installing NVIDIA Docker runtime

NVIDIA Docker runtime is required to support GPU-accelerated Docker containers. Install the NVIDIA Docker runtime by running the following commands:

```
curl -s -L https://nvidia.github.io/nvidia-docker/gpgkey | sudo apt-key add -
distribution=$(. /etc/os-release;echo $ID$VERSION_ID)
curl -s -L https://nvidia.github.io/nvidia-docker/$distribution/nvidia-docker.list | sudo
    tee /etc/apt/sources.list.d/nvidia-docker.list
sudo apt-get update && sudo apt-get install -y nvidia-docker2
sudo systemctl restart docker
```

To verify the NVIDIA-Docker installation, run:

```
sudo docker run --runtime=nvidia --rm nvidia/cuda:10.1-base nvidia-smi
```

A correctly configured system will output the status of the GPU.

```
Output:
+-----------------------------------------------------------------------------+
| NVIDIA-SMI 450.36.06    Driver Version: 450.36.06    CUDA Version: 11.0     |
|-------------------------------+----------------------+----------------------+
| GPU  Name        Persistence-M| Bus-Id        Disp.A | Volatile Uncorr. ECC |
| Fan  Temp  Perf  Pwr:Usage/Cap|         Memory-Usage | GPU-Util  Compute M. |
|===============================+======================+======================|
|   0  GeForce GTX 1080    Off  | 00000000:01:00.0  On |                  N/A |
| 0%   35C    P8     8W / 180W |    411MiB /  8110MiB |      0%      Default |
+-------------------------------+----------------------+----------------------+
```

Step 3: Creating and Running a CUDA Docker Container

To create a CUDA-enabled Docker container, use the official NVIDIA CUDA Docker image as a base. Create a Dockerfile:

```
# Base image
FROM nvidia/cuda:11.0-base

# Add maintainer for the Dockerfile
LABEL maintainer="example@example.com"

# Set working directory
WORKDIR /usr/src/app

# Copy local files to the Docker container
COPY . .

# Install required packages
RUN apt-get update && apt-get install -y \
    build-essential \
    && rm -rf /var/lib/apt/lists/*

# Compile the CUDA code
RUN nvcc hello.cu -o hello

# Command to run when container starts
CMD ["./hello"]
```

An example hello.cu CUDA file:

```
#include <iostream>

__global__ void helloCUDA() {
    printf("Hello from GPU!\\n");
}

int main() {
    helloCUDA<<<1, 1>>>();
    cudaDeviceSynchronize();
    std::cout << "Hello from CPU!" << std::endl;
    return 0;
}
```

To build and run the Docker container, execute:

```
sudo docker build -t cuda-hello-world .
sudo docker run --runtime=nvidia --rm cuda-hello-world
```

```
Output:
Hello from GPU!
Hello from CPU!
```

Benefits of Using Docker for CUDA Development:

- **Reproducibility:** Consistent environments for all collaborators using Docker images.
- **Isolation:** No interference with the host system, avoiding configuration conflicts.
- **Portability:** Seamlessly migrate containers across different systems.
- **Scalability:** Efficient resource usage, especially when scaling applications across clusters.

Ensure the correct configuration of the Docker engine and installed NVIDIA-Docker runtime by verifying the CUDA programming components within the container.

Chapter 4

Understanding CUDA Kernels and Threads

This chapter covers the essentials of CUDA kernels and threads, explaining what CUDA kernels are and how to write and launch them. It discusses thread indexing, mapping, and the role of block and grid dimensions in the execution of parallel tasks. The chapter also addresses thread synchronization and cooperation using shared memory, explores thread divergence issues, and highlights best practices for designing efficient CUDA kernels.

4.1 What is a CUDA Kernel?

A CUDA kernel is a function written in C++, augmented with CUDA-specific extensions, that runs on the GPU rather than the CPU. It is the fundamental building block of CUDA programs, allowing developers to leverage the parallel processing capabilities of NVIDIA GPUs. A CUDA kernel can be executed simultaneously by thousands of threads, making it a powerful tool for performing highly parallel computations.

When a CUDA kernel is called, it is executed N times in parallel by N different threads, as opposed to a standard C++ function which is executed once on the calling thread. These threads are organized into a hierarchy of three levels: grid, blocks, and threads. Each thread within a block can access shared memory, which is specific to that block and has lower latency than global memory. This hierarchical structure is crucial for managing parallel tasks effectively and writing efficient CUDA applications.

To declare a CUDA kernel, the `__global__` keyword is used before the function's return type. The function's arguments are passed similarly to a regular C++ function, but it gets executed on the GPU. An example declaration of a CUDA kernel function is shown below:

```
__global__ void myKernel(int *data, int value) {
    // Kernel code goes here
}
```

Each kernel function must be explicitly called from the host (CPU) code and executed on the device (GPU). The syntax for launching a kernel includes specifying the grid and block dimensions within triple angle brackets `<<< >>>`. An example of launching the previously declared kernel with a certain grid and block configuration is as follows:

```
int main() {
    int *dev_data;
    int value = 10;

    // Allocate memory on the GPU
    cudaMalloc((void**)&dev_data, size * sizeof(int));

    // Specify grid and block dimensions
    dim3 gridDim(1);
    dim3 blockDim(256);

    // Launch the kernel
    myKernel<<<gridDim, blockDim>>>(dev_data, value);

    return 0;
}
```

The dimensions of the grid and blocks specify how the threads are organized when the kernel is executed. The grid is a 2D or 3D array of thread blocks, and each block is a 1D, 2D, or 3D array of threads. This separation into grids and blocks provides a scalable way to map the problem domain effectively, distributing the workload across thousands of threads.

Within the kernel function, each thread has a unique index that can be queried to identify its position within its block and grid. These indices are available through built-in variables such as `threadIdx`, `blockIdx`, and their associated dimensions, `blockDim` and `gridDim`. An example illustrating how to compute a unique thread identifier is shown below:

```
__global__ void myKernel(int *data, int value) {
    int idx = threadIdx.x + blockIdx.x * blockDim.x;
    data[idx] = value;
```

```
}
```

In the example above, each thread computes a unique index idx based on its threadIdx.x and blockIdx.x values, allowing it to access and modify its corresponding element in the data array.

CUDA kernels can also utilize various types of device memory, such as shared memory, constant memory, and texture memory, to optimize their performance. Shared memory, for instance, is a block-specific memory that provides faster access compared to global memory and allows threads within the same block to communicate and collaborate efficiently.

Moreover, CUDA kernels can include synchronization points using the __syncthreads() function, which ensures that all threads within a block reach the synchronization point before any of them proceed. This is critical for avoiding race conditions and ensuring data integrity when threads in a block are working together on a shared dataset.

Understanding the fundamental concepts of a CUDA kernel, such as thread hierarchy, memory types, and synchronization mechanisms, is essential for leveraging the full power of CUDA-enabled GPUs. By effectively utilizing these features, developers can write highly parallelized and optimized applications that perform complex computations much faster than their CPU-only counterparts.

4.2 Writing Your First CUDA Kernel

A CUDA kernel is essentially a function written in C++ that, when called, is executed N times in parallel by N different CUDA threads. These threads are organized into blocks, and the blocks themselves form a grid. The execution configuration, including the number of threads and blocks, must be specified when launching the kernel.

To write your first CUDA kernel, begin by defining the kernel function using the __global__ declaration specifier. This tells the compiler that the function will be executed on the device (GPU) but can be called from the host (CPU).

Here is a simple CUDA kernel that adds two integers:

```
__global__ void add(int *a, int *b, int *c) {
    *c = *a + *b;
}
```

In this example, the __global__ keyword is used to declare the add function as a kernel. The asterisks (*) indicate that the parameters a, b, and c are pointers to integers. This kernel performs a simple addition operation on the values pointed to by a and b, storing the result in the location pointed to by c.

Next, the kernel needs to be invoked (or launched) from the host code. This is done using a specific syntax, where the execution configuration is specified within triple angular brackets. Here is how you would call the kernel:

```
int main() {
    int a, b, c;
    int *d_a, *d_b, *d_c;
    int size = sizeof(int);

    // Allocate memory on the device
    cudaMalloc(&d_a, size);
    cudaMalloc(&d_b, size);
    cudaMalloc(&d_c, size);

    // Initialize host variables
    a = 2;
    b = 7;

    // Copy variables from host to device
    cudaMemcpy(d_a, &a, size, cudaMemcpyHostToDevice);
    cudaMemcpy(d_b, &b, size, cudaMemcpyHostToDevice);

    // Launch the add() kernel on the GPU
    add<<<1, 1>>>(d_a, d_b, d_c);

    // Copy result from device to host
    cudaMemcpy(&c, d_c, size, cudaMemcpyDeviceToHost);

    // Cleanup
    cudaFree(d_a);
    cudaFree(d_b);
    cudaFree(d_c);

    // Print the result
    printf("Result of %d + %d = %d\n", a, b, c);

    return 0;
}
```

First, we allocate memory on the device for the variables d_a, d_b, and d_c using the cudaMalloc function. The sizeof(int) informs the allocator of the amount of memory to be allocated. Next, we initialize host variables, then copy these values to the allocated device memory using the cudaMemcpy function with the cudaMemcpyHostToDevice flag.

The kernel is then launched using the «<1, 1»> execution configuration. The numbers in the triple angular brackets specify the dimensions of the grid and block, respectively. In this case, we are launching a single block with a single thread.

After the kernel has finished executing, we copy the result back to the host memory using cudaMemcpy with the cudaMemcpyDeviceToHost flag. Finally, we free the allocated device memory using cudaFree and print the result.

Here is the expected output when running the program:

```
Result of 2 + 7 = 9
```

This example demonstrates the fundamental steps required to write and launch a CUDA kernel. The key concepts include defining the kernel with __global__, allocating and copying memory between the host and device, and launching the kernel with an appropriate execution configuration. With these basics, you can begin to harness the power of parallel computation on the GPU.

4.3 Launching CUDA Kernels

The launch of CUDA kernels is a crucial aspect of parallel programming with CUDA. To effectively utilize the computational power of GPUs, it is essential to understand how to invoke CUDA kernels correctly and efficiently. In this section, the syntax and mechanics of launching CUDA kernels are discussed in detail, encompassing various parameters and configurations that can significantly impact performance.

A CUDA kernel is launched using triple angle brackets, also known as the *execution configuration* or *«<...»>* syntax. The general form of a kernel launch is as follows:

```
kernel_function<<<num_blocks, num_threads_per_block, shared_mem_bytes,
    stream>>>(kernel parameters);
```

Here, each element within the *«<...»>* brackets defines how the kernel is executed:

- num_blocks: Specifies the number of thread blocks to be used.
- num_threads_per_block: Specifies the number of threads within each block.
- shared_mem_bytes (optional): Allocates dynamic shared memory.

- stream (optional): Specifies the CUDA stream for asynchronous execution.

Consider a simple example where a kernel adds corresponding elements of two arrays:

```
__global__ void vectorAdd(const float *A, const float *B, float *C, int N) {
    int idx = blockIdx.x * blockDim.x + threadIdx.x;
    if (idx < N) {
        C[idx] = A[idx] + B[idx];
    }
}
```

To launch the vectorAdd kernel with, for example, 256 threads per block and an appropriate number of blocks to cover an array size N, the following code can be used:

```
int N = ...; // Assume N is defined
dim3 threadsPerBlock(256);
dim3 numBlocks((N + threadsPerBlock.x - 1) / threadsPerBlock.x);
vectorAdd<<<numBlocks, threadsPerBlock>>>(A, B, C, N);
```

The dim3 type is often used for the num_blocks and num_threads_per_block parameters, allowing specification in up to three dimensions, i.e., x, y, and z. This multi-dimensional configuration supports complex structures like matrices, 3D volumes, and other multi-dimensional data representations.

Dynamic Shared Memory Allocation

The third parameter in the execution configuration, shared_mem_bytes, is used to allocate dynamic shared memory. Dynamic shared memory provides scratchpad memory on a per-block basis, enabling faster access for threads within the same block compared to global memory.

For instance, suppose a kernel involves matrix multiplication, where shared memory is used to hold temporary values. The launch would include the amount of shared memory required:

```
matrixMultiply<<<numBlocks, threadsPerBlock, sharedMemSize>>>(A, B, C, N);
```

The kernel definition can declare dynamic shared memory as follows:

```
__global__ void matrixMultiply(const float *A, const float *B, float *C, int N) {
    extern __shared__ float sharedMemory[];
    // Implementation using sharedMemory for intermediate computations
}
```

CUDA Streams for Asynchronous Execution

CUDA streams allow multiple kernel executions and memory operations to be performed asynchronously, overlapping to utilize the GPU more efficiently. By default, operations are part of the 0 stream, also known as the *default stream*. However, explicit streams can be created and used to manage concurrency:

```
cudaStream_t stream;
cudaStreamCreate(&stream);
vectorAdd<<<numBlocks, threadsPerBlock, 0, stream>>>(A, B, C, N);
cudaStreamDestroy(stream);
```

This code creates a CUDA stream, launches the vectorAdd kernel within this stream, and destroys the stream after the kernel execution. Using streams enhances control over task scheduling, priority, and synchronization between different operations.

Synchronizing Kernel Execution

Although kernels launched in non-default streams may execute asynchronously, i.e., control returns to the CPU before kernel completion, synchronization primitives ensure complete execution before proceeding. CUDA provides cudaDeviceSynchronize() to block the CPU until all preceding operations finish:

```
vectorAdd<<<numBlocks, threadsPerBlock>>>(A, B, C, N);
cudaDeviceSynchronize();
```

Alternatively, cudaStreamSynchronize() waits for operations in a specific stream:

```
vectorAdd<<<numBlocks, threadsPerBlock, 0, stream>>>(A, B, C, N);
cudaStreamSynchronize(stream);
```

Proper synchronization is crucial when subsequent CPU operations depend on the results of kernel executions or when multiple streams need coordinated execution.

Error Handling in Kernel Launches

Kernel launches are asynchronous by default, and errors may not propagate immediately to the host code. cudaGetLastError() helps detect any errors after a kernel launch:

```
vectorAdd<<<numBlocks, threadsPerBlock>>>(A, B, C, N);
cudaError_t err = cudaGetLastError();
if (err != cudaSuccess) {
    printf("CUDA Kernel launch failed: %s\n", cudaGetErrorString(err));
}
```

This method ensures that errors are detected promptly, enabling proper handling and debugging.

Understanding the intricacies of launching CUDA kernels, including configuration parameters, dynamic shared memory, streams, synchronization, and error handling, is fundamental for optimizing GPU utilization and achieving high-performance parallel computing.

4.4 Understanding CUDA Threads

Threads are the fundamental units of execution in CUDA programming. Within the CUDA architecture, threads are lightweight, as they are not associated with any heavy-weight processes. CUDA threads are able to run thousands or even millions simultaneously. This parallelism is the core strength of CUDA and allows for significant acceleration of computationally intensive tasks.

Each thread operates independently but can share data with other threads through various forms of memory, including shared memory and global memory. Understanding the structure and execution model of CUDA threads is essential for writing efficient parallel programs.

Threads in CUDA are organized into a hierarchical structure consisting of blocks and grids. Each kernel execution specifies the number of blocks in a grid and the number of threads in each block. This organization provides a significant amount of flexibility and scalability.

When a CUDA kernel is launched, threads are organized in a three-level hierarchy:

- **Thread:** The smallest execution unit in CUDA.
- **Block:** A collection of threads that can cooperate among themselves through shared memory and have synchronization barriers.
- **Grid:** A collection of blocks that execute the kernel across the entire data set.

Each thread within a block can access shared memory, which is unique to that block, and all threads can access global memory.

To better understand CUDA threads, consider the example of performing element-wise addition of two arrays. Each element addition can be executed by a separate thread, achieving parallelism.

```
__global__ void add(int *a, int *b, int *c) {
```

```
  int index = threadIdx.x;
  c[index] = a[index] + b[index];
}
```

In this example, the threadIdx.x variable is used to identify each thread's unique index within a block. This allows each thread to operate on different elements of the arrays independently.

The threadIdx variable is a built-in 3-dimensional vector available to all threads. Threads can be indexed along the x, y, and z dimensions using threadIdx.x, threadIdx.y, and threadIdx.z respectively. This 3D organization allows programmers to better match the parallel structure of many problems, such as those involving 2D or 3D data arrays.

Within a block, threads can synchronize with each other using the __syncthreads() function. This barrier synchronization ensures that all threads in the block reach the barrier before any thread can proceed beyond it. This is essential when some threads produce results that other threads will consume.

For more complex operations involving multi-dimensional data, the grid organization is leveraged. The built-in variables blockIdx and blockDim are used to manage blocks within a grid.

Consider extending the array addition example to cover a larger array by organizing threads into blocks and grids:

```
__global__ void add(int *a, int *b, int *c, int N) {
  int index = blockIdx.x * blockDim.x + threadIdx.x;
  if (index < N)
    c[index] = a[index] + b[index];
}
```

In this extended example, blocks are indexed by blockIdx.x, and blockDim .x specifies the number of threads per block. The overall thread index in the grid is determined by the combination of blockIdx.x, blockDim.x, and threadIdx.x.

To launch this kernel, the number of blocks and threads per block must be specified:

```
int N = 1024;
int threadsPerBlock = 256;
int blocksPerGrid = (N + threadsPerBlock - 1) / threadsPerBlock;
add<<<blocksPerGrid, threadsPerBlock>>>(a, b, c, N);
```

This configuration ensures that enough threads are created to cover all elements in the arrays. The formula for blocksPerGrid ensures that fractional blocks, which are partially filled, are included in the execution.

Understanding the behavior and organization of threads within blocks and grids, and how they map to large data sets, allows for effective design and execution of parallel algorithms on a CUDA-enabled GPU.

4.5 Thread Indexing and Mapping

In CUDA, threads are organized into a grid of thread blocks, which provides a scalable way to handle massive parallel computations. Each thread within this structure can be uniquely identified by its indices, which are crucial for determining the portion of data it processes. This section dives into the mechanisms of thread indexing and mapping, essential concepts for effectively harnessing the power of CUDA.

Each thread in a CUDA kernel can be identified uniquely through its thread indices. These indices allow threads to select data elements they will operate on, enabling concurrent execution of parallel tasks. CUDA provides three built-in variables to facilitate thread indexing: threadIdx, blockIdx, and blockDim.

threadIdx Refers to the thread's index within its block.

blockIdx Refers to the block's index within the grid.

blockDim Specifies the dimensions of the thread block.

Each of these variables is of type dim3, a three-dimensional vector designed to handle multi-dimensional data structures. The use of dim3 facilitates the decomposition of data processing tasks along three axes: x, y, and z. Here's an example illustrating these variables:

```
// Sample CUDA Kernel
__global__ void exampleKernel() {
    int x = threadIdx.x;
    int y = threadIdx.y;
    int z = threadIdx.z;
    int bx = blockIdx.x;
    int by = blockIdx.y;
    int bz = blockIdx.z;
    int blockDimX = blockDim.x;
    int blockDimY = blockDim.y;
    int blockDimZ = blockDim.z;

    // Each thread prints its unique indices
    printf("Thread (%d, %d, %d) in Block (%d, %d, %d) with BlockDim (%d, %d, %d)
        \n",
        x, y, z, bx, by, bz, blockDimX, blockDimY, blockDimZ);
}
```

Global memory allocation is performed using the cudaMalloc function. This function assigns a specified number of bytes to the device's global memory and returns a pointer to the allocated memory.

```
cudaError_t cudaMalloc(void **devPtr, size_t size);
```

devPtr is a pointer to the allocated device memory, and size denotes the number of bytes to allocate. The function returns an error code of type cudaError_t, where cudaSuccess indicates successful allocation. The allocated memory must be explicitly freed using the cudaFree function to avoid memory leaks.

```
cudaError_t cudaFree(void *devPtr);
```

devPtr is the pointer to memory previously allocated with cudaMalloc.

Example:

Consider the following example that demonstrates memory allocation and deallocation.

```
#include <cuda_runtime.h>
#include <iostream>
#include <vector>

int main() {
    int numElements = 1024;
    size_t size = numElements * sizeof(float);

    // Allocate memory on the GPU
    float *d_array;
    cudaError_t err = cudaMalloc((void**)&d_array, size);

    if (err != cudaSuccess) {
        std::cerr << "Failed to allocate device memory (error code "
                  << cudaGetErrorString(err) << ")!" << std::endl;
        return EXIT_FAILURE;
    }

    // Free the allocated memory
    err = cudaFree(d_array);

    if (err != cudaSuccess) {
        std::cerr << "Failed to free device memory (error code "
                  << cudaGetErrorString(err) << ")!" << std::endl;
        return EXIT_FAILURE;
    }

    return EXIT_SUCCESS;
}
```

In this example, cudaMalloc is used to allocate memory for an array of floats on the device. The allocated memory is then freed using cudaFree.

Pitched Memory Allocation:

For 2D and 3D arrays, it is often beneficial to use pitched memory allocation to ensure proper alignment and efficient memory access. Pitched memory can be allocated using the cudaMallocPitch function.

```
cudaError_t cudaMallocPitch(void **devPtr, size_t *pitch,
                            size_t width, size_t height);
```

devPtr is a pointer to the allocated pitched memory, pitch is the width in bytes of the allocated region (including any padding), width is the requested width of the allocation, and height is the requested height.

Example:

```
#include <cuda_runtime.h>
#include <iostream>

int main() {
    size_t width = 64;
    size_t height = 64;
    float *d_array;
    size_t pitch;

    // Allocate pitched memory
    cudaError_t err = cudaMallocPitch((void**)&d_array, &pitch,
                                      width * sizeof(float), height);

    if (err != cudaSuccess) {
        std::cerr << "Failed to allocate pitched memory (error code "
                  << cudaGetErrorString(err) << ")!" << std::endl;
        return EXIT_FAILURE;
    }

    // Free the allocated pitched memory
    err = cudaFree(d_array);

    if (err != cudaSuccess) {
        std::cerr << "Failed to free pitched memory (error code "
                  << cudaGetErrorString(err) << ")!" << std::endl;
        return EXIT_FAILURE;
    }

    return EXIT_SUCCESS;
}
```

In this example, cudaMallocPitch is utilized to allocate a 2D array with padding to ensure proper memory alignment, which is then freed using cudaFree.

Unified Memory Allocation:

Unified Memory, accessible from both the CPU and GPU, can be allocated using cudaMallocManaged. This simplifies memory management as it reduces the need for explicit memory transfers.

```
        unifiedMemoryPtr[i] = static_cast<float>(i);
    }

    kernel<<<1, 100>>>(unifiedMemoryPtr);
    cudaDeviceSynchronize();

    for (int i = 0; i < 100; ++i) {
        printf("%f\n", unifiedMemoryPtr[i]);
    }

    cudaFree(unifiedMemoryPtr);
    return 0;
}
```

In this code:

- Unified Memory is allocated and initialized on the host.
- A kernel is launched to process the data on the device.
- The host reads back the processed data after synchronization.

Memory Deallocation

Memory allocated with `cudaMallocManaged` should be deallocated using `cudaFree`. For example:

```
cudaFree(unifiedMemoryPtr);
```

This ensures that all the Unified Memory allocated is properly released, avoiding memory leaks.

Performance Considerations

While Unified Memory simplifies programming, it can impose performance overheads due to the automatic migration and coherence mechanisms. To optimize performance, it is essential to consider the following strategies:

- **Prefetching**: Using `cudaMemPrefetchAsync` to explicitly prefetch memory to the device can reduce page faults and improve performance.

  ```
  cudaMemPrefetchAsync(unifiedMemoryPtr, 100 * sizeof(float),
          cudaCpuDeviceId);
  ```

- **Memory Advisory Functions**: Using memory advisory functions like `cudaMemAdvise` to provide hints about the memory usage patterns can assist the CUDA runtime in optimizing data placement and access.

```
cudaMemAdvise(unifiedMemoryPtr, 100 * sizeof(float),
    cudaMemAdviseSetPreferredLocation, cudaCpuDeviceId);
```

- **Access Patterns**: Ensuring that memory access patterns are as regular and sequential as possible can reduce the overhead associated with memory migrations and page faults.

Caveats

Several caveats should be noted while using Unified Memory:

- While Unified Memory simplifies data management, it does not eliminate the need for optimization. Properly managing memory allocation, access, and deallocation is critical for achieving high performance.
- Migration and coherence overheads can impact the performance of memory-bound applications. Profiling tools should be used to identify bottlenecks and optimize memory usage effectively.

Unified Memory is a powerful tool in the CUDA programming model that facilitates easier memory management and data sharing between the host and device. By understanding its functionality and applying best practices, developers can efficiently utilize Unified Memory to enhance the performance and productivity of their CUDA applications.

5.7 Memory Allocation and Deallocation

Memory management in CUDA is fundamental for the effective utilization of the GPU's performance capabilities. Proper allocation and deallocation of memory ensure that resources are used efficiently and that applications do not suffer from memory leaks or performance degradation due to improper handling of memory resources.

The primary functions utilized for memory allocation and deallocation in CUDA are cudaMalloc and cudaFree, respectively. Additionally, there are specialized functions for specific types of memory (e.g., cudaMallocManaged for unified memory and cudaMallocPitch for pitched memory allocations).

Global Memory Allocation:

Constant memory allocation differs from global memory in that it is done statically and has a fixed size set at compile time. Data transfer to constant memory is done from the host using specific CUDA API functions. Below is an example of how to copy data to constant memory from the host:

```
float hostArray[256];
// Initialize hostArray with values
cudaMemcpyToSymbol(constArray, hostArray, sizeof(float) * 256);
```

The cudaMemcpyToSymbol function is employed to copy data from host memory to constant memory. The parameters include the symbol that represents the constant memory array, the source array on the host, and the size of the data to be copied.

When accessing constant memory within a kernel, the following syntactical approach applies:

```
__global__ void kernelFunction()
{
    int idx = threadIdx.x;
    float val = constArray[idx];
    // Utilize val
}
```

Constant memory access is optimized for broadcasting, where multiple threads read the same memory address. However, due to its small size and read-only nature, it is suitable only for specific application use-cases such as lookup tables, constants, and coefficients.

An important aspect is the constant memory cache, which is shared among all multiprocessors on the GPU. When a warp of threads accesses the same address in constant memory, the value is fetched once from device memory and broadcast to all threads in the warp. This broadcast mechanism significantly reduces memory latency compared to global memory accesses. However, if all threads in a warp access different addresses in constant memory, performance may degrade to that of global memory access due to cache thrashing.

Here is a detailed example illustrating the entire process of managing constant memory, including copying data and kernel launch:

```
#include <cuda_runtime.h>
#include <cstdio>

__constant__ float constData[256];

__global__ void constantMemoryKernel(float *output)
{
    int index = threadIdx.x;
    output[index] = constData[index] * 2.0f;
```

```
}

void check_cuda_error(const char* message)
{
    cudaError_t err = cudaGetLastError();
    if (err != cudaSuccess)
    {
        printf("CUDA Error: %s: %s\n", message, cudaGetErrorString(err));
        exit(EXIT_FAILURE);
    }
}

int main()
{
    float hostData[256];
    for (int i = 0; i < 256; ++i)
    {
        hostData[i] = static_cast<float>(i);
    }

    cudaMemcpyToSymbol(constData, hostData, sizeof(float) * 256);

    float *deviceOutput;
    cudaMalloc(&deviceOutput, sizeof(float) * 256);

    constantMemoryKernel<<<1, 256>>>(deviceOutput);
    check_cuda_error("Kernel launch");

    float hostOutput[256];
    cudaMemcpy(hostOutput, deviceOutput, sizeof(float) * 256,
        cudaMemcpyDeviceToHost);
    check_cuda_error("Memory copy from device to host");

    cudaFree(deviceOutput);

    for (int i = 0; i < 256; ++i)
    {
        printf("%f ", hostOutput[i]);
    }

    return 0;
}
```

This example includes a kernel that reads from constant memory, a function to copy data to constant memory, and the necessary code to handle memory on the host and device. The kernel, constantMemoryKernel, accesses the constData array and performs simple operations for demonstration purposes.

Performance considerations for constant memory are crucial. Despite its benefits, constant memory should be used judiciously, keeping in mind its limited size and the nature of its cache. Developers should ensure that bandwidth utilization is optimized by exploiting temporal locality, i.e., designing kernels such that multiple threads access the same or nearby memory locations.

Error handling when dealing with constant memory operations is sim-

- **Calculating Grid and Block Dimensions**

To compute these dimensions, it helps to start with the total number of work items (e.g., pixels in an image). Assume we need to process a 4096x4096 image:

```
int imageWidth = 4096;
int imageHeight = 4096;
dim3 threadsPerBlock(32, 32);
dim3 numBlocks((imageWidth + threadsPerBlock.x - 1) / threadsPerBlock.x,
              (imageHeight + threadsPerBlock.y - 1) / threadsPerBlock.y);
```

The dimensions of numBlocks are computed to cover all work items. The calculations ensure full coverage by rounding up the division. Note that threadsPerBlock.x and threadsPerBlock.y must appropriately divide the problem size, and should these dimensions be suboptimal, the under-utilization of GPU resources or thread contention might occur.

Different configurations of grid and block dimensions can significantly influence performance. It is imperative to experiment with various configurations since the optimal layout depends on hardware capabilities and specific problem constraints.

- **Threads per Block and Block per Grid Considerations**

Several considerations arise when deciding on the number of threads per block and the number of blocks per grid:

- **Resource allocation:** Each thread requires a certain amount of register and shared memory. The combined needs of all threads in a block must not exceed the limits of the GPU's SM (Streaming Multiprocessor). Thus, block size decisions might be constrained by the application's register and shared memory use.
- **Occupancy:** Occupancy is the ratio of active warps to the maximum number of warps supported on an SM. Higher occupancy may lead to better latency hiding, but this relationship is not strictly linear and depends on the workload's complexity.
- **Memory access patterns:** Blocks and thread configurations should ensure coalesced accesses to global memory to maximize memory bandwidth utilization. Poor memory access patterns can degrade performance significantly due to non-coalesced memory accesses leading to memory transaction overhead.

- **Kernel code structure:** The structure of the kernel code may also influence the dimensions. Conditional branches dependent on thread indices or block indices might lead to divergence or warp serialization, reducing overall efficiency.

```
// Kernel that benefits from well-chosen block and grid dimensions
__global__ void processImageKernel(float *input, float *output, int width, int height)
{
    int x = blockIdx.x * blockDim.x + threadIdx.x;
    int y = blockIdx.y * blockDim.y + threadIdx.y;

    if (x < width && y < height) {
        // Process the pixel at (x, y)
        int idx = y * width + x;
        output[idx] = input[idx] * 2.0f; // Example operation
    }
}
```

In this kernel, each thread calculates its coordinates using blockIdx and threadIdx, ensuring correct indexing into the image arrays. The bounds checking with if statements ensures that threads do not access out-of-bounds memory, crucial for avoiding segmentation faults or undefined behaviors.

- **Practical Tips for Choosing Dimensions**

- **Profiling and Testing:** Utilize CUDA profiling tools like NVIDIA Nsight Systems and Nsight Compute to test different configuration setups.

- **Incremental Changes:** Make incremental adjustments to block and grid sizes rather than large changes, observing the performance impact at each step.

- **Application-Specific Tuning:** Some applications benefit from more threads per block, while others do better with more blocks; domain knowledge can guide initial configuration choices.

- **Keep Thread Count Close to Multiples of 32:** The CUDA architecture executes threads in warps of 32. Higher efficiency is often achieved when the total number of threads per block is a multiple of 32, avoiding partially filled warps.

Using these techniques, one can derive optimal grid and block dimensions tailored to specific application needs, ensuring efficient CUDA kernel execution and resource utilization.

When this kernel is launched, each thread will print its unique identifiers, displaying how it fits within the hierarchical structure of threads and blocks.

```
Thread (0, 0, 0) in Block (0, 0, 0) with BlockDim (16, 16, 1)
Thread (1, 0, 0) in Block (0, 0, 0) with BlockDim (16, 16, 1)
Thread (2, 0, 0) in Block (0, 0, 0) with BlockDim (16, 16, 1)
...
```

The indices threadIdx and blockIdx enable threads to uniquely identify themselves within the grid. To effectively map threads to data elements, it's common practice to calculate a unique global index. This global index can be derived as follows for a one-dimensional grid:

```
int globalIndex = blockIdx.x * blockDim.x + threadIdx.x;
```

For more complex multi-dimensional grids, the global index computation can be extended:

```
int globalIndexX = blockIdx.x * blockDim.x + threadIdx.x;
int globalIndexY = blockIdx.y * blockDim.y + threadIdx.y;
int globalIndexZ = blockIdx.z * blockDim.z + threadIdx.z;
```

These calculations allow a thread to operate on the correct data element in one, two, or three-dimensional grids. Let's consider an example where we process a two-dimensional image by mapping each thread to a pixel in the image:

```
// CUDA Kernel for image processing
__global__ void processImageKernel(float* image, int width, int height) {
    int x = blockIdx.x * blockDim.x + threadIdx.x;
    int y = blockIdx.y * blockDim.y + threadIdx.y;

    int index = y * width + x;

    if (x < width && y < height) {
        // Process the pixel (e.g., invert color)
        image[index] = 1.0f - image[index];
    }
}
```

In this example, each thread computes its unique indices x and y to process a corresponding pixel in the two-dimensional image array. The condition ensures that threads outside the image boundaries do not attempt to access invalid memory locations.

Thread mapping becomes particularly significant when dealing with non-contiguous data or when applying more complex operations. Here are a few additional considerations:

- When processing multi-dimensional data, always ensure that the dimensions of blocks and the grid are chosen to cover the entire data structure.

- Avoid thread divergence by ensuring that threads within a warp follow the same execution path whenever possible.

- Utilize shared memory effectively to minimize global memory accesses, enhancing performance.

The concepts of thread indexing and mapping form the cornerstone of efficient CUDA programming. By carefully calculating global indices and considering dimensions, you can unleash powerful parallel processing capabilities to tackle a wide range of computational problems.

4.6 Block and Grid Dimensions

The execution model of CUDA hinges significantly on the structure and organization of threads into blocks and blocks into grids. This hierarchical organization enables scalable parallelism and efficient execution on the NVIDIA GPU architecture. Understanding and effectively utilizing block and grid dimensions is key to designing high-performing CUDA applications.

CUDA threads are organized into a grid which is, in turn, composed of blocks. Each of these blocks can be one-dimensional (1D), two-dimensional (2D), or three-dimensional (3D). The choice of dimensionality depends on the nature of the problem being solved. Each block can host up to 1024 threads, in any combination of dimensions that do not exceed this limit.

```
// Example of defining block and grid dimensions
dim3 numBlocks(16, 16, 1); // Defining a 2D grid of 16x16 blocks
dim3 threadsPerBlock(32, 32, 1); // Each block has 32x32 threads
```

Here, dim3 is a built-in CUDA data type used for specifying dimensions. In this snippet, numBlocks defines a 2D grid with 16 blocks along the x and y axes and a single block along the z-axis. Similarly, threadsPerBlock defines a block size with 32 threads along both the x and y axes and a single thread along the z-axis. The product of these dimensions must not exceed the hardware limit of 1024 threads per block.

The grid's configuration is crucial because it must be selected based on the problem size. For instance, if processing a 2D image, a 2D grid and 2D blocks simplify thread indexing and data access.

4.7 Synchronizing Threads

In the context of CUDA programming, thread synchronization is a critical concept that ensures the correct execution and coordination of threads within a block. Synchronization allows threads to wait for each other at specific points in the program to ensure all threads have reached the same state before proceeding. This is particularly important when threads share data and need to prevent race conditions that can arise from concurrent data access.

CUDA provides a simple yet effective mechanism for thread synchronization within a block using the __syncthreads() function. This function acts as a barrier at which all threads in a block must wait until every thread reaches that point in the code. Only then can they all proceed. This mechanism is vital for coordinating shared memory usage among threads.

The __syncthreads() function can be used as follows:

```
__global__ void kernelFunction(int *data) {
    int idx = threadIdx.x;

    // Perform some calculations
    data[idx] += 5;

    // Synchronize threads
    __syncthreads();

    // Further calculations that depend on synchronized data
    if (idx == 0) {
        for (int i = 1; i < blockDim.x; i++) {
            data[0] += data[i];
        }
    }
}
```

In this example, the initial computation updates the data array without requiring synchronization. However, before the second computation stage, __syncthreads() ensures that all threads have completed the first stage. This is imperative because the second stage involves aggregating results from all threads, and any premature access to unsynchronized data could lead to incorrect results.

Proper usage of __syncthreads() avoids race conditions, where multiple threads simultaneously access and modify shared data, leading to unpredictable outcomes. Consider the following:

```
int sharedData[BLOCK_SIZE];

__global__ void raceConditionExample(int *data) {
```

```
    int idx = threadIdx.x;

    // Unsynchronized write-read operations
    if (idx == 0) {
        sharedData[0] = 0;
    }

    sharedData[idx] = data[idx];

    // Potential race condition: multiple threads access sharedData[0]
    int temp = sharedData[0];
    sharedData[0] += temp;

    // Unsynchronized update might result in different values each run
    data[idx] = sharedData[0];
}
```

The above code demonstrates a race condition, as the assignment to sharedData[0] is not synchronized. Various threads might read and write to sharedData[0] at the same time, resulting in an indeterminate final value.

Applying __syncthreads() ensures correctness:

```
int sharedData[BLOCK_SIZE];

__global__ void correctSynchronizationExample(int *data) {
    int idx = threadIdx.x;

    // Prevent race condition with synchronization
    if (idx == 0) {
        sharedData[0] = 0;
    }

    __syncthreads(); // Ensure sharedData[0] is initialized before proceeding

    sharedData[idx] = data[idx];

    __syncthreads(); // Ensure sharedData[idx] is written before any thread reads

    int temp = sharedData[0];
    sharedData[0] += temp;

    __syncthreads(); // Ensure all additions are complete before writing back

    data[idx] = sharedData[0];
}
```

In this corrected version, __syncthreads() guarantees that the initialization of sharedData[0] by thread 0 is completed before other threads access it. Subsequent synchronizations ensure that updates to sharedData are visible to all threads at appropriate stages. This approach eliminates race conditions and ensures a consistent output.

It's important to note that __syncthreads() can only be used within a block; it cannot synchronize threads across different blocks. For applications requiring synchronization across multiple blocks, further strategies beyond the basic CUDA synchronization primitives, such as using atomic operations or explicit parallel reduction techniques, may be necessary.

Another consideration when using __syncthreads() is its correct placement in the control flow. Conditional branches involving __syncthreads() can lead to deadlocks if not all threads execute the synchronization point correctly. For instance:

```
__global__ void conditionalSyncExample(int *data) {
    int idx = threadIdx.x;

    if (idx % 2 == 0) {
        __syncthreads(); // Deadlock possibility: not all threads execute
    }
}
```

Only even-indexed threads will call __syncthreads() in this example, causing those threads to wait indefinitely for odd-indexed threads that never reach the synchronization point. Such misuses must be avoided to prevent deadlocks and ensure program correctness.

For optimal performance, the use of __syncthreads() should be minimized and only applied when absolutely necessary, as it can introduce latency by halting all threads until synchronization is achieved. These considerations also inform the broader design of efficient CUDA kernels.

Properly synchronized threads facilitate the correct and efficient execution of parallel tasks, ensuring data integrity and enabling effective utilization of shared memory resources. Addressing synchronization at a fundamental level is therefore essential for robust and reliable CUDA programming.

4.8 Shared Memory and Thread Cooperation

Shared memory in CUDA plays a pivotal role in enabling efficient cooperation among threads within the same block. Unlike global memory, shared memory offers low-latency access and can be employed to dramatically enhance the performance of CUDA applications. This section delves into the mechanics of shared memory, the benefits it provides, and how threads can cooperate using this memory space.

CUDA provides each thread block with a small, programmable space called shared memory. This memory is on-chip, making it significantly faster than global memory. Shared memory can be used to share data among threads in the same block, which is particularly useful for tasks requiring frequent data exchanges or coordination between threads.

To declare shared memory within a CUDA kernel, the __shared__ qualifier is used. The shared memory is visible to all the threads within the block and remains persistent for the lifetime of the block. The following example demonstrates the declaration of shared memory:

```
__global__ void myKernel() {
    __shared__ int sharedData[256];
    // Kernel code here
}
```

In this example, sharedData is an array of 256 integers allocated in shared memory. Each thread within the block can read from and write to this array.

Utilizing Shared Memory for Thread Cooperation

To understand how shared memory facilitates thread cooperation, consider the task of summing an array of numbers using parallel reduction. Reduction often requires threads to share intermediate results, which is efficiently handled using shared memory.

Here is a simplified example of a parallel reduction operation using shared memory:

```
__global__ void reduce(int *input, int *output, int size) {
    __shared__ int sdata[256];

    unsigned int tid = threadIdx.x;
    unsigned int i = blockIdx.x * blockDim.x + threadIdx.x;

    if (i < size)
        sdata[tid] = input[i];
    else
        sdata[tid] = 0;

    __syncthreads();

    for (unsigned int s = blockDim.x / 2; s > 0; s >>= 1) {
        if (tid < s)
            sdata[tid] += sdata[tid + s];
        __syncthreads();
    }

    if (tid == 0)
        output[blockIdx.x] = sdata[0];
}
```

In this kernel:

- sdata is an array to hold intermediate sums.
- Each thread loads one element from the global input array into the shared memory.
- The __syncthreads() function ensures all threads have loaded their elements before any thread proceeds with the reduction.
- The reduction is performed in-place within the shared memory array.
- The final reduced value from each block is written to the output array.

Synchronizing Threads

Proper synchronization is critical when using shared memory to ensure accuracy and prevent race conditions. The __syncthreads() function is a barrier synchronization function used to synchronize all threads in a block. When a thread reaches __syncthreads(), it waits until all threads within the block have reached this point before continuing.

Here is an illustration of its importance:

```
__global__ void unsafeKernel(int *data) {
    __shared__ int sdata[256];

    unsigned int tid = threadIdx.x;
    sdata[tid] = data[tid] + 1;

    // Missing __syncthreads could lead to undefined behavior
    sdata[tid] = sdata[tid] * 2;
}
```

In this unsafe kernel example, if we miss the __syncthreads() call, it is possible that some threads might read the shared data before other threads have written to it, resulting in undefined behavior. Adding __syncthreads() after updating sdata[tid] ensures all threads have completed their write operations before any thread proceeds to the next step:

```
__global__ void safeKernel(int *data) {
    __shared__ int sdata[256];

    unsigned int tid = threadIdx.x;
    sdata[tid] = data[tid] + 1;

    __syncthreads();

    sdata[tid] = sdata[tid] * 2;
}
```

Shared Memory and Bank Conflicts

Shared memory is divided into equally sized memory modules, called banks, that allow multiple simultaneous accesses as long as there are no conflicts. If multiple threads access different memory banks simultaneously, the accesses can be serviced in parallel. However, if multiple threads access the same memory bank, a bank conflict occurs, which serializes the accesses and reduces performance.

For instance:

```
__global__ void bankConflictExample() {
    __shared__ int sharedArray[32];

    int tid = threadIdx.x;
    sharedArray[tid] = tid;

    __syncthreads();

    // Reading from shared memory, potential for bank conflicts
    int value = sharedArray[tid * 2];
}
```

In the above example, accesses like sharedArray[tid * 2] could lead to bank conflicts if tid * 2 maps multiple threads to the same bank. To avoid bank conflicts, stride accesses or padding can be employed.

Conclusion Subtly Integrated

Efficient use of shared memory can dramatically improve the performance of CUDA kernels by minimizing global memory accesses and enabling fast data sharing among threads. Proper synchronization using __syncthreads() is essential to ensure data consistency and avoid race conditions. Understanding the concept of bank conflicts and how to mitigate them is crucial for optimizing the use of shared memory. As we design CUDA kernels, leveraging shared memory appropriately allows us to harness the full potential of the massive parallelism offered by modern GPUs.

4.9 Thread Divergence

Thread divergence arises when threads of the same warp, which is a group of 32 threads in CUDA, follow different execution paths. This condition can significantly reduce the performance of CUDA programs. To ensure optimal performance, understanding and managing thread divergence is crucial.

In CUDA, threads within a warp execute instructions in a SIMT (Single Instruction, Multiple Threads) manner. When threads take different branches of a conditional statement, execution paths diverge, and the warp must serialize the execution of each branch. This process leads to increased instruction counts and degraded performance.

Consider the following example:

```
__global__ void divergent_kernel(int *data) {
    int idx = threadIdx.x + blockDim.x * blockIdx.x;
    if (idx % 2 == 0) {
        data[idx] *= 2;
    } else {
        data[idx] += 1;
    }
}
```

In this kernel, threads with even indices execute the first branch ('data[idx] *= 2'), while threads with odd indices execute the second branch ('data[idx] += 1'). When executed in a warp, this code causes thread divergence because not all threads follow the same path.

To handle thread divergence, consider restructuring your algorithm to minimize branching inside warps. For example, using predication, which replaces conditional branches with arithmetic operations, can sometimes help. The following code illustrates predication by computing both operations and selecting the result using a conditional assignment:

```
__global__ void predicated_kernel(int *data) {
    int idx = threadIdx.x + blockDim.x * blockIdx.x;
    int oldVal = data[idx];
    int newVal1 = oldVal * 2;
    int newVal2 = oldVal + 1;
    data[idx] = (idx % 2 == 0) ? newVal1 : newVal2;
}
```

Although predication can eliminate divergence, it should be applied judiciously. The arithmetic intensity of operations and the nature of the application should be considered to determine if the benefits outweigh the costs.

Another strategy involves organizing data to align with warp boundaries, ensuring threads within a warp follow the same path. The following example demonstrates processing even and odd indices separately with two kernel launches:

```
__global__ void even_indices_kernel(int *data) {
    int idx = threadIdx.x + blockDim.x * blockIdx.x;
    if (idx * 2 < N) {
        data[2 * idx] *= 2;
```

```
    }
}

__global__ void odd_indices_kernel(int *data) {
    int idx = threadIdx.x + blockDim.x * blockIdx.x;
    if (idx * 2 + 1 < N) {
        data[2 * idx + 1] += 1;
    }
}

// Host side code to launch both kernels
int main() {
    int *d_data;
    // Allocation and initialization code here
    even_indices_kernel<<<gridSize, blockSize>>>(d_data);
    odd_indices_kernel<<<gridSize, blockSize>>>(d_data);
}
```

This approach ensures that each kernel processes data uniformly, avoiding divergence within each warp. However, launching multiple kernels has its trade-offs, including potential overhead and increased complexity.

Thread divergence also occurs in loops. Consider the following example:

```
__global__ void loop_divergence_kernel(int *data) {
    int idx = threadIdx.x + blockDim.x * blockIdx.x;
    for (int i = 0; i < idx; ++i) {
        data[idx] *= 2;
    }
}
```

The loop iteration count varies per thread, causing divergence. In such cases, techniques to reduce iteration variability or loop unrolling, as shown below, might be effective:

```
__global__ void loop_unrolled_kernel(int *data) {
    int idx = threadIdx.x + blockDim.x * blockIdx.x;
    if (idx >= 4) {
        data[idx] *= 2; // Unroll the loop for first few iterations
        data[idx] *= 2;
        data[idx] *= 2;
        data[idx] *= 2;
    } else {
        for (int i = 0; i < idx; ++i) {
            data[idx] *= 2;
        }
    }
}
```

This kernel unrolls the loop for the initial iterations, decreasing divergence as threads execute similarly for the majority of iterations.

Efficient CUDA programming requires balancing access patterns, avoiding divergence, and utilizing hardware effectively. Recognizing points of divergence and applying optimization techniques can significantly enhance program performance.

4.10 Best Practices for Designing CUDA Kernels

Designing efficient CUDA kernels is crucial for achieving optimal performance in parallel computing applications. The key to efficient kernel design entails careful consideration of memory access patterns, thread organization, and the minimization of performance bottlenecks. Adhering to best practices in these areas can significantly enhance the execution speed and resource utilization of your CUDA programs.

Memory Access Patterns:

Optimal memory access patterns are essential for achieving high memory throughput. The following guidelines can help in designing effective memory access strategies:

- **Coalesced Access:** Ensure that global memory accesses by threads within a warp are coalesced. This means that consecutive threads in a warp should access consecutive memory locations. This consolidated access reduces the number of memory transactions and maximizes bandwidth utilization.

```
__global__ void addVectors(float *a, float *b, float *c, int n) {
    int index = threadIdx.x + blockIdx.x * blockDim.x;
    if (index < n)
        c[index] = a[index] + b[index];
}
```

- **Shared Memory Usage:** Use shared memory to reduce the latency of accessing data that is reused within a block. Shared memory is significantly faster than global memory and can be used to store intermediate results or frequently accessed data.

```
__global__ void matrixMultiplyShared(float *a, float *b, float *c, int N) {
    __shared__ float Asub[TILE_SIZE][TILE_SIZE];
    __shared__ float Bsub[TILE_SIZE][TILE_SIZE];
    int tx = threadIdx.x, ty = threadIdx.y;
    int Row = blockIdx.y * blockDim.y + ty;
    int Col = blockIdx.x * blockDim.x + tx;
    float Cvalue = 0.0;

    for (int m = 0; m < (N / TILE_SIZE); ++m) {
        Asub[ty][tx] = a[Row * N + (m * TILE_SIZE + tx)];
```

```
        Bsub[ty][tx] = b[(m * TILE_SIZE + ty) * N + Col];
        __syncthreads();
        for (int k = 0; k < TILE_SIZE; ++k)
            Cvalue += Asub[ty][k] * Bsub[k][tx];
        __syncthreads();
    }
    c[Row * N + Col] = Cvalue;
}
```

- **Avoid Bank Conflicts:** When using shared memory, ensure that bank conflicts are minimized. Bank conflicts occur when multiple threads access the same memory bank simultaneously, causing serialization of accesses. Access patterns should be designed so that threads access different memory banks.

```
__shared__ float sharedData[32];
int index = threadIdx.x * 4;
sharedData[index] = 1.0f; // Avoids bank conflicts
```

Thread Organization:

Efficient organization of threads within blocks and grids is critical. Consider the following strategies:

- **Select Appropriate Block Size:** The size of the thread block should be selected based on the capabilities of the GPU and the nature of the computation. Ensure that the block size is a multiple of the warp size (32 threads on NVIDIA GPUs) to maximize occupancy.

```
dim3 blockSize(16, 16); // 256 threads per block
dim3 gridSize((N + blockSize.x - 1) / blockSize.x, (N + blockSize.y - 1) /
    blockSize.y);
matrixMultiplyShared<<<gridSize, blockSize>>>(deviceA, deviceB, deviceC,
    N);
```

- **Occupancy Considerations:** High occupancy (the ratio of active warps to the maximum number of warps supported by a multiprocessor) may help hide latency of memory accesses. However, beyond a certain point, increasing occupancy does not significantly benefit performance and can even degrade it due to resource contention. Profile and tune occupancy accordingly.

```
cudaOccupancyMaxPotentialBlockSize(&minGridSize, &blockSize,
    matrixMultiplyShared, 0, 0);
gridSize = (N + blockSize - 1) / blockSize;
```

- **Load Balancing:** Ensure that the workload is evenly distributed across threads and blocks to prevent some threads from being idle while others are still processing. This can be achieved by designing kernel grids and blocks that match the problem's dimension.

```
__global__ void addVectors(float *a, float *b, float *c, int n) {
    int idx = blockIdx.x * blockDim.x + threadIdx.x;
    if (idx < n)
        c[idx] = a[idx] + b[idx];
}
int threadsPerBlock = 256;
int blocksPerGrid = (n + threadsPerBlock - 1) / threadsPerBlock;
addVectors<<<blocksPerGrid, threadsPerBlock>>>(a, b, c, n);
```

Minimizing Bottlenecks:

Performance bottlenecks can degrade the efficiency of CUDA kernels. The following practices can help in minimizing such bottlenecks:

- **Avoid Branch Divergence:** Ensure that threads within the same warp follow the same execution path. Divergence occurs when different threads take different branches, causing serialization of execution and reducing parallel efficiency.

```
__global__ void compute(float *data, int n) {
    int idx = threadIdx.x + blockIdx.x * blockDim.x;
    if (idx < n) {
        float value = data[idx];
        if (value > 0)
            data[idx] = sqrt(value);
        else
            data[idx] = value * value;
    }
}
```

- **Use Asynchronous Memory Transfers:** Utilize asynchronous memory transfers between host and device to overlap data transfer and computation. This can be achieved with CUDA streams.

```
cudaStream_t stream;
cudaStreamCreate(&stream);
cudaMemcpyAsync(deviceA, hostA, size, cudaMemcpyHostToDevice, stream);
kernel<<<grid, block, 0, stream>>>(deviceA, deviceB);
cudaMemcpyAsync(hostB, deviceB, size, cudaMemcpyDeviceToHost, stream);
cudaStreamSynchronize(stream);
cudaStreamDestroy(stream);
```

- **Hardware Utilization:** Fully utilize the computational resources of the GPU. Ensure that a sufficient number of threads are launched to fully load the GPU's cores. Be mindful of resource limits such as registers and shared memory per block.

```
int minGridSize, blockSize;
cudaOccupancyMaxPotentialBlockSize(&minGridSize, &blockSize, kernel, 0, 0);
dim3 gridSize((size + blockSize - 1) / blockSize);
kernel<<<gridSize, blockSize>>>(deviceData);
```

Attention to these areas when designing CUDA kernels can lead to significant performance improvements and better resource utilization. These best practices serve as guidelines that should be considered and adapted based on the specific requirements and constraints of your parallel computing tasks.

Chapter 5

Memory Management in CUDA

This chapter provides a comprehensive overview of the various memory types in CUDA, including global, shared, constant, texture, and unified memory. It covers memory allocation and deallocation practices, as well as memory transfer techniques between host and device. Additionally, it discusses strategies for optimizing memory access patterns to enhance performance and addresses common pitfalls and error handling related to memory management.

5.1 Overview of Memory Types in CUDA

CUDA exposes several types of memory, each with unique properties and usage scenarios. To harness the full potential of CUDA, it's essential to understand these memory types and how they can be utilized effectively in various computational workloads. The primary memory types in CUDA include global memory, shared memory, constant memory, texture memory, and unified memory.

Global memory is the most abundant memory available on the GPU. It is accessible by all threads and across different kernel launches, making it highly versatile. However, access to global memory is relatively slow compared to other memory types due to its high latency, which can impact overall performance if not managed correctly. Therefore, optimizing the usage of global memory through coalescing—where memory accesses are grouped to form fewer transactions—is vital for achieving higher bandwidth utilization.

Shared memory is a faster, on-chip memory shared among threads within the same thread block. It is significantly faster than global memory and is particularly useful for reducing the latency of memory accesses when threads in a block need to share data. Shared memory enables efficient parallel algorithms such as parallel reductions, where intermediate results are stored in shared memory before being combined. Proper synchronization with __syncthreads() is crucial to avoid race conditions when multiple threads access shared memory.

Constant memory is a read-only memory space that remains constant throughout the execution of a kernel. It is cached and thus provides fast read access when all threads in a warp access the same memory location. Constant memory is limited in size but is suitable for storing variables that do not change during kernel execution, such as coefficients in a mathematical formula or lookup tables.

Texture memory provides a way to fetch memory using dedicated hardware that can perform specific operations, such as linear interpolation, automatically. Texture memory is read-only and cached, making it ideal for applications involving 2D or 3D spatial data such as image processing or volume rendering. CUDA also offers surface memory, which is writable and provides similar benefits in terms of caching and spatial locality.

Unified memory introduces a more flexible memory management model by allowing pointers that can be accessed from both the host (CPU) and the device (GPU). This eliminates the need for explicit memory copies between the host and the device, simplifying memory management in GPU-accelerated applications. Unified memory is particularly beneficial in scenarios where data structures need to be shared between the CPU and GPU or where dynamic memory allocation during execution is required.

To summarize the importance of understanding each memory type's characteristics, consider a typical scenario where optimizing memory access patterns can lead to significant performance improvements. For example, suppose the data required for computation does not fit entirely into the faster memory spaces, such as shared or constant memory. In that case, segmenting data and strategically placing it into appropriate memory spaces can yield better performance compared to using global memory alone.

Effective memory management is a cornerstone of high-performance CUDA programming. Understanding the memory hierarchy and leveraging the strengths of each memory type ensures computational efficiency and accelerates application performance. Each memory type serves specific purposes and has distinct advantages, making them pivotal elements in designing algorithms that fully utilize the capabilities of CUDA-enabled GPUs.

```
// Example: Allocating and using shared memory within a kernel
__global__ void matrixMul(float *A, float *B, float *C, int N) {
    extern __shared__ float sharedMem[];
    float *As = sharedMem;
    float *Bs = &sharedMem[N * blockDim.x];

    int tx = threadIdx.x;
    int ty = threadIdx.y;
    int bx = blockIdx.x;
    int by = blockIdx.y;

    float Cvalue = 0.0;
    for (int m = 0; m < (N / blockDim.x); ++m) {
        As[ty * blockDim.x + tx] = A[(by * blockDim.y + ty) * N + (m * blockDim.x +
            tx)];
        Bs[ty * blockDim.x + tx] = B[(m * blockDim.x + ty) * N + (bx * blockDim.x +
            tx)];
        __syncthreads();

        for (int k = 0; k < blockDim.x; ++k) {
            Cvalue += As[ty * blockDim.x + k] * Bs[k * blockDim.x + tx];
        }
        __syncthreads();
    }
    C[(by * blockDim.y + ty) * N + (bx * blockDim.x + tx)] = Cvalue;
}
```

Efficiently utilizing shared memory, as shown in the example above, demonstrates how performance can be significantly improved by using memory types suited to the access patterns and computation needs of the task at hand.

5.2 Global Memory Management

Global memory in CUDA refers to the large, off-chip memory space available on the GPU. It is the primary memory resource for storing data that is accessed by both the host (CPU) and the device (GPU). Understanding how to effectively manage global memory is crucial for optimizing the performance of CUDA applications.

When managing global memory, several key aspects need to be considered, including allocation, deallocation, memory access patterns, and data transfer between the host and device. We discuss each of these factors in detail below.

1. Allocation and Deallocation of Global Memory

To allocate memory on the GPU, the CUDA Runtime API provides the cudaMalloc function. This function allocates a specified number of bytes on the device and returns a pointer to the allocated memory.

```
cudaError_t cudaMalloc(void** devPtr, size_t size);
```

Here, devPtr is the pointer to the allocated memory, and size is the number of bytes to allocate. The function returns a cudaError_t error code indicating whether the allocation was successful.

Example:

```
// Allocate array on GPU
int *d_array;
size_t size = 10 * sizeof(int);
cudaError_t err = cudaMalloc((void**)&d_array, size);
if (err != cudaSuccess) {
    printf("cudaMalloc failed: %s\n", cudaGetErrorString(err));
}
```

After memory is allocated on the device, it must be freed when it is no longer needed to avoid memory leaks. The cudaFree function is used for this purpose.

```
cudaError_t cudaFree(void* devPtr);
```

Example:

```
// Free memory on GPU
cudaFree(d_array);
```

2. Data Transfer Between Host and Device

Transferring data between the host and device is essential for utilizing global memory effectively. The CUDA Runtime API provides the cudaMemcpy function for this purpose.

```
cudaError_t cudaMemcpy(void* dst, const void* src, size_t count, cudaMemcpyKind
    kind);
```

The parameters are as follows: - dst: Destination memory address. - src: Source memory address. - count: Size in bytes of data to copy. - kind: Type of transfer, specified with one of the following enumerators:

- cudaMemcpyHostToHost

- cudaMemcpyHostToDevice
- cudaMemcpyDeviceToHost
- cudaMemcpyDeviceToDevice

Example:

```
// Copy data from host to device
int h_array[10] = {...};
cudaMemcpy(d_array, h_array, size, cudaMemcpyHostToDevice);

// Copy data from device to host
cudaMemcpy(h_array, d_array, size, cudaMemcpyDeviceToHost);
```

The cudaMemcpyAsync function can be used for asynchronous memory transfers, allowing the CPU and GPU to execute concurrently. Proper synchronization mechanisms must be used to ensure data integrity when employing asynchronous transfers.

```
cudaError_t cudaMemcpyAsync(void* dst, const void* src, size_t count,
    cudaMemcpyKind kind, cudaStream_t stream = 0);
```

Example:

```
// Asynchronously copy data from host to device
cudaMemcpyAsync(d_array, h_array, size, cudaMemcpyHostToDevice);
```

3. Optimizing Memory Access Patterns

Effective utilization of global memory is paramount to achieving high performance in CUDA applications. The performance of global memory access can be dramatically influenced by how data is accessed. Here are important considerations for optimizing global memory access:

Coalesced Accesses: Global memory accesses are most efficient when they are coalesced. This means that data is accessed by threads in a manner that combines multiple memory requests into a single transaction. Coalescing requirements vary between different compute capabilities, but generally, it involves ensuring that threads in a warp access contiguous memory addresses.

Example:

```
__global__ void add(int *a, int *b, int *c) {
    int index = threadIdx.x + blockIdx.x * blockDim.x;
    c[index] = a[index] + b[index];
}
```

Memory Alignment: Ensure that data structures are aligned to the boundary that enables optimal memory transactions. Using types like float4 and int4 can help in achieving alignment naturally.

Avoiding Unnecessary Memory Transfers: Minimize the frequency and volume of data transfers between the host and device. Whenever possible, perform computations directly on the GPU to utilize its parallel processing capabilities fully.

Memory Access Patterns: Structuring memory access patterns to allow for sequential rather than random access can further enhance memory performance.

Caching Mechanisms: Modern GPUs incorporate L1 and L2 caches, which can significantly boost performance if data reuse within the cache is maximized. Awareness of cache behavior and ensuring data locality can have a considerable impact on the efficiency of memory transactions.

Efficient global memory management involves appropriate allocation and deallocation, awareness and reduction of memory transfer overheads, and careful optimization of memory access patterns. By adhering to these principles, the performance and efficiency of CUDA applications can be significantly enhanced.

5.3 Shared Memory Management

Shared memory in CUDA is an exceptionally fast memory space that supports efficient data sharing among threads within the same block. It is implemented on-chip, offering much lower latency than global memory. However, the scope of shared memory is limited to the lifetime of the block, and it is not accessible to threads in other blocks.

To declare a shared memory array, the __shared__ keyword is used. Below is an example of declaring and using shared memory in a CUDA kernel:

```
__global__ void matrixMultiplyShared(float *A, float *B, float *C, int N) {
    // Define tile size
    const int TILE_SIZE = 16;

    // Allocate shared memory
    __shared__ float sharedA[TILE_SIZE][TILE_SIZE];
    __shared__ float sharedB[TILE_SIZE][TILE_SIZE];

    // Calculate thread row and column within matrix C
    int row = blockDim.y * blockIdx.y + threadIdx.y;
    int col = blockDim.x * blockIdx.x + threadIdx.x;

    float value = 0;
```

```
    // Loop over all tiles
    for (int t = 0; t < (N / TILE_SIZE); ++t) {
        // Load data into shared memory
        sharedA[threadIdx.y][threadIdx.x] = A[row * N + t * TILE_SIZE + threadIdx.
            x];
        sharedB[threadIdx.y][threadIdx.x] = B[(t * TILE_SIZE + threadIdx.y) * N +
            col];

        // Synchronize to make sure the tiles are loaded
        __syncthreads();

        // Perform computation for the current tile
        for (int k = 0; k < TILE_SIZE; ++k) {
            value += sharedA[threadIdx.y][k] * sharedB[k][threadIdx.x];
        }

        // Synchronize to make sure computation is done before loading new tile data
        __syncthreads();
    }

    // Write the result back to global memory
    C[row * N + col] = value;
}
```

In this kernel for matrix multiplication, shared memory is used to load sub-tiles of the matrices, reducing redundant global memory accesses. The __syncthreads() function is employed to synchronize threads within a block, ensuring that all data needed for computation is loaded before computation begins and that all computations are completed before the next tile is loaded.

It is critical to properly synchronize threads when using shared memory to avoid race conditions and ensure correctness of the data. The __syncthreads() intrinsic synchronizes all threads within a block, ensuring all shared memory operations are completed before any thread proceeds.

Shared memory has a size limit which is device-specific. You can query the amount of shared memory available per block using:

```
cudaDeviceProp prop;
cudaGetDeviceProperties(&prop, device);
printf("Shared memory per block: %ld bytes\n", prop.sharedMemPerBlock);
```

Efficient use of shared memory also requires avoiding bank conflicts. Shared memory is divided into 32 banks that can be accessed simultaneously. However, if multiple threads access different addresses within the same bank, conflicts will occur, leading to serialization of accesses and reduced performance. The following example illustrates how bank conflicts can be avoided:

```
__global__ void avoidBankConflicts(float *input, float *output, int size) {
```

```
    __shared__ float sData[32][32 + 1]; // Padding to avoid bank conflicts

    int x = blockDim.x * blockIdx.x + threadIdx.x;
    int y = blockDim.y * blockIdx.y + threadIdx.y;

    if (x < size && y < size) {
        // Load data from global memory to shared memory
        sData[threadIdx.y][threadIdx.x] = input[y * size + x];
        __syncthreads();

        // Output in transposed order
        output[x * size + y] = sData[threadIdx.x][threadIdx.y];
    }
}
```

In this kernel, the shared memory array is padded to avoid conflicts. The added dimension ensures that adjacent threads access different memory banks, thereby avoiding conflicts.

Shared memory plays a vital role in performance critical kernels. Proper management of shared memory, including allocation, synchronization, and avoidance of bank conflicts, is essential to fully leverage its benefits. As with any optimization, developers should profile their code using tools like NVIDIA Nsight Compute to understand if and where shared memory can provide performance benefits.

5.4 Constant Memory Management

Constant memory in CUDA is a type of read-only memory that is cached on the device. It is specifically optimized for scenarios where multiple threads access the same memory location, offering reduced latency compared to global memory due to its caching mechanism. CUDA provides constant memory specifically to improve performance for read-only data that does not change over the course of kernel execution. This section delves deeply into the nuances of managing constant memory, including its allocation, access, and performance considerations.

Constant memory is declared using the `__constant__` qualifier, and it can be accessed within device code similarly to how global memory is accessed. However, it comes with certain restrictions and optimizations. The size of constant memory is limited to 64KB, which necessitates efficient usage.

The declaration of constant memory in the global scope is straightforward. Here is an example:

```
__constant__ float constArray[256];
```

```
    int x = threadIdx.x + blockIdx.x * blockDim.x;
    int y = threadIdx.y + blockIdx.y * blockDim.y;
    float value;
    surf2Dread(&value, surf, x * sizeof(float), y);
    ...
    surf2Dwrite(value, surf, x * sizeof(float), y);
}
```

Surface memory is particularly advantageous when operations need to be performed repeatedly on the same memory locations, as it allows for efficient read-modify-write cycles. Applications like stencil computations, image convolutions, and data rearrangement routines can benefit from using surface memory.

Best Practices and Considerations

The use of texture and surface memory should consider the following best practices and design principles:

- *Access Patterns*: Ensure access patterns leverage spatial locality to maximize cache efficiency.
- *Interpolation and Filtering*: Utilize hardware interpolation features for efficient sampling.
- *Memory Binding*: Properly handle binding and unbinding of textures and surfaces to avoid resource leaks.
- *Performance Analysis*: Use profiling tools to measure the performance impact and adjust memory access patterns accordingly.
- *Error Checking*: Implement thorough error checking for all CUDA memory operations to handle potential errors effectively.

Understanding texture and surface memory mechanisms, alongside appropriate usage, can lead to substantial performance gains and scalable GPU programming practices.

5.6 Unified Memory in CUDA

Unified Memory in CUDA simplifies memory management by providing a single memory space that can be accessed by both the host and the device. With Unified Memory, developers do not need to manually copy data between the host and device, as the CUDA runtime system automatically handles data migration and coherence.

Unified Memory was introduced in CUDA 6 and has evolved to include various optimizations and features to enhance development efficiency and performance. It abstracts the complexity of managing separate memory spaces on the host and device, providing an easier programming model, especially for applications with complex memory access patterns.

Unified Memory Allocation

Memory in Unified Memory is allocated using the cudaMallocManaged function. This function returns a pointer to the allocated memory that can be accessed by both the host and the device. The syntax is as follows:

```
cudaError_t cudaMallocManaged(void **devPtr, size_t size, unsigned int flags =
    cudaMemAttachGlobal);
```

- devPtr is the pointer to the allocated memory.
- size is the size of memory to allocate, in bytes.
- flags are optional and by default, should be set to cudaMemAttachGlobal, indicating global visibility of the memory.

Here is an example of how to use cudaMallocManaged:

```
float *unifiedMemoryPtr;
cudaMallocManaged(&unifiedMemoryPtr, 100 * sizeof(float));
```

In this example, unifiedMemoryPtr points to an array of 100 float elements in Unified Memory.

Data Access and Consistency

When Unified Memory is accessed by the host, it behaves like regular system memory. When accessed by the device, it behaves like device memory. The CUDA runtime ensures data consistency between host and device by migrating pages of the memory to the appropriate processor and keeping copies coherent.

Consider the following situation:

```
__global__ void kernel(float *data) {
    int idx = threadIdx.x + blockIdx.x * blockDim.x;
    data[idx] = data[idx] * 2.0f;
}

int main() {
    float *unifiedMemoryPtr;
    cudaMallocManaged(&unifiedMemoryPtr, 100 * sizeof(float));

    for (int i = 0; i < 100; ++i) {
```

```
cudaError_t cudaMallocManaged(void **devPtr, size_t size,
                              unsigned int flags = cudaMemAttachGlobal);
```

devPtr is a pointer to the allocated memory, size is the number of bytes to allocate, and flags can control attachment (e.g., cudaMemAttachGlobal or cudaMemAttachHost).

Example:

```
#include <cuda_runtime.h>
#include <iostream>

int main() {
    int numElements = 1024;
    size_t size = numElements * sizeof(float);

    // Allocate unified memory
    float *array;
    cudaError_t err = cudaMallocManaged(&array, size);

    if (err != cudaSuccess) {
        std::cerr << "Failed to allocate unified memory (error code "
                  << cudaGetErrorString(err) << ")!" << std::endl;
        return EXIT_FAILURE;
    }

    // Free the allocated unified memory
    err = cudaFree(array);

    if (err != cudaSuccess) {
        std::cerr << "Failed to free unified memory (error code "
                  << cudaGetErrorString(err) << ")!" << std::endl;
        return EXIT_FAILURE;
    }

    return EXIT_SUCCESS;
}
```

In this example, cudaMallocManaged is used to allocate unified memory, enabling the same pointer to be used for accessing data on both the host and the device. The memory is deallocated using cudaFree.

It's essential to handle memory allocation and deallocation with care to prevent memory leaks or access violations that can lead to undefined behavior and application crashes. By understanding and properly utilizing the CUDA memory management functions, efficient and reliable GPU programming can be achieved.

5.8 Memory Transfers Between Host and Device

Memory transfer between the host (CPU) and the device (GPU) is a fundamental operation in CUDA programming. Effective memory transfer strategies are crucial for optimizing performance, as the PCIe bus—typically used for data transfer between the host and the device—has significantly lower bandwidth compared to the GPU's global memory. This section explores how to efficiently manage these transfers, the functions available for memory transfer, and best practices to minimize their impact on overall application performance.

CUDA provides several API functions to facilitate memory transfers. These functions are declared in the cuda.h header file and are part of the CUDA runtime API. The primary functions for memory transfer are:

- cudaMemcpy
- cudaMemcpyAsync

The cudaMemcpy function is blocking and synchronous, meaning it will not return control to the host until the copy operation is complete. Syntax and usage examples are provided below:

```
cudaError_t cudaMemcpy(
    void* dst,
    const void* src,
    size_t count,
    cudaMemcpyKind kind
);

// Example:
// Copy 1MB of data from host to device
cudaMemcpy(device_ptr, host_ptr, 1024*1024, cudaMemcpyHostToDevice);

// Copy 1MB of data from device to host
cudaMemcpy(host_ptr, device_ptr, 1024*1024, cudaMemcpyDeviceToHost);
```

The cudaMemcpyKind parameter specifies the direction of the copy. The values can be:

- cudaMemcpyHostToDevice
- cudaMemcpyDeviceToHost
- cudaMemcpyDeviceToDevice
- cudaMemcpyHostToHost

ilarly important. Functions such as cudaGetLastError help detect and debug issues related to constant memory transfers and kernel execution.

Understanding the balance between various types of memory in CUDA is vital for efficient GPU programming. Utilizing constant memory appropriately, taking into account its advantages and limitations, can lead to significant performance gains in CUDA applications.

5.5 Texture Memory and Surface Memory

Texture memory and surface memory are specialized types of memory in CUDA designed to optimize certain kinds of data access patterns, particularly those involving spatial locality and interpolation. These memory types leverage the texture and surface caches in the GPU, which can significantly improve performance for specific applications, such as image processing and computational fluid dynamics.

Texture Memory

Texture memory allows for efficient spatially-coherent memory access by providing texture fetching capabilities. Textures in CUDA are read-only memory spaces bound to linear memory on the device and accessed through a texture reference. They facilitate desired operations such as linear interpolation, addressing modes (clamping, wrapping), and normalized coordinate access.

To utilize texture memory, a developer needs to go through the following primary steps:

1. **Define and Allocate Linear Memory:**

Before binding texture memory, the developer must allocate the linear memory that will hold the texture data on the device.

```
float* d_data;
cudaMalloc(&d_data, width * height * sizeof(float));
cudaMemcpy(d_data, h_data, width * height * sizeof(float),
        cudaMemcpyHostToDevice);
```

2. **Bind Memory to a Texture Reference:**

The next step involves defining a texture reference and binding the previously allocated linear memory to this texture reference.

```
texture<float, 2, cudaReadModeElementType> texRef;
cudaChannelFormatDesc channelDesc = cudaCreateChannelDesc<float>();
```

```
cudaBindTexture2D(0, &texRef, d_data, &channelDesc, width, height, width *
    sizeof(float));
```

3. **Access Texture Memory:**

In the CUDA kernel, texture fetching is performed using the 'tex2D' function for 2D textures, which retrieves elements from the texture cache.

```
__global__ void kernel(TextureObject texObj, ...) {
    int x = threadIdx.x + blockIdx.x * blockDim.x;
    int y = threadIdx.y + blockIdx.y * blockDim.y;
    float value = tex2D(texObj, x, y);
    ...
}
```

Importantly, texture memory is cached, and fetches from it can be extremely fast when spatial locality is exploited. Texture memory also supports hardware-accelerated interpolation, allowing for efficient sampling at non-integer coordinates, a critical feature for applications involving image scaling, transformations, and fluid-simulation interpolation tasks.

Surface Memory

Surface memory in CUDA is analogous to texture memory but allows for both read and write operations. Surfaces are useful for scenarios where data needs to be manipulated on the GPU and the resulting modifications need to be read subsequently.

Like textures, surfaces also require linear memory allocation followed by a binding step, but they operate through surface references instead of texture references.

1. **Define and Allocate Linear Memory:**

```
float* d_surfaceData;
cudaMalloc(&d_surfaceData, width * height * sizeof(float));
cudaMemcpy(d_surfaceData, h_surfaceData, width * height * sizeof(float),
    cudaMemcpyHostToDevice);
```

2. **Bind Memory to a Surface Reference:**

```
surface<void, 2> surfRef;
cudaChannelFormatDesc channelDesc = cudaCreateChannelDesc<float>();
cudaBindSurfaceToArray(surfRef, d_surfaceData, &channelDesc);
```

3. **Access Surface Memory:**

The surface memory can be accessed using 'surf2Dread' and 'surf2Dwrite' for reading and writing, respectively.

```
__global__ void surfaceKernel(surface<void, 2> surf, ...) {
```

For cases where non-blocking behavior is desired, cudaMemcpyAsync should be used. This function is asynchronous with respect to the host, enabling the host to proceed with other tasks while the memory transfer is in progress. It requires a stream to operate, offering fine-grained control over execution timelines.

```
cudaError_t cudaMemcpyAsync(
    void* dst,
    const void* src,
    size_t count,
    cudaMemcpyKind kind,
    cudaStream_t stream = 0
);

// Example:
// Asynchronous copy 1MB of data from host to device
cudaMemcpyAsync(device_ptr, host_ptr, 1024*1024, cudaMemcpyHostToDevice,
    stream);

// Asynchronous copy 1MB of data from device to host
cudaMemcpyAsync(host_ptr, device_ptr, 1024*1024, cudaMemcpyDeviceToHost,
    stream);
```

The stream argument allows for overlap of computation and communication, making efficient use of available resources.

When multiple streams and transfers are involved, cudaStreamSynchronize and cudaDeviceSynchronize functions can be used to ensure that tasks are correctly ordered and completed. Example usage:

```
cudaStream_t stream1, stream2;
cudaStreamCreate(&stream1);
cudaStreamCreate(&stream2);

// Asynchronous memory transfer using stream1
cudaMemcpyAsync(device_ptr1, host_ptr1, 1024*1024, cudaMemcpyHostToDevice,
    stream1);

// Asynchronous memory transfer using stream2
cudaMemcpyAsync(device_ptr2, host_ptr2, 1024*1024, cudaMemcpyHostToDevice,
    stream2);

// Synchronize stream1
cudaStreamSynchronize(stream1);

// Synchronize stream2
cudaStreamSynchronize(stream2);

// Destroy streams
cudaStreamDestroy(stream1);
cudaStreamDestroy(stream2);
```

Stream Synchronization ensures correct order and completion of tasks.

Page-locked (also known as pinned) memory can provide significant performance improvements for memory transfers. By locking a region of host memory, the operating system ensures that the memory is pre-allocated and non-swappable, reducing the overhead of memory paging and allowing the GPU to access data directly via DMA (Direct Memory Access).

```
cudaError_t cudaHostAlloc(
    void** pHost,
    size_t size,
    unsigned int flags );

// Example:
// Allocate 1MB of pinned memory
cudaHostAlloc(&host_ptr, 1024*1024, cudaHostAllocDefault);
```

Pinned memory should be used judiciously as it reduces the available physical memory for other processes, potentially impacting overall system performance.

Parallelizing both data transfers and computations can further optimize performance. Using multiple CUDA streams allows performing kernel execution concurrently with data transfers. Effective overlap of data transfer with computation can significantly reduce the perceived latency of data transfers.

Another advanced technique involves using Unified Memory, which abstracts away the explicit copying of memory between the host and the device. This feature, introduced in CUDA 6, allows the programmer to allocate memory that is automatically managed and migrated by the CUDA runtime as needed.

```
cudaError_t cudaMallocManaged(
    void **devPtr,
    size_t size,
    unsigned int flags = cudaMemAttachGlobal);

// Example:
// Allocate 1MB of Unified Memory
cudaMallocManaged(&unified_ptr, 1024*1024);
```

When using Unified Memory on systems without NVLink, it is still beneficial to prefetch data to the preferred location to optimize access patterns using cudaMemPrefetchAsync.

```
cudaError_t cudaMemPrefetchAsync(
    void *devPtr,
    size_t count,
    int dstDevice,
    cudaStream_t stream = 0);

// Example:
// Prefetching Unified Memory to device
cudaMemPrefetchAsync(unified_ptr, 1024*1024, cudaGetDevice(), 0);
```

Proper error handling is essential when performing memory transfers. For every memory transfer function call while programming in CUDA, it is recommended to check the return status using cudaError_t and handle any errors appropriately. Example:

```
cudaError_t err = cudaMemcpy(device_ptr, host_ptr, 1024*1024,
    cudaMemcpyHostToDevice);

if (err != cudaSuccess) {
    // Handle the error
    printf("CUDA error: %s\n", cudaGetErrorString(err));
}
```

Understanding and applying these memory transfer techniques effectively ensures that data movement does not become a bottleneck in CUDA applications, allowing full utilization of the GPU's computational capabilities.

5.9 Optimizing Memory Access Patterns

In CUDA programming, memory access patterns play a vital role in determining overall application performance. Improper memory access can lead to high latency and inefficient use of the memory bandwidth. To mitigate these issues and enhance performance, it is crucial to optimize memory access patterns. This section discusses various techniques and strategies to achieve optimal memory access in CUDA applications.

One of the fundamental concepts in optimizing memory access patterns is **coalesced memory access**. When threads in a warp access consecutive memory addresses, these accesses can be coalesced into a single memory transaction, significantly improving memory throughput. Conversely, if threads access memory in a scattered fashion, the memory transactions become serialized, leading to performance degradation.

Consider the following example, demonstrating a coalesced and an uncoalesced access pattern in a simple CUDA kernel:

```
__global__ void coalescedAccess(float *d_out, float *d_in) {
    int idx = threadIdx.x + blockDim.x * blockIdx.x;
    // Coalesced access
    d_out[idx] = d_in[idx];
}

__global__ void uncoalescedAccess(float *d_out, float *d_in, int stride) {
    int idx = threadIdx.x + blockDim.x * blockIdx.x;
    // Uncoalesced access
```

```
    d_out[idx] = d_in[idx * stride];
}

int main() {
    // Define variables and allocate memory
    float *d_in, *d_out;
    cudaMalloc((void**)&d_in, N * sizeof(float));
    cudaMalloc((void**)&d_out, N * sizeof(float));

    // Call kernels
    coalescedAccess<<<blocks, threads>>>(d_out, d_in);
    uncoalescedAccess<<<blocks, threads>>>(d_out, d_in, stride);

    // Free memory
    cudaFree(d_in);
    cudaFree(d_out);

    return 0;
}
```

In the coalescedAccess kernel, each thread accesses consecutive memory elements, resulting in coalesced memory transactions. On the other hand, the uncoalescedAccess kernel accesses memory elements with a stride, resulting in non-coalesced memory accesses, which reduce performance.

Another critical consideration is the **use of shared memory**. Shared memory is a limited yet high-speed memory region that can be shared among threads within the same block. Utilizing shared memory effectively can reduce redundant global memory accesses and increase data reuse. For example, consider a matrix multiplication kernel:

```
__global__ void matrixMulShared(float *A, float *B, float *C, int N) {
    __shared__ float As[BLOCK_SIZE][BLOCK_SIZE];
    __shared__ float Bs[BLOCK_SIZE][BLOCK_SIZE];

    int tx = threadIdx.x;
    int ty = threadIdx.y;
    int row = blockIdx.y * BLOCK_SIZE + ty;
    int col = blockIdx.x * BLOCK_SIZE + tx;

    float value = 0.0f;

    for (int m = 0; m < (N / BLOCK_SIZE); ++m) {
        As[ty][tx] = A[row * N + (m * BLOCK_SIZE + tx)];
        Bs[ty][tx] = B[(m * BLOCK_SIZE + ty) * N + col];
        __syncthreads();

        for (int k = 0; k < BLOCK_SIZE; ++k) {
            value += As[ty][k] * Bs[k][tx];
        }
        __syncthreads();
    }

    C[row * N + col] = value;
}
```

Here, the kernel uses shared memory to load sub-blocks of the matrices A and B into As and Bs, respectively. This reduces the number of global memory accesses and takes advantage of the high-speed shared memory for intermediate calculations.

Minimizing **divergent memory accesses** is also essential. Divergent memory accesses occur when threads in a warp follow different execution paths due to branch instructions, causing serialized memory transactions. While the CUDA hardware is designed to handle some level of divergence, excessive divergence can severely impact performance.

Additionally, **memory alignment** should be considered. Memory accesses are most efficient when the data structures are aligned to the memory boundaries. For instance, 32-bit (4-byte) and 64-bit (8-byte) types should be aligned to 4-byte and 8-byte boundaries, respectively. Misaligned accesses result in additional memory transactions, decreasing performance.

The following restructuring ensures aligned accesses:

```
struct AlignedData {
    float x;
    float y;
    float z;
    float w; // Ensure 16-byte alignment for float4
};

__global__ void processAligned(float4 *d_data, int N) {
    int idx = threadIdx.x + blockDim.x * blockIdx.x;
    if (idx < N) {
        float4 value = d_data[idx];
        // Processing value
    }
}
```

Ensuring data is naturally aligned minimizes inefficient memory transactions.

Finally, the **use of texture memory** can optimize memory access for certain types of data, particularly when detiling matrices. Texture memory is cached and can provide efficient, non-coalesced access patterns beneficial for graphics and certain scientific computations. Using cudaTextureObject_t and surface object APIs can leverage these advantages.

In practice, balancing and combining these strategies—coalesced access, shared memory utilization, minimizing divergence, ensuring alignment, and leveraging texture memory—are key to optimizing memory access patterns in CUDA. Focusing on these areas will significantly improve the computational performance and efficiency of CUDA applications.

5.10 Avoiding and Handling Memory Errors

Memory errors in CUDA can arise from various sources, resulting in unpredictable behavior, crashes, or incorrect results. Addressing these issues requires understanding common pitfalls, employing best practices, and utilizing built-in tools and techniques for debugging and error handling.

A frequent source of memory errors is **out-of-bounds access**, where an array or pointer exceeds its allocated memory space. In CUDA, this can occur in device code if the grid or block dimensions are incorrectly computed, or if index calculations within a kernel exceed array boundaries. Monitoring these parameters carefully and using assertions can help catch such errors early.

It's crucial to ensure that all **memory allocations** are adequate for the expected data sizes. Under-allocations lead to writes or reads outside the designated memory, while over-allocations waste valuable memory resources. Here's an example code segment illustrating proper memory allocation in CUDA:

```
int n = 1024;
float *d_array;
cudaError_t status = cudaMalloc(&d_array, n * sizeof(float));
if (status != cudaSuccess) {
    fprintf(stderr, "cudaMalloc failed: %s\n", cudaGetErrorString(status));
    // Handle error appropriately
}
```

An essential technique for avoiding memory errors involves the systematic use of **cudaMemcpy** for transferring data between host and device. Ensure the correct direction of transfer and appropriate data sizes:

```
cudaMemcpy(d_array, h_array, n * sizeof(float), cudaMemcpyHostToDevice);
// Verify the transfer was successful
status = cudaGetLastError();
if (status != cudaSuccess) {
    fprintf(stderr, "cudaMemcpy failed: %s\n", cudaGetErrorString(status));
    // Handle error appropriately
}
```

Another critical aspect is the correct utilization of **cudaFree** to deallocate memory that is no longer needed. Failure to do so can result in memory leaks, exhausting device memory over time. Proper deallocation looks as follows:

```
status = cudaFree(d_array);
if (status != cudaSuccess) {
    fprintf(stderr, "cudaFree failed: %s\n", cudaGetErrorString(status));
    // Handle error appropriately
}
```

Memory alignment is another potential source of errors and inefficiencies. For best performance, memory accesses should be aligned to 128 bytes when possible. Misaligned accesses can lead to performance penalties or hardware exceptions. Using cudaMallocPitch is advisable for allocating 2D arrays as it ensures proper alignment:

```
size_t pitch;
float *d_matrix;
cudaMallocPitch(&d_matrix, &pitch, width * sizeof(float), height);
```

Tools such as **cuda-memcheck**, part of the CUDA toolkit, are invaluable for detecting and diagnosing memory errors. It helps to identify invalid memory accesses, uninitialized memory reads, and various other memory-related issues. An example of running cuda-memcheck on a compiled CUDA program is shown below:

```
$ cuda-memcheck ./my_cuda_program
========= CUDA-MEMCHECK
========= Program hit error 1: invalid global read
=========     at 0x00000128 in kernel.cu:45
...
```

Implementing **error handling mechanisms** involves checking the status returned by CUDA runtime functions and taking appropriate actions in case of failures. Use assert or condition checks to monitor these statuses:

```
cudaError_t status = cudaMemcpy(d_array, h_array, n * sizeof(float),
      cudaMemcpyHostToDevice);
assert(status == cudaSuccess);

if (status != cudaSuccess) {
    fprintf(stderr, "cudaMemcpy failed: %s\n", cudaGetErrorString(status));
    // Implement recovery or exit strategy
}
```

Synchronization errors occur when there is a mismatch in the expected sequence of execution, leading to race conditions or incorrect results. Ensuring proper synchronization using __syncthreads() within kernels and cudaDeviceSynchronize() between host and device actions can mitigate these issues.

Efficient handling also involves best practices such as consolidating memory transfers, using page-locked host memory for faster transfers, and avoiding excessive memory allocation and deallocation within performance-critical sections.

Finally, consider utilizing more advanced features like **managed memory** in CUDA Unified Memory to reduce explicit memory management burdens. While this can simplify programming, it still requires attention to usage patterns to avoid pitfalls related to data locality and performance impacts.

Understanding and systematically applying these strategies and tools will significantly reduce the likelihood of encountering memory errors in CUDA applications, leading to more robust and efficient programs.

Chapter 6

CUDA Parallel Programming Models

This chapter introduces various parallel programming models in CUDA, including Single Instruction Multiple Threads (SIMT), thread and data parallelism, and domain decomposition. It covers task and hybrid parallelism models, and explains the use of streams for parallel execution. The chapter also delves into hierarchical grid execution and multi-GPU programming, providing best practices for selecting and implementing the most suitable parallel programming model for different types of computational tasks.

6.1 Introduction to Parallel Programming Models

Parallel programming models are critical for leveraging the full computational power of modern GPUs. These models specify how to decompose a problem into tasks that can be executed simultaneously, efficiently managing the resources provided by CUDA's architecture. Understanding various models is essential for optimizing performance and achieving scalability in complex applications.

The fundamental concept behind parallel programming models is the decomposition of computational tasks into sub-tasks that can be executed concurrently. This decomposition is generally classified into three primary types: task parallelism, data parallelism, and domain decomposition.

Task parallelism involves the concurrent execution of different tasks or functions. Each task performs a distinct operation, and multiple tasks can run independently across different computational units. In CUDA, task parallelism is typically implemented by launching multiple kernels, each executing a unique task. This model is particularly advantageous when the tasks have varying computational requirements and do not need to communicate frequently.

Data parallelism focuses on performing the same operation across a large dataset. In CUDA, this is achieved by dividing the data into chunks that are processed in parallel by different threads. Each thread executes the same instruction set but on different pieces of data. This model is highly efficient for large-scale computations, such as matrix multiplications, where the same operation is repeated over numerous elements.

Domain decomposition is a strategy where a computational domain is divided into smaller regions, each processed independently. This technique, often combined with data parallelism, is useful in simulations and finite element analysis, where a large problem space can be subdivided into smaller, more manageable sections. Each section can be processed in parallel, and the results are combined to obtain the final solution.

```
// Example illustrating data parallelism in CUDA
__global__ void vectorAdd(const float* A, const float* B, float* C, int N) {
    int idx = blockIdx.x * blockDim.x + threadIdx.x;
    if (idx < N) {
        C[idx] = A[idx] + B[idx];
    }
}

int main() {
    int N = 1000000;
    float *d_A, *d_B, *d_C;

    // Allocate device memory
    cudaMalloc((void**)&d_A, N * sizeof(float));
    cudaMalloc((void**)&d_B, N * sizeof(float));
    cudaMalloc((void**)&d_C, N * sizeof(float));

    // Kernel launch with N blocks of 512 threads each
    vectorAdd<<<(N + 511) / 512, 512>>>(d_A, d_B, d_C, N);

    cudaDeviceSynchronize();

    // Free device memory
    cudaFree(d_A);
```

```
    cudaFree(d_B);
    cudaFree(d_C);

    return 0;
}
```

Another key aspect is the management of thread hierarchy and synchronization. CUDA employs a hierarchical model of threads organized into blocks and grids. Each grid consists of multiple blocks, and each block contains multiple threads. This hierarchy allows for scalable and flexible parallelism. Threads within a block can communicate and synchronize using shared memory and synchronization barriers, enabling fine-grained parallelism.

```
// Understanding thread hierarchy
__global__ void exampleKernel() {
    int threadID = threadIdx.x;
    int blockID = blockIdx.x;
    int blockDim = blockDim.x;
    int globalID = blockID * blockDim + threadID;

    printf("Thread %d in block %d has global ID %d\n", threadID, blockID, globalID);
}

int main() {
    exampleKernel<<<4, 8>>>(); // 4 blocks with 8 threads each
    cudaDeviceSynchronize();

    return 0;
}
```

```
Output:
Thread 0 in block 0 has global ID 0
Thread 1 in block 0 has global ID 1
...
Thread 7 in block 0 has global ID 7
Thread 0 in block 1 has global ID 8
Thread 1 in block 1 has global ID 9
...
Thread 7 in block 1 has global ID 15
...
```

Memory hierarchies and data locality, essential for optimizing parallel execution, must be considered. CUDA offers multiple types of memory: global, shared, and local, each with different access times and scope. Understanding and efficiently exploiting these memory types can significantly impact performance.

Global Memory is accessible by all threads but has higher latency. It is suitable for data that needs to be shared across the grid but should be minimized to reduce memory access time.

Shared Memory, with lower latency, is accessible only by threads within the same block. It is used for frequently accessed data and to enable communication between threads in the same block.

Local Memory is private to each thread and primarily used for register spilling when there are not enough registers available for a thread's variables.

When choosing a parallel programming model, consider the problem domain, computational characteristics, and resource constraints. Properly aligning the computational problem with an appropriate model and effectively utilizing CUDA's hierarchical threading and memory architecture can lead to substantial performance improvements. Understanding these foundational principles paves the way for exploring more advanced models and techniques in CUDA parallel programming.

6.2 Single Instruction Multiple Threads (SIMT)

Single Instruction Multiple Threads (SIMT) is a cornerstone of CUDA's execution model, fundamentally shaping how parallelism is managed and leveraged on NVIDIA's GPUs. SIMT represents a paradigm where multiple threads execute the same instruction simultaneously but on different data elements. This model aligns concepts from traditional SIMD (Single Instruction, Multiple Data) with the flexibility and scalability required for modern GPU architectures.

SIMT Architecture Overview

Under the SIMT model, CUDA threads are organized into blocks, and these blocks are further grouped into a grid. Each block contains multiple threads, which are the basic units of computation in CUDA. These threads execute in a lockstep fashion, meaning they follow the same instruction path but operate on their own data. The execution units within the GPU, known as streaming multiprocessors (SMs), manage these threads.

The SIMT model emerges from the ability of SMs to execute a single instruction across a warp of threads. A warp typically consists of 32 threads, which execute together in an SIMD fashion. When a CUDA kernel is launched, the grid of thread blocks is distributed across the available SMs. Each SM schedules warps from multiple blocks for execution, balancing resource usage while maintaining high throughput.

Illustratively, consider the following CUDA kernel performing vector addition:

```
__global__ void vectorAdd(const float *A, const float *B, float *C, int N) {
    int i = threadIdx.x + blockIdx.x * blockDim.x;
    if (i < N) {
        C[i] = A[i] + B[i];
    }
}
```

In the kernel above, each thread computes one element of the resulting vector C. When launched with appropriate grid and block dimensions, each thread will operate on different elements of vectors A and B, concurrently adding values and storing the results in C.

Warp Execution and Divergence

While threads in a warp execute the same instruction simultaneously, branching can lead to a phenomenon known as warp divergence. Warp divergence occurs when threads within the same warp take different execution paths, typically due to conditional statements (e.g., if-else). This divergence can impact performance, as the scheduler must serialize the divergent paths, causing some threads to idle while others execute.

Consider the following modified example with a conditional statement:

```
__global__ void vectorAddConditional(const float *A, const float *B, float *C, int N)
    {
    int i = threadIdx.x + blockIdx.x * blockDim.x;
    if (i < N) {
        if (A[i] > 0) {
            C[i] = A[i] + B[i];
        } else {
            C[i] = 0;
        }
    }
}
```

In this example, conditional execution within the kernel function could result in warp divergence. Threads where $A[i] > 0$ will execute a different path than those where $A[i] \leq 0$, leading to efficiency losses. Optimizing for minimal branching and ensuring that all threads within a warp follow the same execution path can enhance performance.

Memory Access Patterns

Efficient memory access is a critical factor in maximizing performance under the SIMT model. Memory coalescing is a technique to enhance throughput by ensuring that memory accesses by threads within a warp fall into contiguous memory locations. Coalesced memory access allows the GPU to fetch data for all threads in a warp with fewer memory transactions, significantly improving bandwidth utilization.

For instance, the vector addition kernel exhibits memory coalescing when threads access consecutive array indices. However, non-coalesced memory accesses can arise if threads access memory in a scattered pattern. An example of such inefficiency is:

```
__global__ void scatteredAccess(const float *A, float *B, int *indices, int N) {
    int i = threadIdx.x + blockIdx.x * blockDim.x;
    if (i < N) {
        B[i] = A[indices[i]];
    }
}
```

In this kernel, accessing A through an arbitrary indices array can lead to scattered memory access patterns, reducing overall memory throughput. Reorganizing data to promote contiguous access patterns should be a key consideration during kernel implementation.

Synchronization

An essential aspect of threading in CUDA is synchronization. Threads within a block can synchronize using the $\_\_\text{syncthreads}()$ function, which acts as a barrier, ensuring all threads in the block reach the synchronization point before any are allowed to proceed. This capability is crucial for coordinating shared memory access and mitigating race conditions.

Here is an example illustrating thread synchronization:

```
__global__ void reduceSum(float *input, float *result, int N) {
    extern __shared__ float sharedData[];
    int tid = threadIdx.x;
    int idx = blockIdx.x * blockDim.x + tid;
    sharedData[tid] = (idx < N) ? input[idx] : 0.0f;
    __syncthreads();

    for (int s = blockDim.x / 2; s > 0; s >>= 1) {
        if (tid < s) {
            sharedData[tid] += sharedData[tid + s];
        }
        __syncthreads();
    }

    if (tid == 0) {
        result[blockIdx.x] = sharedData[0];
    }
}
```

This reduction kernel accumulates the sum of elements within each block using shared memory and synchronization. Each thread loads data into shared memory, syncs to ensure all data is loaded, and then performs a reduction in a step-wise manner. Proper usage of synchronization functions is critical for accurate and efficient parallel computations.

Single Instruction Multiple Threads (SIMT) offers a robust model for exploiting data parallelism on GPU architectures. Understanding warp execution, optimizing memory access patterns, and correctly applying synchronization primitives are fundamental aspects of leveraging this model to achieve high-performance CUDA applications.

6.3 Thread and Data Parallelism

Thread and data parallelism are fundamental concepts in CUDA programming that enable efficient utilization of the GPU hardware. Understanding the distinctions and the implementation techniques for both thread and data parallelism is crucial for achieving optimal performance.

Thread parallelism, also known as task parallelism, involves distributing different tasks or functions across multiple threads. This means that each thread operates independently and can execute different instructions simultaneously. Thread parallelism is particularly advantageous in scenarios where tasks are heterogeneous, requiring different computational workloads.

Conversely, data parallelism involves the same operation being performed concurrently across different data elements. This is particularly well-suited for SIMD (Single Instruction Multiple Data) architectures like GPUs, where the same instruction set can be efficiently broadcast to multiple processing elements. Data parallelism leverages the GPU's capability to provide significant speedup in applications such as image processing, numerical simulations, and matrix operations where the same operation is applied to each element of a dataset.

```
__global__ void addKernel(int *c, const int *a, const int *b) {
    int i = threadIdx.x;
    c[i] = a[i] + b[i];
}

int main() {
    const int arraySize = 5;
    const int a[arraySize] = {1, 2, 3, 4, 5};
    const int b[arraySize] = {10, 20, 30, 40, 50};
    int c[arraySize] = {0};

    int *dev_a = 0;
    int *dev_b = 0;
    int *dev_c = 0;
```

```
    // Allocate GPU buffers for three vectors (two input, one output)
    cudaMalloc((void**)&dev_c, arraySize * sizeof(int));
    cudaMalloc((void**)&dev_a, arraySize * sizeof(int));
    cudaMalloc((void**)&dev_b, arraySize * sizeof(int));

    // Copy input vectors from host memory to GPU buffers.
    cudaMemcpy(dev_a, a, arraySize * sizeof(int), cudaMemcpyHostToDevice);
    cudaMemcpy(dev_b, b, arraySize * sizeof(int), cudaMemcpyHostToDevice);

    // Launch a kernel on the GPU with one thread for each element.
    addKernel<<<1, arraySize>>>(dev_c, dev_a, dev_b);

    // Copy output vector from GPU buffer to host memory.
    cudaMemcpy(c, dev_c, arraySize * sizeof(int), cudaMemcpyDeviceToHost);

    // Display resulting vector
    for (int i = 0; i < arraySize; ++i)
        printf("%d ", c[i]);

    // Free GPU buffers
    cudaFree(dev_c);
    cudaFree(dev_a);
    cudaFree(dev_b);

    return 0;
}
```

In the code provided, data parallelism is illustrated through an example where the same operation (addition) is concurrently applied to elements of arrays a and b. Each thread handles a single element from the arrays, operating in parallel with other threads. The addKernel function is invoked with arraySize threads, each adding corresponding elements from arrays a and b and storing the result in array c.

The main function sets up the environment by allocating memory on the GPU for the arrays and copying data from host memory to these arrays. The kernel is then launched and each thread performs the addition operation on the GPU. After computation, the results are copied back to the host memory and printed out. The memory allocated on the GPU is subsequently freed.

- Task parallelism can be implemented similarly, but instead of applying the same operation across data elements, each thread could be assigned a different task. This is less common in classical CUDA programming but can be useful when implementing complex algorithms requiring different operations.

- It's essential to understand how CUDA fosters thread and data parallelism through its hierarchical threading model. Threads are organized into blocks, and blocks are organized into grids. This model enables developers to leverage both fine-grained and coarse-grained parallelism. For instance, blocks of threads can handle different data chunks (coarse-grained), while individual threads in a block handle elements within those chunks (fine-grained).

- To effectively exploit parallelism, take advantage of shared memory within thread blocks to reduce global memory accesses and synchronization overhead. Shared memory allows threads within the same block to share data efficiently. Synchronization mechanisms like __syncthreads() are available to ensure accurate data sharing among threads.

Integrating both thread and data parallelism into your CUDA programs involves identifying independent tasks and homogeneous data operations and organizing them into threads and blocks appropriately. Fine-tuning the number of threads per block can impact performance significantly due to the GPU's architecture, including considerations like warp size and memory coalescing. When executed efficiently, combining thread and data parallelism leads to optimized GPU resource utilization, enhancing computational throughput for diverse applications.

6.4 Domain Decomposition

Domain decomposition is a critical technique in parallel computing that refers to dividing a large computational problem into smaller subproblems that can be solved concurrently on multiple processors or threads. When implementing domain decomposition in CUDA, the goal is to exploit the parallel architecture of GPUs to distribute work effectively and minimize inter-thread communication overhead.

In CUDA programming, domain decomposition involves spatially or functionally partitioning the problem domain. The choice of decomposition strategy depends on the nature of the problem and the computational resources available. The two primary techniques are spatial domain decomposition and functional domain decomposition.

Spatial Domain Decomposition

Spatial domain decomposition involves dividing the computational domain into smaller regions, with each region assigned to a different GPU thread or block. This technique is particularly useful for problems where the workload is relatively uniform across the domain, such as the numeric simulation of partial differential equations (PDEs).

Consider a simple example of a 2D heat diffusion problem represented by a grid. The domain decomposition strategy would divide the grid into smaller subgrids, each processed by a separate thread block. Let us define the grid size as NX by NY, and assume the use of a CUDA block size of BLOCKDIM_X by BLOCKDIM_Y. The following code snippet illustrates this spatial domain decomposition:

```
__global__ void heat_diffusion(float *temperature, float *new_temperature,
                               int NX, int NY, float alpha) {
    int ix = blockIdx.x * blockDim.x + threadIdx.x;
    int iy = blockIdx.y * blockDim.y + threadIdx.y;

    if (ix > 0 && ix < NX-1 && iy > 0 && iy < NY-1) {
        int idx = iy * NX + ix;
        float tx = temperature[idx + 1] - 2.0f * temperature[idx] + temperature[idx - 1];
        float ty = temperature[idx + NX] - 2.0f * temperature[idx] + temperature[idx -
            NX];
        new_temperature[idx] = temperature[idx] + alpha * (tx + ty);
    }
}
```

In this example, the spatial domain decomposition strategy ensures that each thread computes the new temperature value for a single grid point based on its neighbors. The use of blockIdx and threadIdx allows the problem domain to be partitioned dynamically based on the block and thread dimensions specified at runtime.

The performance of the spatial domain decomposition relies heavily on the balance of workload among threads and the overhead of synchronizing boundary data. Proper handling of boundary conditions is critical to ensure accurate computations and avoid race conditions. Using shared memory to store boundary values can reduce global memory accesses and improve performance.

Functional Domain Decomposition

Functional domain decomposition, in contrast, divides the computation into distinct tasks or functions, with each task performed by different threads or thread blocks. This approach is suitable for problems where different subtasks can be executed in parallel without significant interaction.

For example, in a physics simulation involving different phases like collision detection, force calculation, and object updates, each phase can be handled by a separate set of threads. Here, functional decomposition leverages the independence of tasks to achieve parallel execution.

Consider the following CUDA kernels representing different functional phases of a physics simulation:

```
__global__ void detect_collisions(Object *objects, int num_objects) {
    // Collision detection logic
}

__global__ void calculate_forces(Object *objects, int num_objects) {
    // Force calculation logic
}

__global__ void update_objects(Object *objects, int num_objects, float dt) {
    int idx = blockIdx.x * blockDim.x + threadIdx.x;
    if (idx < num_objects) {
        // Object update logic based on calculated forces
    }
}
```

In the above code, three different kernels are defined for collision detection, force calculation, and object updates, respectively. By launching these kernels in separate streams or using CUDA's asynchronous execution features, the entire simulation can benefit from functional parallelism.

```
detect_collisions<<<num_blocks, blockDim>>>(d_objects, num_objects);
cudaDeviceSynchronize();

calculate_forces<<<num_blocks, blockDim>>>(d_objects, num_objects);
cudaDeviceSynchronize();

update_objects<<<num_blocks, blockDim>>>(d_objects, num_objects, dt);
cudaDeviceSynchronize();
```

Proper scheduling and synchronization are essential in functional domain decomposition to prevent race conditions and ensure that data dependencies between tasks are respected. CUDA streams and events can be utilized to manage these dependencies effectively.

In both spatial and functional domain decomposition, profiling tools like nvprof and Nsight can help identify performance bottlenecks, guiding further optimization efforts. Analyzing memory access patterns, computational load balance, and synchronization overhead is key to refining the decomposition strategy.

Overall, domain decomposition remains an indispensable technique in leveraging the full potential of CUDA-enabled GPUs, allowing the decomposition of complex computational problems into manageable and executable units. Through careful planning and implementation, significant performance gains and computational efficiency can be achieved.

6.5 Task Parallelism

Task parallelism is a parallel programming model that focuses on distributing tasks across multiple computing processors. Unlike data parallelism, which involves performing identical operations on different data elements concurrently, task parallelism involves executing different tasks, potentially on the same or different data elements, in parallel. In the CUDA architecture, task parallelism allows the execution of different kernel functions or the same kernel function with different parameters concurrently.

A practical application of task parallelism often involves division of a large computational problem into multiple, smaller tasks. Each of these tasks can then be assigned to a different GPU thread block or even to different streams within the same CUDA application. This model is particularly useful for applications where different operations need to be performed simultaneously, or where the workload is heterogeneous.

To illustrate task parallelism in CUDA, consider the scenario where we need to perform different processing steps on different parts of a dataset. Suppose we have a dataset that needs to undergo image processing, analysis, and classification. These operations are distinct and thus can be executed concurrently.

```
__global__ void processImageKernel(int *imageData) {
    // Kernel to perform image processing
}

__global__ void analyzeDataKernel(int *analyzedData) {
    // Kernel to perform data analysis
}

__global__ void classifyDataKernel(int *classificationResults) {
    // Kernel to classify data
}

void performTaskParallelism(int *imageData, int *analyzedData, int *
      classificationResults) {
    // Launch kernels to perform tasks in parallel
    processImageKernel<<<numBlocks, numThreads>>>(imageData);
    analyzeDataKernel<<<numBlocks, numThreads>>>(analyzedData);
    classifyDataKernel<<<numBlocks, numThreads>>>(classificationResults);
}
```

In the above code example, three separate kernels are defined, each corresponding to a different task: image processing, data analysis, and data classification. The function performTaskParallelism launches these kernels concurrently. In actual CUDA code, proper synchronization mechanisms such as CUDA streams or events should be utilized to manage task dependencies and ensure correct execution order.

Streams in CUDA are a powerful feature that allows concurrent execution of kernels from different streams. By creating multiple streams, tasks can be issued and executed in parallel without waiting for other tasks in different streams to complete. Here's how streams can be effectively used to implement task parallelism:

```
void performTaskParallelismWithStreams(int *imageData, int *analyzedData, int *
      classificationResults) {
    cudaStream_t stream1, stream2, stream3;
    cudaStreamCreate(&stream1);
    cudaStreamCreate(&stream2);
    cudaStreamCreate(&stream3);

    processImageKernel<<<numBlocks, numThreads, 0, stream1>>>(imageData);
    analyzeDataKernel<<<numBlocks, numThreads, 0, stream2>>>(analyzedData);
    classifyDataKernel<<<numBlocks, numThreads, 0, stream3>>>(
          classificationResults);

    cudaStreamSynchronize(stream1);
    cudaStreamSynchronize(stream2);
    cudaStreamSynchronize(stream3);

    cudaStreamDestroy(stream1);
    cudaStreamDestroy(stream2);
    cudaStreamDestroy(stream3);
}
```

In this example, three CUDA streams are created, and each kernel is launched in its respective stream. The cudaStreamSynchronize function is called to ensure that each stream completes its tasks before the program proceeds. By dividing tasks across different streams, CUDA can overlap data transfers and computations, effectively utilizing the GPU's resources for improved performance.

Task parallelism also plays an essential role in multi-GPU programming, where different GPUs can perform separate tasks simultaneously. This approach is beneficial for scaling computational tasks across multiple GPUs to achieve faster execution times. Implementing task parallelism across multiple GPUs involves distributing different tasks to each GPU and ensuring proper synchronization and data management.

The following code demonstrates a basic example of task parallelism using two GPUs:

```
void performTaskParallelismMultiGPU(int *imageData1, int *imageData2) {
    int deviceCount;
    cudaGetDeviceCount(&deviceCount);
    if (deviceCount < 2) {
        printf("Need at least 2 GPUs for this example.\n");
        return;
    }
```

```
    cudaSetDevice(0);
    cudaStream_t stream1;
    cudaStreamCreate(&stream1);
    processImageKernel<<<numBlocks, numThreads, 0, stream1>>>(imageData1);
    cudaStreamSynchronize(stream1);
    cudaStreamDestroy(stream1);

    cudaSetDevice(1);
    cudaStream_t stream2;
    cudaStreamCreate(&stream2);
    processImageKernel<<<numBlocks, numThreads, 0, stream2>>>(imageData2);
    cudaStreamSynchronize(stream2);
    cudaStreamDestroy(stream2);
}
```

In this multi-GPU example, the cudaSetDevice function is used to select the active GPU, and different tasks (in this case, different segments of image processing) are assigned to separate GPUs. Proper synchronization is ensured using CUDA streams. This approach not only facilitates better resource utilization but also significantly reduces execution time for large-scale computations.

Task parallelism in CUDA programming leverages the GPU's capability to execute multiple, independent tasks concurrently. By effectively dividing tasks and managing their execution through streams and multi-GPU configurations, substantial performance improvements can be achieved. Task parallelism is crucial in scenarios where heterogeneous computations need to be processed simultaneously, making it an indispensable part of high-performance CUDA programming.

6.6 Hybrid Parallelism Models

Hybrid parallelism models in CUDA programming entail combining multiple parallelism strategies to optimize performance for complex computational tasks. This approach leverages the strengths of different models to address their individual limitations, providing a more flexible and efficient execution model. We will explore the implementation of hybrid parallel strategies by examining the integration of task parallelism with data parallelism and the usage of streams to synchronize multiple operations concurrently.

First, consider a scenario where both data parallelism and task parallelism are essential. Data parallelism involves decomposing a large dataset into smaller chunks that can be processed concurrently by different threads. On the other hand, task parallelism focuses on breaking down computational tasks or functions that can run parallelly. Combining these two forms of parallelism allows you to execute different kernels simultaneously while managing numerous data computations in parallel.

In a typical application, tasks might require performing distinct operations on different parts of a dataset. Let's examine an example that demonstrates this integration:

```
__global__ void processPartA(float* data, int size) {
    int idx = blockDim.x * blockIdx.x + threadIdx.x;
    if (idx < size) {
        data[idx] = data[idx] * 2.0f;
    }
}

__global__ void processPartB(float* data, int size) {
    int idx = blockDim.x * blockIdx.x + threadIdx.x;
    if (idx < size) {
        data[idx] = data[idx] + 1.0f;
    }
}

int main() {
    const int dataSize = 1024;
    float* d_data;
    cudaMalloc((void**)&d_data, dataSize * sizeof(float));

    // Launching processPartA and processPartB kernels on separate streams
    cudaStream_t stream1, stream2;
    cudaStreamCreate(&stream1);
    cudaStreamCreate(&stream2);

    processPartA<<<(dataSize + 255) / 256, 256, 0, stream1>>>(d_data, dataSize);
    processPartB<<<(dataSize + 255) / 256, 256, 0, stream2>>>(d_data, dataSize);

    // Synchronize the streams
    cudaStreamSynchronize(stream1);
    cudaStreamSynchronize(stream2);

    cudaStreamDestroy(stream1);
    cudaStreamDestroy(stream2);
    cudaFree(d_data);
    return 0;
}
```

In this example, two separate kernels processPartA and processPartB are executed concurrently using two streams, stream1 and stream2. By employing streams, different parts of the dataset can undergo distinct operations simultaneously. This hybrid approach combines the data parallel calculations within each kernel with the task parallelism of running different kernels concurrently.

The efficiency of this model is determined by balancing the computational workload across tasks and ensuring proper synchronization. CUDA streams facilitate asynchronous execution, reducing idle times of the GPU by overlapping computations. The synchronization functions like cudaStreamSynchronize are critical to guarantee that all tasks are completed before proceeding to subsequent operations, thereby maintaining the correct order of execution.

Another way to harness hybrid parallelism is to dynamically allocate computational resources based on the task requirements. For instance, some tasks might require more computational power, while others may need less. Adjusting resources such as the number of threads or blocks for each task can optimize performance.

Consider an example where we combine task parallelism with adaptive resource allocation:

```
__global__ void heavyComputation(float* data, int size) {
    int idx = blockDim.x * blockIdx.x + threadIdx.x;
    if (idx < size) {
        for (int i = 0; i < 100; ++i) {
            data[idx] += sin(data[idx]);
        }
    }
}

__global__ void lightComputation(float* data, int size) {
    int idx = blockDim.x * blockIdx.x + threadIdx.x;
    if (idx < size) {
        data[idx] *= 0.5f;
    }
}

int main() {
    const int dataSize = 1024;
    float* d_data;
    cudaMalloc((void**)&d_data, dataSize * sizeof(float));

    // Launch kernels with different resource allocations
    heavyComputation<<<(dataSize + 255) / 256, 256>>>(d_data, dataSize);
    lightComputation<<<(dataSize + 63) / 64, 64>>>(d_data, dataSize);

    cudaDeviceSynchronize();
    cudaFree(d_data);
    return 0;
}
```

Here, heavyComputation and lightComputation kernels are launched with different numbers of blocks and threads based on their computational intensity. heavyComputation requires more processing and thus utilizes a larger number of threads per block, whereas lightComputation involves relatively simpler operations, needing fewer threads. This flexibility in resource assignment is pivotal in maximizing utilization and enhancing throughput.

Moreover, leveraging the CUDA dynamic parallelism (CDP) feature enables kernel functions to launch additional kernels. Such a capability is particularly useful in recursive algorithms or when the workload can be dynamically resolved at runtime. Combining dynamic parallelism within a hybrid model can offer advanced optimization strategies tailored to complex applications.

The following example demonstrates a hybrid model integrating CUDA dynamic parallelism:

```
__global__ void parentKernel(float* data, int size) {
    int idx = blockDim.x * blockIdx.x + threadIdx.x;
    if (idx < size / 2) {
        float* subData = data + idx * (size / blockDim.x);
        childKernel<<<1, 256>>>(subData, size / 2);
        cudaDeviceSynchronize();
    }
}

__global__ void childKernel(float* data, int size) {
    int idx = blockDim.x * blockIdx.x + threadIdx.x;
    if (idx < size) {
        data[idx] = sqrt(data[idx]);
    }
}

int main() {
    const int dataSize = 1024;
    float* d_data;
    cudaMalloc((void**)&d_data, dataSize * sizeof(float));

    parentKernel<<<4, 256>>>(d_data, dataSize);

    cudaDeviceSynchronize();
    cudaFree(d_data);
    return 0;
}
```

In the above code, the parentKernel launches the childKernel using dynamic parallelism. This capability allows childKernel to be executed on subsets of the data managed by parentKernel. The synchronization within the parent kernel ensures sequential consistency across launched kernels.

Hybrid Parallelism Models significantly enhance CUDA's efficiency by synchronizing the execution of heterogeneous kernel tasks, making this approach fundamental for optimizing high-performance computing applications. Properly orchestrating data and task parallel executions—along with adaptive resource allocations and dynamic parallelism—ensures maximal GPU utilization and minimizes execution time.

6.7 Using Streams for Parallel Execution

In CUDA, streams provide a mechanism for concurrent execution of kernel functions, independent memory transfers, and the overlap of computation with data transfers. A stream is essentially a sequence of operations that are executed in order, but different streams can potentially execute concurrently. Exploiting streams effectively can lead to significant performance improvements, especially when overlapping computations with memory transfers.

To create and use streams, the CUDA runtime API provides several functions. The primary functions used for managing streams include cudaStreamCreate(), cudaStreamDestroy(), and cudaStreamSynchronize(). Below is a concise example demonstrating how to create and destroy a stream:

```
cudaStream_t stream;
cudaStreamCreate(&stream);

// Execute kernel in stream
myKernel<<< gridSize, blockSize, 0, stream >>>(d_data);

// Synchronize stream
cudaStreamSynchronize(stream);

// Destroy stream
cudaStreamDestroy(stream);
```

In this example, a stream is created using cudaStreamCreate(). The kernel myKernel is then launched in the created stream. Synchronization is performed to ensure that all operations in the stream have completed with cudaStreamSynchronize(), and finally, the stream is destroyed using cudaStreamDestroy().

When utilizing streams, it's important to understand the concept of stream dependencies and asynchronous execution. Memory transfers and kernel executions can be issued to different streams to achieve overlap. Here is an example to illustrate this aspect:

```
cudaStream_t stream1, stream2;
cudaStreamCreate(&stream1);
cudaStreamCreate(&stream2);

cudaMemcpyAsync(d_data1, h_data1, dataSize, cudaMemcpyHostToDevice, stream1);
cudaMemcpyAsync(d_data2, h_data2, dataSize, cudaMemcpyHostToDevice, stream2);

myKernel<<< gridSize, blockSize, 0, stream1 >>>(d_data1);
myKernel2<<< gridSize, blockSize, 0, stream2 >>>(d_data2);

cudaMemcpyAsync(h_result1, d_result1, dataSize, cudaMemcpyDeviceToHost, stream1
    );
```

```
cudaMemcpyAsync(h_result2, d_result2, dataSize, cudaMemcpyDeviceToHost, stream2
    );

cudaStreamSynchronize(stream1);
cudaStreamSynchronize(stream2);

cudaStreamDestroy(stream1);
cudaStreamDestroy(stream2);
```

In this example, two streams, stream1 and stream2, are created. Memory transfers and kernel executions are issued to these streams using cudaMemcpyAsync() and typical kernel launch syntax, respectively. Asynchronous memory operations allow data transfers to occur concurrently with kernel execution, provided that the operations target different streams and do not overlap solely on the same device resources.

Effects of using streams depend heavily on the actual hardware capabilities, such as the number of supported concurrent execution contexts and the architecture of the GPU scheduler. Overlapping memory transfers with kernel computations is particularly effective on GPUs that support concurrent copy and compute operations. For example, NVIDIA GPUs starting from the Fermi architecture (CC 2.x) have this capability.

Effective stream management also involves ensuring that operations targeting the same resources are correctly synchronized. Attempts to read or write from/to the same memory locations from multiple streams can lead to race conditions and undefined behavior. It is essential to respect the program's data dependencies and use appropriate synchronization methods to safeguard the integrity of data.

An additional technique for optimizing stream usage involves the use of cudaEvent_t objects, which can be employed for more precise synchronization across streams. Events in CUDA serve as markers in streams and can be used to record when specific operations have been completed. This is useful for creating explicit dependencies between operations in different streams without full blocking synchronization. The following example demonstrates basic usage of events:

```
cudaStream_t stream1, stream2;
cudaStreamCreate(&stream1);
cudaStreamCreate(&stream2);

cudaEvent_t event;
cudaEventCreate(&event);

cudaMemcpyAsync(d_data1, h_data1, dataSize, cudaMemcpyHostToDevice, stream1);
cudaEventRecord(event, stream1);

myKernel<<< gridSize, blockSize, 0, stream1 >>>(d_data1);
cudaEventRecord(event, stream1);
```

```
cudaStreamWaitEvent(stream2, event, 0);
myKernel2<<< gridSize, blockSize, 0, stream2 >>>(d_data2);

cudaStreamSynchronize(stream1);
cudaStreamSynchronize(stream2);

cudaEventDestroy(event);
cudaStreamDestroy(stream1);
cudaStreamDestroy(stream2);
```

Here, an event is created and recorded in stream1 after a memory copy operation and a kernel launch. The second stream, stream2, is instructed to wait for this event, effectively synchronizing its operations to occur after the event has been recorded. This approach allows for finer control over the order of execution among different streams without completely blocking the host thread.

Understanding and leveraging streams effectively can significantly improve application performance by enabling concurrent execution of tasks and better utilization of GPU resources. Proper synchronization and stream management are crucial for harnessing the full power of CUDA streams for parallel execution.

6.8 Hierarchical Grid Execution

Hierarchical grid execution in CUDA allows the organization of threads into a multi-level grid structure, which can be leveraged to exploit parallelism efficiently at multiple levels. This section expounds on the concepts foundational to hierarchical grid execution, discusses its benefits, and illustrates practical examples of implementing this model in CUDA programming.

The grid structure in CUDA consists of three primary components: grids, blocks, and threads. Each grid comprises one or more blocks, and each block consists of multiple threads. Blocks are organized in a two-dimensional array (a grid) while threads within a block are arranged in three-dimensional arrays. This hierarchical organization is crucial for matching the hardware architecture, which contains multiple streaming multiprocessors (SMs) within a GPU. Each SM can run multiple blocks simultaneously, allowing a high degree of parallelism.

Grid: A collection of thread blocks that execute a given kernel.

Block: A group of threads that can cooperate with each other by sharing data through shared memory and synchronizing their execution to coordinate memory access.

Thread: The smallest unit of execution in CUDA that performs operations sequentially. Each thread has its own set of registers and local memory.

The hierarchical grid execution model enables flexibility not only in terms of managing parallel tasks but also in terms of optimizing memory access patterns and reducing inter-thread communication overhead.

To initialize hierarchical grid execution in CUDA, the following syntax is used to define the grid and block dimensions when launching a kernel:

```
kernel<<<gridDim, blockDim>>>(...);
```

Here, gridDim defines the dimensions of the grid and blockDim defines the dimensions of each block. Both parameters can be specified as dim3 type, which accommodates three dimensions (x, y, z).

Consider the following example, which illustrates a simple vector addition using hierarchical grid execution:

```
__global__ void vectorAdd(const float *A, const float *B, float *C, int N) {
    int idx = blockIdx.x * blockDim.x + threadIdx.x;
    if (idx < N) {
        C[idx] = A[idx] + B[idx];
    }
}

int main() {
    int N = 1000;
    size_t size = N * sizeof(float);

    float *h_A, *h_B, *h_C;
    float *d_A, *d_B, *d_C;

    // Allocate host memory
    h_A = (float *)malloc(size);
    h_B = (float *)malloc(size);
    h_C = (float *)malloc(size);

    // Initialize host arrays
    for (int i = 0; i < N; ++i) {
        h_A[i] = static_cast<float>(i);
        h_B[i] = static_cast<float>(i);
    }

    // Allocate device memory
    cudaMalloc((void **)&d_A, size);
    cudaMalloc((void **)&d_B, size);
    cudaMalloc((void **)&d_C, size);

    // Copy host memory to device
    cudaMemcpy(d_A, h_A, size, cudaMemcpyHostToDevice);
    cudaMemcpy(d_B, h_B, size, cudaMemcpyHostToDevice);

    // Define grid and block dimensions
```

```
    dim3 blockDim(256);
    dim3 gridDim((N + blockDim.x - 1) / blockDim.x);

    // Launch the kernel
    vectorAdd<<<gridDim, blockDim>>>(d_A, d_B, d_C, N);

    // Copy result back to host
    cudaMemcpy(h_C, d_C, size, cudaMemcpyDeviceToHost);

    // Verify the result
    for (int i = 0; i < N; ++i) {
        if (fabs(h_C[i] - (h_A[i] + h_B[i])) > 1e-5) {
            printf("Error at index %d\n", i);
            break;
        }
    }

    // Free device memory
    cudaFree(d_A);
    cudaFree(d_B);
    cudaFree(d_C);

    // Free host memory
    free(h_A);
    free(h_B);
    free(h_C);

    return 0;
}
```

This example demonstrates the computation of vector addition, where each element in the result vector C is the sum of the corresponding elements in vectors A and B.

The block and grid dimensions are essential in CUDA programming as they influence performance and hardware utilization. Efficient mapping of threads to GPU cores requires careful consideration of hardware details such as the number of available SMs, the maximum number of threads per block, and the memory hierarchy.

When working with hierarchical grid execution, memory optimization techniques like coalesced memory access can significantly enhance performance. Threads within the same block can leverage shared memory to reduce global memory access latency. Shared memory is on-chip memory that provides higher bandwidth compared to global memory, thereby facilitating faster inter-thread communication within a block.

Another optimization strategy involves the use of warp divergence control. In CUDA, threads are executed in groups of 32, called warps. To avoid performance degradation due to warp divergence, it is crucial to ensure that all threads in a warp follow the same execution path. Conditional statements within kernels should be designed to minimize divergence among threads within a warp.

Understanding and leveraging hierarchical grid execution is pivotal in devising efficient and scalable CUDA programs. Effective utilization of the grid structure aligns with harnessing the full computational power of GPUs, thereby accelerating a wide range of scientific and engineering applications.

6.9 Multi-GPU Parallel Programming

Multi-GPU parallel programming involves the simultaneous utilization of multiple Graphics Processing Units (GPUs) to perform complex computational tasks, significantly enhancing computational performance and scalability. This section elucidates the methodologies and intricacies associated with multi-GPU programming within the CUDA framework. By distributing workloads across several GPUs, one can achieve higher throughput, reduced computation time, and manage more extensive data sets effectively.

To effectively leverage multiple GPUs, it is crucial to understand the underlying architecture and communication mechanisms. The CUDA programming model provides various APIs and constructs to facilitate multi-GPU programming. These include device management functions, memory management functions, and peer-to-peer communication functions.

Device Management Functions: The first step in multi-GPU programming involves identifying the available GPUs and managing the context for each GPU. The following CUDA API functions are essential:

```
// Get the number of available GPUs
int deviceCount;
cudaGetDeviceCount(&deviceCount);
std::cout << "Number of GPUs: " << deviceCount << std::endl;
```

Each GPU is identified by a device ID. To set the active GPU that the current host thread will execute on, use the cudaSetDevice() function:

```
// Set the active GPU to device 0
cudaSetDevice(0);
```

It is essential to check for device properties to determine the most suitable tasks for each GPU. The cudaGetDeviceProperties() function retrieves information about the specific GPU such as the compute capability, total global memory, and the number of multiprocessors:

```
cudaDeviceProp deviceProp;
cudaGetDeviceProperties(&deviceProp, device);
std::cout << "Device " << device << " has compute capability "
        << deviceProp.major << "." << deviceProp.minor << std::endl;
```

Memory Management: Proper memory management across multiple GPUs is a critical aspect of performance optimization. Standard memory allocation functions such as cudaMalloc() and cudaFree() can be used, but operations must be explicitly directed to the appropriate device context:

```
float *d_A;
cudaSetDevice(0);
cudaMalloc((void **)&d_A, size);
```

Once memory is allocated, data needs to be transferred from the host to the respective GPU memory using cudaMemcpy():

```
// Copy data from host to GPU 0
cudaSetDevice(0);
cudaMemcpy(d_A, h_A, size, cudaMemcpyHostToDevice);
```

Kernel Execution and Synchronization: With multiple GPUs, kernels can execute concurrently, significantly speeding up the computation process. Each GPU operates independently, executing kernels defined for specific parts of the computation. It is crucial to synchronize these operations to ensure correct results:

```
// Launch kernel on GPU 0
cudaSetDevice(0);
Kernel<<<grid, block>>>(d_A);

// Synchronize GPU 0
cudaDeviceSynchronize();
```

This model allows effective overlap of computation and data transfer between the host and multiple GPUs.

Peer-to-Peer Communication: Peer-to-peer (P2P) memory copy allows direct data transfer between the memory spaces of different GPUs, bypassing the host and improving performance. To enable P2P memory transfer, use cudaDeviceEnablePeerAccess():

```
// Enable peer access between GPU 0 and GPU 1
cudaSetDevice(0);
cudaDeviceEnablePeerAccess(1, 0);
```

Once P2P access is enabled, data can be transferred directly between the GPUs using cudaMemcpyPeer():

```
// Copy data from GPU 0 to GPU 1
cudaMemcpyPeer(d_B, 1, d_A, 0, size);
```

Multi-GPU Programming Models: Several models can be implemented for multi-GPU programming, including data parallelism and task parallelism. In data parallelism, different chunks of data are processed on different GPUs, while in task parallelism, different tasks or stages of computation are distributed across GPUs.

For example, in data parallelism:

```
// Assuming we have num_gpus GPUs
for (int i = 0; i < num_gpus; i++) {
    cudaSetDevice(i);
    size_t offset = i * chunk_size;
    cudaMemcpy(d_A + offset, h_A + offset, chunk_size, cudaMemcpyHostToDevice);
    Kernel<<<grid, block>>>(d_A + offset);
    cudaMemcpy(h_A + offset, d_A + offset, chunk_size, cudaMemcpyDeviceToHost);
}
```

Multi-GPU programming significantly boosts computational capabilities by harnessing the collective power of multiple devices. By efficiently managing device contexts, memory, kernel execution, and utilizing peer-to-peer communication, one can achieve substantial performance improvements suitable for large-scale scientific computations and data-intensive applications.

6.10 Best Practices for Choosing a Parallel Programming Model

Choosing an optimal parallel programming model in CUDA requires careful consideration of various factors, including the nature of the computational task, the available hardware resources, and the desired performance characteristics. This section outlines best practices to guide the selection process to achieve efficient and effective parallel execution.

Understand the Task at Hand
Identify the nature of the computational workload. Tasks can broadly fall into categories such as data parallelism, task parallelism, or a combination of both. Data parallelism is suitable for problems where the same operation is performed on multiple data elements independently, which aligns well with CUDA's architecture through SIMT (Single Instruction Multiple Threads) execution. Task parallelism is appropri-

ate for problems that can be decomposed into independent or semi-independent tasks, which may suit concurrent kernel executions or the use of multiple streams.

Analyze Memory Access Patterns
Efficient memory access is critical for achieving high performance. Understanding and optimizing the memory access patterns can significantly impact the performance of the parallel program. Coalesced memory access, where contiguous threads access contiguous memory locations, should be targeted to minimize memory latency. Use shared memory judiciously to store frequently accessed data, reducing global memory accesses. Assess whether data transfer between the host and device can be minimized or overlapped with computation using CUDA streams.

Consider Scalability
The parallel programming model chosen should scale with the problem size and available hardware. Models that overly depend on specific hardware configurations might limit scalability. Ensure that the model can efficiently utilize additional computational resources, whether through an increased number of threads, streaming multiprocessors, or multiple GPUs.

Balance Load Among Resources
Load balancing is essential for maximizing resource utilization. Both static and dynamic load balancing techniques can be used to distribute computational work evenly across threads and blocks. Strategies such as domain decomposition can distribute different parts of a problem across multiple GPUs or streams, ensuring that no single resource becomes a bottleneck.

Leverage Hierarchical Grid Execution
Use hierarchical grid execution to organize computations into a grid of thread blocks. Each block executes concurrently, and threads within a block can cooperate using shared memory and synchronization mechanisms. This hierarchical approach allows more efficient management of resources and can be optimized based on the problem's specific needs.

Incorporate Stream-Based Parallel Execution
Streams can be used to overlap computation and communication, improving the overall efficiency. By partitioning tasks into different streams, it is possible to execute multiple kernels concurrently while simultaneously managing memory transfers between the host and device. This asynchronous execution can significantly reduce idle times

and make better use of the GPU resources.

Deploy Multi-GPU Strategies
For tasks that exceed the computational capacity of a single GPU, multi-GPU parallel programming models can be employed. Distribute the workload effectively among multiple GPUs to enhance performance. Utilize NVIDIA's NVLink or GPUDirect RDMA for efficient inter-GPU communication, minimizing the overhead associated with data transfers.

Employ Task Parallelism and Hybrid Models
Many real-world applications exhibit both data and task parallelism, making hybrid parallel programming models advantageous. By combining different models, such as SIMT for data parallel parts and task-based parallelism for control flow, it is possible to achieve higher performance. Hybrid models leverage the strengths of each approach, providing flexibility and scalability.

Optimize Resource Utilization
Monitor and profile the resource utilization to identify bottlenecks and optimize accordingly. Use tools such as NVIDIA Visual Profiler (nvprof) or Nsight Systems to gain insights into GPU performance, memory usage, and kernel execution timelines. Fine-tune kernel launches, memory allocations, and usage patterns based on the profiling data to achieve maximum efficiency.

Follow Established Best Practices
Adhere to established best practices within the CUDA programming community. Keep up-to-date with CUDA documentation, tutorials, and community forums. Incorporate feedback and optimization techniques suggested by other experienced practitioners to continuously improve and refine the parallel programming model employed.

Choosing an appropriate parallel programming model is critical for leveraging the full potential of CUDA-enabled hardware. By systematically analyzing the task requirements, memory access patterns, scalability, and resource utilization, and by applying hybrid models where suitable, developers can achieve significant performance gains and efficient computation.

Chapter 7

Optimizing CUDA Performance

This chapter focuses on techniques for optimizing CUDA performance, starting with profiling CUDA applications to identify bottlenecks. It explores optimizing memory access patterns, reducing memory transfers, and improving instruction throughput. The chapter also covers strategies for optimizing kernel launch configurations, latency hiding techniques, caching, and shared memory usage. Additional topics include maximizing occupancy and resource utilization, as well as balancing load and reducing divergence to achieve higher performance in CUDA applications.

7.1 Introduction to CUDA Performance Optimization

In high-performance computing, achieving optimal performance in CUDA applications necessitates a methodical approach to identify and eliminate bottlenecks. Optimization is not a one-size-fits-all task; rather, it requires a deep understanding of the CUDA programming model and the architecture of NVIDIA GPUs. Ensuring that your application fully utilizes the underlying hardware capabilities is crucial for achieving high performance.

The process begins with profiling CUDA applications to pinpoint areas where performance can be improved. Profiling tools like nvprof and Nsight Compute provide insights into how your application interacts with the GPU. These tools help identify hotspots, inefficient memory access patterns, and other performance impediments. Understanding the results from profiling guides subsequent optimization efforts.

Memory access patterns play a significant role in CUDA performance. Global memory accesses, which are typically non-coalesced, can introduce substantial latency. Ensuring that memory accesses are coalesced where possible helps reduce this latency. Techniques such as memory alignment and using shared memory to avoid redundant global memory accesses are critical in optimizing memory performance. Shared memory, being closer to the multiprocessor, has much lower latency compared to global memory, and its judicious use can lead to considerable performance gains.

Reducing memory transfers between the host and the device is another pivotal optimization strategy. These transfers are relatively slow compared to on-device memory transactions. By minimizing these transfers, especially in time-critical sections of the code, one can significantly enhance the overall application throughput. Strategies include overlapping data transfers with computation using streams and zero-copy memory techniques, where the host and device can simultaneously access the same memory space.

Improving instruction throughput involves ensuring efficient utilization of the GPU's arithmetic units. This optimization can be achieved by maximizing the number of floating-point operations per second (FLOPS). Techniques include optimizing mathematical operations, minimizing branching to avoid warp divergence, and leveraging intrinsic functions for computational efficiency. Additionally, understanding the interplay between instruction types and their execution units is essential.

Optimizing kernel launch configurations is critical for leveraging the full computational capabilities of the GPU. Factors such as the number of threads per block, the number of blocks per grid, and the use of shared memory per block must be finely tuned. Balancing these parameters requires understanding the specific GPU architecture, as different GPUs have different capabilities and limitations in terms of thread and block counts.

Latency hiding techniques are employed to maximize the work done by the GPU while waiting for data transfers or other operations to complete. Techniques such as asynchronous kernel execution and overlapping kernel executions with data transfers are beneficial in this realm. The effective use of CUDA streams can lead to significant improvements in latency hiding.

Caching and shared memory techniques further augment the performance by reducing the number of accesses to the slower global memory. Using shared memory to store frequently accessed data, utilizing constant memory for read-only data, and minimizing L2 cache misses ensure that the GPU spends less time waiting for data and more time performing computations.

Maximizing occupancy and resource utilization involves ensuring that the GPU's computational resources are fully engaged. This includes optimizing the register usage and shared memory allocation such that the maximum number of warps can be in-flight. However, maximizing occupancy should not be done at the expense of increased register spilling to local memory or inappropriate shared memory usage, which could negate the benefits.

Load balancing and reducing divergence in the GPU workload ensure that all threads within a warp and all warps within a block perform work efficiently. Load imbalance and warp divergence are common pitfalls in CUDA programming. Intelligent kernel design, memory access patterns, and dynamic parallelism are keys to an evenly distributed load that minimizes idle computational resources.

Understanding and leveraging these techniques in conjunction with a thorough profiling and iterative testing process forms the bedrock of effective CUDA performance optimization.

7.2 Profiling CUDA Applications

Profiling is an essential process for identifying performance bottlenecks and inefficiencies in CUDA applications. Precise profiling enables developers to understand how their code utilizes hardware resources and where potential improvements can be made. Profiling CUDA applications involves several tools and techniques designed to monitor and analyze a wide range of runtime metrics.

CUDA Profiling Tools

NVIDIA provides several tools for profiling CUDA applications. These tools include the NVIDIA Visual Profiler, nvprof, and the Nsight suite, which offer capabilities for collecting and visualizing performance data.

- **NVIDIA Visual Profiler**: A graphical profiling tool that provides a detailed timeline display, enabling developers to visualize and analyze the CUDA application's execution flow.
- **nvprof**: A command-line profiling tool that offers a comprehensive set of metrics and events, useful for automated analysis and scripting.
- **Nsight Compute and Nsight Systems**: Advanced profiling tools that provide fine-grained performance analysis and system-level profiling capabilities, including GPU, CPU, and memory interactions.

Using nvprof for Profiling

nvprof is a powerful tool for initial performance analysis. It collects various metrics and events from the CUDA application and generates a comprehensive report. Below is an example command to profile a CUDA application using nvprof:

```
nvprof --metrics achieved_occupancy,kernel_duration a.out
```

nvprof outputs metrics such as achieved occupancy and kernel duration, allowing for a detailed analysis of the performance characteristics.

```
== PROFILES ==
Metric Name                  Metric Value
------------------------------ -------------
achieved_occupancy             0.75
kernel_duration              455.23 ms
```

Interpreting Output Metrics

Interpreting the profiling output involves understanding the significance of different metrics:

- **Achieved Occupancy**: Reflects the ratio of active warps to the maximum number of warps supported on a multiprocessor. Higher occupancy often correlates with better resource utilization but does not always guarantee optimal performance.
- **Kernel Duration**: Indicates the total time taken by a kernel to execute. A lower duration suggests better performance, but it must be considered alongside instruction throughput, memory bandwidth, and other factors.

Using NVIDIA Visual Profiler

The NVIDIA Visual Profiler provides a GUI-based approach to profiling. By running a CUDA application within this tool, developers can capture a detailed execution trace, which includes timelines for kernel launches, memory transfers, and synchronization activities. For instance, to start profiling, launch the application within the profiler:

- Open the Visual Profiler and select File -> New Session.
- Specify the application executable and arguments.
- Start profiling and wait for the data collection to complete.

The profiling session will produce a timeline visualization, which highlights the execution order of kernels and memory transfers, identifies idle periods, and allows for the examination of dependencies and concurrency.

Nsight Compute and Nsight Systems

For more advanced profiling needs, Nsight Compute and Nsight Systems offer in-depth analysis features:

- **Nsight Compute**: Focuses on GPU kernel performance metrics, including detailed warp state analysis, memory throughput, and instruction counts.
- **Nsight Systems**: Provides a holistic view of system-wide performance, capturing interactions between the CPU, GPU, and other system components. It supports multi-process application profiling and can be particularly useful for optimizing complex pipelines.

An example of initializing a profiling session using Nsight Compute:

```
nv-nsight-cu-cli --kernel-id ::regex:"myKernel*" ./myCudaApplication
```

The output provides detailed insights into kernel performance:

```
== PROFILES ==
Kernel Name                    Duration   Warp State Analysis
------------------------------ ---------- --------------------
myKernel                       235.12 ms  Active, Stalled
```

Best Practices for Profiling

There are several best practices to follow when profiling CUDA applications to ensure accurate and meaningful results:

- **Run Multiple Profiling Sessions**: Conduct multiple profiling sessions under different input conditions and system states to capture a comprehensive performance profile.
- **Minimize Overhead**: Be aware that profiling introduces overhead. Use lightweight profiling runs and selective metric collection to reduce the impact.
- **Analyze Different Kernels Separately**: Different kernels may have varying performance characteristics. Profile and optimize them individually for finer control over resource utilization.
- **Correlate Profiling Data with Source Code**: Link performance data back to the source code to identify and address specific performance bottlenecks.

Profiling forms the foundation for all subsequent optimization efforts. By leveraging profiling tools effectively, developers gain the insights necessary to optimize memory access patterns, reduce memory transfers, and improve instruction throughput—all pivotal for achieving superior CUDA application performance.

7.3 Optimizing Memory Access Patterns

Efficient memory access patterns are crucial to achieving high performance in CUDA applications. Memory access patterns directly influence the throughput by determining how effectively the GPU memory system can serve the simultaneous memory requests issued by threads. Optimizing these patterns often involves aligning memory accesses to exploit coalescing in global memory, maximizing use of shared memory, and minimizing memory latency.

Memory coalescing is a fundamental concept that profoundly impacts performance. Coalesced memory accesses occur when a warp of 32 threads accesses consecutive memory locations. This results in fewer, wider memory transactions rather than multiple, smaller ones. For instance, consider a scenario where each thread in a warp accesses consecutive elements in an array:

```
__global__ void coalescedAccess(float* data) {
    int idx = threadIdx.x + blockIdx.x * blockDim.x;
    data[idx] = data[idx] * 2.0f;
}
```

In this example, given that ‘threadIdx.x‘ spans from 0 to 31 within a warp, and assuming ‘blockDim.x‘ is a multiple of 32, each thread accesses a consecutive float element in the ‘data‘ array. This alignment allows the accesses to be coalesced, significantly reducing the number of separate memory transactions needed.

Misaligned or non-coalesced memory accesses result in multiple memory transactions for each warp, greatly increasing memory latency and reducing overall throughput. Consider the following example where the access pattern is non-coalesced:

```
__global__ void nonCoalescedAccess(float* data) {
    int idx = threadIdx.x + blockIdx.x * blockDim.x;
    data[idx * 2] = data[idx * 2] * 2.0f; // Non-coalesced access
}
```

Here, each thread accesses elements that are spaced two floats apart, preventing coalescence and leading to inefficient memory utilization.

Shared memory is a low-latency memory space that enables highly efficient inter-thread communication within a block. Appropriate use of shared memory can substantially optimize memory access patterns by reducing global memory accesses. As an example, consider a matrix multiplication kernel. Utilizing shared memory to store tile sub-matrices can reduce the number of global memory accesses:

```
__global__ void matrixMulSharedMem(const float* A, const float* B, float* C, int N)
    {
    __shared__ float Asub[32][32];
    __shared__ float Bsub[32][32];

    int tx = threadIdx.x, ty = threadIdx.y;
    int row = blockIdx.y * 32 + ty;
    int col = blockIdx.x * 32 + tx;
    float Cvalue = 0;

    for (int m = 0; m < N / 32; ++m) {
        Asub[ty][tx] = A[row * N + (m * 32 + tx)];
        Bsub[ty][tx] = B[(m * 32 + ty) * N + col];
        __syncthreads();

        for (int k = 0; k < 32; ++k) {
            Cvalue += Asub[ty][k] * Bsub[k][tx];
        }
        __syncthreads();
    }

    C[row * N + col] = Cvalue;
}
```

In this example, the tiles of matrices A and B are loaded into shared memory, significantly reducing the number of global memory accesses by reusing each element loaded into shared memory multiple times.

To further reduce memory latency, it is essential to utilize the memory hierarchy effectively. The CUDA memory hierarchy includes registers, shared memory, L1 cache, L2 cache, and global memory. Registers are the fastest but have limited size. Shared memory provides much higher bandwidth compared to global memory but is still limited in size and scope to a single block. L1 and L2 caches offer a compromise with greater sizes but slightly higher access latencies compared to shared memory.

Effective use of these various memory spaces requires careful consideration of data locality, size, and access patterns. For instance, if temporary variables are used repeatedly in a kernel, ensuring they are stored in registers or shared memory can dramatically reduce access latency. Moreover, optimizing thread block and grid dimensions to fully utilize shared memory without exceeding its limits is essential.

It is noteworthy that excessive use of shared memory can lead to lower occupancy if the memory requirements of each block are significant. Thus, a balance must be struck between using shared memory and other types of memory to maximize overall performance. The CUDA occupancy calculator can be a helpful tool for determining this balance by simulating different resource allocation scenarios.

A third significant strategy for optimizing memory access patterns involves reducing memory divergence. Memory divergence occurs when threads in a single warp follow different execution paths due to conditional statements or different memory access patterns. Reducing divergence yields higher memory throughput as all threads in a warp can access memory simultaneously. Consider the following example that causes memory divergence:

```
__global__ void divergentWarp(float* data) {
    int idx = threadIdx.x + blockIdx.x * blockDim.x;
    if ((idx % 2) == 0) {
        data[idx] = data[idx] * 2.0f;
    } else {
        data[idx] = data[idx] * 3.0f;
    }
}
```

The different conditions within the same warp lead to divergent execution paths, resulting in inefficient memory access and execution. By restructuring the code to avoid these conditional divergences, one can improve the warp execution efficiency.

Understanding and optimizing these aspects of memory access patterns are critical to achieving high-performance CUDA applications.

Efficiently managing global memory coalescence, maximizing shared memory usage, and minimizing memory divergence collectively contribute to reduced memory latency and increased overall throughput.

7.4 Reducing Memory Transfers

Data transfer between the host (CPU) and the device (GPU) is one of the primary bottlenecks in CUDA applications. Reducing memory transfers can significantly enhance the performance and efficiency of CUDA programs. This section discusses several techniques to minimize and optimize memory transfer between the host and the device.

Asynchronous Memory Transfer is one approach to mitigate the overhead of data transfer. CUDA allows for asynchronous data transfers, using streams to overlap computation and communication. By transferring data in smaller chunks, and overlapping these transfers with kernel execution, the application can utilize both the CPU and GPU more effectively. Below is an example illustrating asynchronous memory transfers using CUDA Streams:

```
// Asynchronous memory transfer example
cudaStream_t stream;
cudaStreamCreate(&stream);

cudaMemcpyAsync(d_data, h_data, size, cudaMemcpyHostToDevice, stream);
// Launch kernel in the same stream
myKernel<<<numBlocks, blockSize, 0, stream>>>(d_data);

// Asynchronous memory transfer back to host
cudaMemcpyAsync(h_result, d_data, size, cudaMemcpyDeviceToHost, stream);

cudaStreamSynchronize(stream);
cudaStreamDestroy(stream);
```

Using *Unified Memory* is another strategy to reduce memory transfer overhead. Unified Memory allows a single memory address space accessible by both the CPU and the GPU, automatically migrating data between host and device as needed. This reduces the need for explicit data transfers, simplifying the code and reducing the potential for data transfer bottlenecks. Example of Unified Memory usage:

```
// Unified Memory example
int *unified_data;
cudaMallocManaged(&unified_data, size);

myKernel<<<numBlocks, blockSize>>>(unified_data);

// CUDA synchronizes unified memory transfer behind the scenes
cudaDeviceSynchronize();
```

Optimizing the *Data Layout* can further minimize memory transfers. By organizing data structures to make efficient use of GPU memory and favor contiguous memory patterns, one can reduce the overall volume of data needing transfer. For instance, using Structure of Arrays (SoA) over Array of Structures (AoS) often results in a more efficient memory transaction due to better coalescing.

```
// Structure of Arrays for better memory coalescing
struct SoA {
    float* x;
    float* y;
    float* z;
};

void initializeData(SoA &data, int n) {
    cudaMalloc(&data.x, n * sizeof(float));
    cudaMalloc(&data.y, n * sizeof(float));
    cudaMalloc(&data.z, n * sizeof(float));
}
```

Further, leveraging *Page-Locked Host Memory* can improve data transfer rates. Page-locked (or pinned) memory prevents the host memory from being paged out, allowing for faster data transfers compared to pageable memory. This technique is especially useful when large amounts of data need to be transferred frequently.

```
// Page-locked memory allocation
float *h_data;
cudaMallocHost(&h_data, size); // Allocates page-locked host memory

cudaMemcpy(d_data, h_data, size, cudaMemcpyHostToDevice); // Faster transfer
```

Another method for reducing memory transfers involves *Employing Zero-Copy Memory*. Zero-copy memory provides a mechanism for the GPU to directly access host memory without copying it to the device memory first. It is particularly useful for applications where the dataset is small or when frequent updates of data are necessary.

```
// Zero-copy memory example
float *h_data;
cudaHostAlloc(&h_data, size, cudaHostAllocMapped);

float *d_data;
cudaHostGetDevicePointer(&d_data, h_data, 0);

myKernel<<<numBlocks, blockSize>>>(d_data);
```

Choosing an appropriate *Memory Copy Mode* for specific needs also helps optimize memory transfers. CUDA provides three types of memory copies: memory copy, asynchronous memory copy, and mapped memory. Analyzing the application's requirements and selecting the correct copy mode can yield significant performance improvements.

Lastly, analyzing and minimizing data transfers through *Profiling Tools* such as NVIDIA's Visual Profiler (nvprof) and Nsight Systems can identify transfer bottlenecks. Profiling helps in understanding the timing and frequency of transfers, allowing for targeted optimization based on empirical data.

Here is a sample command to profile a CUDA application:

```
nvprof --print-gpu-trace ./myCudaApplication
```

Analyzing the output will provide insights into memory transfer efficiencies and areas that require optimization.

```
==1234== NVPROF is profiling ./myCudaApplication...
==1234== Profiling application: ./myCudaApplication
==1234== Profiling result:
            Type  Time(%)      Time     Calls       Avg       Min       Max  Name
 GPU activities:   98.86%  47.527ms         2  23.764ms  23.764ms  23.764ms  myKernel
                    1.14%  548.97us         2  274.49us  274.21us  274.74us  [CUDA memcpy HtoD]
==1234== API calls:
      API calls:   52.04%  47.558ms         2  23.779ms  23.778ms  23.780ms  cudaMemcpy
                    ...
```

Integration of these techniques can help reduce memory transfers, enhancing the overall performance of CUDA applications. By employing asynchronous transfers, Unified Memory, page-locked memory, zero-copy memory, and using appropriate profiling tools, CUDA programs can achieve more efficient memory usage and reduced data transfer latency.

7.5 Improving Instruction Throughput

Improving instruction throughput is a critical aspect in optimizing CUDA applications. Instruction throughput defines how many instructions are executed per unit time and directly impacts the performance of CUDA kernels. Various techniques can be employed to enhance instruction throughput, ranging from compiler optimizations to manual tuning of the code. This section explores several effective strategies.

Compiler Optimizations

The first step towards improving instruction throughput is to leverage compiler optimizations. CUDA compilers, such as nvcc, provide multiple optimization flags that can influence instruction scheduling and register usage. The commonly used optimization flag -O3 enables high-level optimizations, including loop unrolling, inlining functions, and other optimizations that can reduce instruction count and improve throughput.

```
nvcc -O3 my_kernel.cu -o my_kernel
```

Additionally, the use of -maxrregcount can limit the number of registers used by each thread, potentially increasing occupancy and therefore improving throughput:

```
nvcc -O3 --maxrregcount=32 my_kernel.cu -o my_kernel
```

Loop Unrolling

Manual loop unrolling can also enhance instruction throughput by reducing the overhead associated with loop control instructions. When loops are unrolled, the number of iterations is explicitly written out, thereby decreasing the loop's computational complexity and increasing the performance.

Consider the following example where a loop iterates 8 times:

```
for (int i = 0; i < 8; i++) {
    output[i] = input[i] * 2.0f;
}
```

The manually unrolled version of the above loop:

```
output[0] = input[0] * 2.0f;
output[1] = input[1] * 2.0f;
output[2] = input[2] * 2.0f;
output[3] = input[3] * 2.0f;
output[4] = input[4] * 2.0f;
output[5] = input[5] * 2.0f;
output[6] = input[6] * 2.0f;
output[7] = input[7] * 2.0f;
```

While this method can significantly reduce the control overhead, care must be taken to ensure register pressure does not increase excessively, which might negate the benefits of loop unrolling.

Instruction Scheduling

Instruction scheduling is another vital element for enhancing instruction throughput. The CUDA compiler attempts to schedule instructions efficiently to utilize the pipeline fully. However, manual intervention is sometimes necessary, particularly in the case of dependencies between consecutive instructions. To avoid pipeline stalling, dependent instructions should be separated by other independent instructions, thereby allowing the GPU to execute operations in parallel.

Consider the following code where instructions are too closely tied, creating dependencies:

```
float a = input[threadIdx.x];
float b = a * 2.0f;
float c = b + 3.0f;
output[threadIdx.x] = c;
```

Instead, one could separate dependent instructions with other independent operations, as shown:

```
float a = input[threadIdx.x];
float temp = otherArray[threadIdx.x]; // Independent operation
float b = a * 2.0f;
float c = b + 3.0f;
output[threadIdx.x] = c;
```

This approach can help to hide the latency of dependent instructions by filling the pipeline with other operations.

Reducing Divergence

Instruction throughput can be severely impacted by control flow divergence, where different threads in a warp follow different execution paths. This divergence causes the warp to serialize the divergent paths, reducing the effective throughput. To minimize divergence, ensure that threads within a warp follow the same execution path as much as possible.

For instance, instead of divergent code like this:

```
if (threadIdx.x < 16) {
    // Path A
    output[threadIdx.x] = input[threadIdx.x] * 2.0f;
} else {
    // Path B
    output[threadIdx.x] = input[threadIdx.x] + 3.0f;
}
```

One might reorder or refactor the code to minimize divergence:

```
float result = (threadIdx.x < 16) ? input[threadIdx.x] * 2.0f : input[threadIdx.x] + 3.0f;
output[threadIdx.x] = result;
```

Ensuring warp coherence can dramatically enhance instruction throughput.

Utilizing CUDA Streams

CUDA streams allow concurrent execution of kernels and memory operations, which can improve instruction throughput. By overlapping compute operations with memory transfers or other compute kernels, the throughput can be maximized.

Here is an example of using CUDA streams for overlapping kernel execution and memory transfers:

```
cudaStream_t stream1, stream2;
cudaStreamCreate(&stream1);
cudaStreamCreate(&stream2);

float *d_A, *d_B;
cudaMalloc((void**)&d_A, size);
cudaMalloc((void**)&d_B, size);

cudaMemcpyAsync(d_A, h_A, size, cudaMemcpyHostToDevice, stream1);
kernel<<<gridSize, blockSize, 0, stream1>>>(d_A);
cudaMemcpyAsync(h_B, d_B, size, cudaMemcpyDeviceToHost, stream2);

cudaStreamSynchronize(stream1);
cudaStreamSynchronize(stream2);

cudaStreamDestroy(stream1);
cudaStreamDestroy(stream2);
```

By employing these strategies, it is possible to maximize the instruction throughput of CUDA applications, thereby deriving efficient and high-performance kernels.

7.6 Optimizing Kernel Launch Configuration

Optimal kernel launch configuration plays a crucial role in achieving peak performance for CUDA applications. It directly affects how well the hardware resources of the GPU are utilized. The kernel launch configuration, specified by the number of thread blocks, the number of threads per block, and the amount of shared memory per block, impacts factors like occupancy, memory usage, and execution efficiency. Correctly configuring these parameters can minimize idle hardware resources, maximize throughput, and reduce execution time.

The «<blocks, threads»> syntax in CUDA is used to specify the number of blocks and the number of threads per block for a kernel launch. The goal is to find an optimal configuration that leverages the full computational power of the GPU.

```
kernel<<<numBlocks, numThreadsPerBlock>>>(...);
```

Choosing the Number of Threads per Block

A fundamental guideline is to make the size of each block a multiple of the warp size, 32 threads. This ensures efficient execution on NVIDIA GPUs, where warps are the unit of thread scheduling. Common choices include 32, 64, 128, 256, and 512 threads per block. However, the choice is constrained by the capabilities of the GPU, particularly the maximum number of threads per block, which can vary between different architectures.

Considerations for determining the number of threads per block include:

- **Resource Utilization**: Each block consumes resources like registers and shared memory. When the number of threads per block is too high, it can lead to resource exhaustion, reducing the number of active warps and thus occupancy.
- **Occupancy**: This refers to the ratio of active warps per multiprocessor to the maximum number of warps. Higher occupancy generally means better utilization of GPU resources, though very high occupancy does not always equate to better performance due to other factors.
- **Shared Memory and Registers**: Blocks must share hardware resources such as shared memory and registers. If a block requires a large amount of shared memory or registers, fewer blocks can reside on the same multiprocessor, potentially reducing occupancy.
- **Compute Capability**: Different generations of GPUs (compute capabilities) have varying limits for the number of threads per block, the amount of shared memory per block, and other architectural features. It is critical to consult the GPU's specific documentation for limitations.

Example

Consider a simple kernel to add two vectors. Suppose we want to determine the optimal number of threads per block for this kernel.

```
// Kernel for vector addition
__global__ void vectorAdd(float *A, float *B, float *C, int N) {
    int idx = blockIdx.x * blockDim.x + threadIdx.x;
    if (idx < N) {
        C[idx] = A[idx] + B[idx];
    }
}
```

For optimal performance, we need to experiment with various block sizes. The theoretical maximum block size is 1024 threads, but practical experimentation with sizes 128, 256, and 512 may yield better real-world performance. Each configuration should be profiled to find the most efficient setup.

Choosing the Number of Blocks

The number of blocks should be chosen such that the entire dataset is processed and GPU resources are fully utilized. Generally, a good practice is to launch enough blocks to ensure that all streaming multiprocessors (SMs) are occupied.

The number of blocks can be calculated as follows:

```
int numBlocks = (N + numThreadsPerBlock - 1) / numThreadsPerBlock;
```

This calculation ensures that all elements are processed, accounting for the case where N is not perfectly divisible by the number of threads per block.

Dynamic Parallelism

In more complex scenarios, kernels might need to launch other kernels. CUDA Dynamic Parallelism allows a kernel to launch other kernels, thereby adding flexibility and potentially optimizing performance for nested parallelism scenarios. Configuring kernel launches dynamically can help maintain high GPU utilization across different execution phases.

```
// Example of dynamic parallelism
__global__ void parentKernel(...) {
    // Some computations
    ...
    // Launch another kernel from within a kernel
    childKernel<<<childBlocks, childThreadsPerBlock>>>(...);
}
```

While this feature adds complexity, it can sometimes simplify algorithm implementation and improve performance when optimized correctly.

Profiling and Tuning

Profiling tools such as NVIDIA Nsight Systems and Nsight Compute provide invaluable insights into the performance characteristics of different kernel configurations. Through profiling, developers can observe metrics such as kernel execution time, memory utilization, and occupancy to make informed decisions on kernel launch configurations.

```
Profiling output:
-----------------
Kernel          Time (ms)    Occupancy (%)   ...
--------------------------------------------------
vectorAdd         1.23         75             ...
vectorAdd         1.10         80             ...
```

Iterative tuning, combined with empirical performance measurement, is crucial in identifying the optimal kernel launch configuration. Small adjustments in the configuration parameters can lead to significant performance improvements.

Balancing the trade-offs between thread block size, resource utilization, and occupancy allows for achieving efficient parallel computation on CUDA-enabled GPUs. Understanding the interplay of these factors and leveraging profiling tools can guide the iterative process of optimizing kernel launch configurations for peak performance.

7.7 Latency Hiding Techniques

Latency in CUDA programming refers to the delay incurred when data is transferred from one memory location to another or when an instruction waits to complete due to various reasons, such as memory accesses or synchronization delays. Effective latency hiding is crucial for optimizing CUDA performance since it helps mitigate the performance impact of these delays. Several techniques can be employed to enhance latency hiding, including leveraging warp schedulers, employing asynchronous operations, and utilizing instruction-level parallelism effectively.

A core concept in CUDA performance optimization is attempting to keep the CUDA cores busy with useful work while other operations, particularly memory operations, are delayed or latent. The CUDA runtime employs warp schedulers, which manage the simultaneous execution of threads within a warp. A key feature of these schedulers is their ability to switch to another warp when the current warp is stalled due to latency (e.g., waiting for a memory fetch operation to complete).

Consider the following kernel code snippet that demonstrates warp-level latency hiding:

```
// Kernel function demonstrating warp-level latency hiding
__global__ void simpleKernel(float *data) {
    int idx = blockIdx.x * blockDim.x + threadIdx.x;
    // Perform memory fetch
    float val = data[idx];
    // Perform a computation on the fetched data
    data[idx] = val * val;
}
```

In the example above, the memory fetch (float val = data[idx];) typically involves latency as the data is fetched from the global memory. During this waiting period, the warp scheduler can switch to another warp that is ready to execute, effectively hiding the latency.

To further alleviate latency, asynchronous memory operations can be employed. CUDA provides asynchronous memory copy operations (e.g., cudaMemcpyAsync) which allow data transfers to take place concurrently with other computations. This is particularly beneficial when overlapping memory transfer with kernel execution. The CUDA streams mechanism plays a pivotal role here, as it allows organizing a sequence of operations into a pipeline to achieve greater concurrency.

The following code demonstrates the use of asynchronous memory copy operations within a CUDA stream which enables latency hiding:

```
cudaStream_t stream;
cudaStreamCreate(&stream);

float *deviceData, *hostData;

// Allocate memory on the device and host
cudaMalloc((void **)&deviceData, sizeof(float) * N);
hostData = (float *)malloc(sizeof(float) * N);

// Asynchronous data transfer from host to device
cudaMemcpyAsync(deviceData, hostData, sizeof(float) * N, cudaMemcpyHostToDevice,
    stream);

// Launch kernel asynchronously within the stream
simpleKernel<<<gridSize, blockSize, 0, stream>>>(deviceData);

// Asynchronous data transfer from device to host
cudaMemcpyAsync(hostData, deviceData, sizeof(float) * N, cudaMemcpyDeviceToHost,
    stream);

cudaStreamSynchronize(stream);
cudaStreamDestroy(stream);
```

In this example, the use of cudaMemcpyAsync alongside a CUDA stream (cudaStream_t stream) facilitates the concurrent execution of memory transfers and kernel execution. The cudaStreamSynchronize function ensures that all tasks within the stream are completed before proceeding.

Another effective latency hiding technique is employing instruction-level parallelism (ILP). ILP maximizes the overlap of instructions by arranging them in such a way that independent instructions can be executed simultaneously. Compilers and programmers play a vital role by ensuring instructions that have no data dependencies run in parallel.

Consider this adjusted kernel function that demonstrates generating ILP:

```
__global__ void ILPKernel(float *data1, float *data2) {
    int idx = blockIdx.x * blockDim.x + threadIdx.x;

    // Independent memory fetches
    float val1 = data1[idx];
    float val2 = data2[idx];

    // Independent computations
    data1[idx] = val1 * val1;
    data2[idx] = val2 * val2;
}
```

In this kernel, two independent memory fetches float val1 = data1[idx] and float val2 = data2[idx] are followed by independent computations. This lack of dependency between operations allows them to be executed concurrently by the CUDA cores, thus effectively hiding latency by taking advantage of ILP.

Lastly, latency hiding can be enhanced by optimizing memory access patterns. Optimal utilization of shared memory, caching, and coalesced memory accesses ensure minimal delays in data movement. For example, shared memory, being significantly faster than global memory, can be used to store frequently accessed data, thus reducing the latency of memory fetch operations:

```
__global__ void sharedMemKernel(float *data) {
    __shared__ float sharedData[BLOCK_SIZE];

    int idx = blockIdx.x * blockDim.x + threadIdx.x;
    int tid = threadIdx.x;

    // Load data into shared memory
    sharedData[tid] = data[idx];
    __syncthreads();

    // Perform computation using shared memory
    sharedData[tid] = sharedData[tid] * sharedData[tid];
    __syncthreads();

    // Write result back to global memory
    data[idx] = sharedData[tid];
}
```

In this kernel, using shared memory (__shared__ float sharedData[BLOCK_SIZE];) minimizes global memory accesses. Threads within a block collaboratively load data into shared memory, perform computations, and write back results—reducing overall latency due to faster memory accessibility.

These latency hiding techniques can significantly boost the performance of CUDA applications by optimizing how operations overlap and make full use of the CUDA hardware capabilities. Efficiently employing warp schedulers, asynchronous operations, instruction-level parallelism, and optimizing memory access patterns helps in achieving higher throughput and reduced execution time in CUDA applications.

7.8 Caching and Shared Memory Techniques

CUDA architecture provides multiple memory types to leverage for optimal performance. In this section, we delve into caching mechanisms and shared memory techniques that can significantly enhance the performance of CUDA applications.

Caching is a fundamental technique to enhance data locality and reduce memory latency. CUDA devices are equipped with an L1 cache, an L2 cache, and a read-only data cache. The L1 cache is closer to the cores and is therefore faster but smaller, whereas the L2 cache is larger but slower. The read-only data cache serves as a specialized cache for read-only data optimized for broadcast scenarios. Understanding the utilization and configuration of these caches is crucial for achieving high performance.

The L1 cache is configurable and can be sized to balance between L1 cache and shared memory. By default, an NVIDIA GPU will allocate 48 KB for shared memory and 16 KB for L1 cache. However, you can change this configuration to suit your application's demands. For instance, if shared memory requirements are high, you might allocate 48 KB to shared memory and 16 KB to L1 cache, or vice versa.

```
cudaFuncSetCacheConfig(myKernel, cudaFuncCachePreferShared);
cudaFuncSetCacheConfig(myKernel, cudaFuncCachePreferL1);
```

Shared memory is another essential resource provided by the CUDA architecture, serving as a manually managed cache. It is an on-chip memory with much lower latency than global memory. Utilizing shared memory can lead to substantial performance improvements, particularly for algorithms with data reuse patterns.

Consider the following example: a matrix multiplication kernel that leverages shared memory for tiles. Each thread block is responsible for computing a tile of the result matrix, loading the required data into shared memory to minimize redundant global memory accesses.

```
__global__ void matrixMultiplyShared(float* A, float* B, float* C, int N) {
    __shared__ float shared_A[TILE_SIZE][TILE_SIZE];
    __shared__ float shared_B[TILE_SIZE][TILE_SIZE];

    int bx = blockIdx.x;
    int by = blockIdx.y;
    int tx = threadIdx.x;
    int ty = threadIdx.y;

    int row = by * blockDim.y + ty;
    int col = bx * blockDim.x + tx;

    float value = 0.0;

    for (int m = 0; m < (N + TILE_SIZE - 1) / TILE_SIZE; ++m) {
        if (row < N && m * TILE_SIZE + tx < N)
            shared_A[ty][tx] = A[row * N + m * TILE_SIZE + tx];
        else
            shared_A[ty][tx] = 0.0;

        if (col < N && m * TILE_SIZE + ty < N)
            shared_B[ty][tx] = B[(m * TILE_SIZE + ty) * N + col];
        else
            shared_B[ty][tx] = 0.0;

        __syncthreads();

        for (int k = 0; k < TILE_SIZE; ++k)
            value += shared_A[ty][k] * shared_B[k][tx];

        __syncthreads();
    }

    if (row < N && col < N)
        C[row * N + col] = value;
}
```

In this kernel, the global memory loads are minimized by loading tiles of matrix A and B into shared memory. The tiles are then processed by simple matrix multiplication within shared memory, reducing the number of global memory transactions.

Bank conflicts are critical to consider when using shared memory. Shared memory is divided into banks, and bank conflicts occur when multiple threads access different addresses within the same bank in the same transaction. This leads to serialization and degraded performance. As of CUDA 3.1, shared memory is organized into 32 banks.

Ensuring that shared memory access patterns are designed to avoid conflicts can substantially boost performance.

A technique to avoid bank conflicts is to carefully align data structures in shared memory. Stride accesses should be matched to the bank width to prevent aligned memory accesses. The modification to our example kernel to avoid bank conflicts might involve padding.

```
__global__ void matrixMultiplySharedWithPadding(float* A, float* B, float* C, int N
    ) {
    __shared__ float shared_A[TILE_SIZE][TILE_SIZE + 1];
    __shared__ float shared_B[TILE_SIZE][TILE_SIZE + 1];

    // Remaining code similar to the previous kernel, with shared_A and shared_B
    // using the padded dimensions.
}
```

In this adjusted kernel, padding is added to the shared memory declarations to prevent bank conflicts by ensuring that each row and column accesses different memory banks.

Additionally, preloading data into the read-only cache using the __ldg intrinsic can be advantageous in read-heavy scenarios. This optimization is particularly useful for global memory accesses that do not change through the kernel's execution. Implementing the __ldg intrinsic can be as follows:

```
float x = __ldg(&A[i]);
```

Leveraging caching mechanisms and shared memory efficiently is a delicate balance that requires diligent profiling and understanding of access patterns. Significant performance gains are achievable by mitigating memory latency and reducing redundant memory accesses through these techniques.

7.9 Occupancy and Resource Utilization

Occupancy in CUDA refers to the ratio of active warps per multiprocessor to the maximum number of warps that the multiprocessor can support. Higher occupancy does not necessarily mean better performance, but insufficient occupancy can lead to poor performance due to underutilization of the GPU resources. Resource utilization, on the other hand, pertains to the efficient employment of various hardware resources such as registers, shared memory, and warp schedulers to achieve high performance. Optimizing both factors is crucial for achieving the best possible performance in CUDA applications.

Factors Affecting Occupancy:

1. **Active Warps:** The number of active warps is influenced by the thread block size and the number of thread blocks allocated per multiprocessor. The hardware limits the total number of threads per multiprocessor to a specific maximum, which indirectly determines the maximum number of active warps.

2. **Registers Per Thread:** Each thread utilizes a certain number of registers, and the total register usage per thread block can limit the number of thread blocks that can be active concurrently. Each multiprocessor has a finite number of registers; hence, an excessive number of registers per thread can reduce occupancy.

3. **Shared Memory Per Block:** Similar to registers, the shared memory allocated per thread block also impacts the number of concurrent thread blocks that can be active on a multiprocessor. The total shared memory available per multiprocessor is fixed, thus an increased shared memory requirement per block reduces the number of blocks that can be active.

4. **Thread Block Size:** Choosing the optimal thread block size is essential because it must align with hardware limits and simultaneously ensure high occupancy. Thread blocks that are too small or too large may lead to suboptimal occupancy.

Calculating Occupancy:

The occupancy can be computed using the equation:

$$\text{Occupancy} = \frac{\text{Number of Active Warps per Multiprocessor}}{\text{Maximum Number of Warps per Multiprocessor}}$$

To facilitate this calculation, NVIDIA provides an Occupancy Calculator that allows users to input parameters such as threads per block, registers per thread, and shared memory per block to estimate the occupancy.

Example: Calculating Occupancy

Consider a kernel with the following parameters:

- Threads per block: 256
- Registers per thread: 32

- Shared memory per block: 1024 bytes

Assume the target GPU has the following specifications:

- Maximum threads per multiprocessor: 2048
- Maximum warps per multiprocessor: 64
- Maximum shared memory per multiprocessor: 48 KB
- Maximum registers per multiprocessor: 65536

Given these specifications, let us compute the occupancy step-by-step:

1. **Thread Blocks per Multiprocessor:**

   The total thread capacity per multiprocessor divided by the threads per block gives the upper limit of thread blocks:

   $$\text{Thread Blocks per Multiprocessor} = \frac{2048}{256} = 8$$

   However, this is only a rough estimate and other factors like register and shared memory usage could lower this number.

2. **Register Limitation:**

   Total registers used per thread block:

   $$\text{Total Registers per Block} = 256 \times 32 = 8192$$

   The number of blocks constrained by register limits:

   $$\text{Blocks by Registers} = \frac{65536}{8192} = 8$$

3. **Shared Memory Limitation:**

   The number of thread blocks constrained by shared memory:

   $$\text{Blocks by Shared Memory} = \frac{49152}{1024} = 48$$

   This value suggests that shared memory is not the limiting factor.

4. **Effective Blocks per Multiprocessor:**

   The actual number of thread blocks per multiprocessor is limited by the smallest value among thread blocks, registers, and shared memory constraints:

$$\text{Effective Blocks} = \text{min}(8, 8, 48) = 8$$

5. **Effective Warps per Multiprocessor:**

   Since each block has 256 threads, and each warp contains 32 threads:

$$\text{Warps per Block} = \frac{256}{32} = 8$$

   Therefore, effective warps per multiprocessor:

$$\text{Effective Warps} = 8 \times 8 = 64$$

6. **Occupancy:**

   Finally, the occupancy is obtained by dividing the number of effective warps by the maximum warps supported per multiprocessor:

$$\text{Occupancy} = \frac{64}{64} = 1.0$$

Thus, the occupancy is found to be 100%, indicating an optimal scenario where all hardware resources are fully utilized. However, achieving high occupancy does not always equate to maximum performance, as it is crucial to balance occupancy with other factors like memory bandwidth, instruction throughput, and latency hiding.

Resource Utilization Strategies:

Improving resource utilization involves optimizing the use of registers and shared memory and ensuring efficient warp scheduling:

- **Register Spilling:** Reducing excessive register usage to prevent register spilling, which can lead to performance penalties as spilled registers are stored in local memory.

```
__global__ void optimizedKernel(int *data) {
    int index = threadIdx.x;
    int temp; // Declare necessary variables
    // Kernel code ensuring minimal register use
}
```

- **Shared Memory Allocation:** Efficiently allocating and managing shared memory to maximize its utilization and reduce latency.

```
__global__ void sharedMemoryKernel(int *data) {
    extern __shared__ int sharedData[];
    int index = threadIdx.x;
    sharedData[index] = data[index]; // Efficient shared memory usage
}
```

- **Optimal Thread Block Size:** Choosing an optimal thread block size that maximizes occupancy without oversaturating resources.

- **Warp Divergence:** Minimizing warp divergence to ensure that all threads within a warp follow the same execution path.

```
__global__ void noDivergenceKernel(int *data) {
    int index = threadIdx.x;
    if (index % 2 == 0) {
        // Code path for even index
    } else {
        // Code path for odd index
    }
}
```

Effective resource utilization requires an understanding of the underlying hardware and balancing different factors to achieve maximum performance. Advanced profiling tools provided by NVIDIA, such as NVIDIA Nsight Systems and NVIDIA Nsight Compute, can aid in pinpointing bottlenecks and optimizing resource usage in CUDA applications.

7.10 Load Balancing and Reducing Divergence

Effective load balancing and minimizing divergence are crucial to achieving optimal performance in CUDA applications. Load balancing ensures that all threads perform computational work uniformly, preventing some threads from idling while others are overloaded. Reducing divergence, particularly in warp execution, ensures efficient execution of threads concurrently.

In CUDA, threads are organized into warps, typically consisting of 32 threads. Each warp executes instructions in a SIMD (Single Instruction, Multiple Data) fashion. Divergence occurs when threads within a warp follow different execution paths due to conditional branches, which can significantly degrade performance. Addressing both load imbalance and divergence can help maximize resource utilization and execution efficiency.

To begin with, consider the following example of load imbalance caused by non-uniform workloads:

```
__global__ void imbalanceKernel(int *data, int N) {
    int idx = blockIdx.x * blockDim.x + threadIdx.x;
    if (idx < N && data[idx] % 2 == 0) {
        // Simulated workload: even indices perform more work
        for (int i = 0; i < 1000; ++i) {
            data[idx] *= 2;
        }
    } else if (idx < N) {
        // Odd indices perform less work
        data[idx] += 1;
    }
}
```

In this kernel, even indices perform significantly more work compared to odd indices, leading to work imbalance. To ameliorate this, we can aim for more uniform work distribution. One strategy is to use dynamic parallelism or adjust the computation sequences such that threads have similar workloads. For instance:

```
__global__ void balancedKernel(int *data, int N) {
    int idx = blockIdx.x * blockDim.x + threadIdx.x;
    if (idx < N) {
        // Ensure each thread performs a comparable amount of work
        for (int i = 0; i < (data[idx] % 2 == 0 ? 1000 : 1); ++i) {
            data[idx] = (data[idx] % 2 == 0) ? data[idx] * 2 : data[idx] + 1;
        }
    }
}
```

Now turning to the issue of divergence, consider a scenario where threads within a warp execute different branches due to a conditional statement:

```
__global__ void divergentKernel(int *data, int N) {
    int idx = blockIdx.x * blockDim.x + threadIdx.x;
    if (idx < N) {
        if (data[idx] < 100) {
            data[idx] *= 2;
        } else {
            data[idx] += 50;
        }
    }
}
```

In this kernel, divergence occurs since threads can take different execution paths based on the condition $\text{data}[\text{idx}] < 100$. One way to mitigate this is by structuring code to minimize conditional branches within warps. For example:

```
__global__ void lessDivergentKernel(int *data, int N) {
    int idx = blockIdx.x * blockDim.x + threadIdx.x;
    if (idx < N) {
        int isBelow100 = (data[idx] < 100);
        data[idx] = isBelow100 * (data[idx] * 2) + (!isBelow100 * (data[idx] + 50));
    }
}
```

The above kernel reduces divergence by calculating both potential outcomes and then selecting the appropriate result using boolean arithmetic, ensuring that all threads in a warp follow a more uniform execution path.

Thread Mapping and Sensible Indexing

Optimizing thread mapping and indexing is another crucial technique. Optimal thread to data mappings can reduce both load imbalance and divergence. For instance, avoiding direct use of blockDim.x or threadIdx.x in favor of more sophisticated mappings that consider data locality and uniformity can yield performance improvements:

```
__global__ void optimizedMappingKernel(int *data, int N) {
    int idx = (blockIdx.x * blockDim.x + threadIdx.x) * 2;
    if (idx < N) {
        data[idx] += data[idx + 1];
    }
}
```

Using Shared Memory to Balance Load

Shared memory can be employed to further balance the load and enhance performance. Threads within a block can collaborate using shared memory, reducing redundant global memory accesses and smoothing out discrepancies in workloads:

```
__global__ void sharedMemoryKernel(int *data, int N) {
    __shared__ int sdata[BLOCK_SIZE];
    int tid = threadIdx.x;
    int idx = blockIdx.x * blockDim.x + tid;

    if (idx < N) {
        sdata[tid] = data[idx];
        __syncthreads();

        if (tid % 2 == 0 && idx + 1 < N) {
            sdata[tid] += data[idx + 1];
        } else if (tid % 2 == 1) {
            sdata[tid]++;
        }
        data[idx] = sdata[tid];
    }
}
```

This kernel allows even threads to collaborate and perform workload balancing more effectively by utilizing shared memory.

Ensuring load balance and reducing divergence not only improve individual kernel performance but also lead to more efficient resource utilization across the GPU. Employing these strategies allows for more consistent and faster execution of CUDA applications.

Chapter 8

Advanced CUDA Programming Techniques

This chapter delves into advanced CUDA programming techniques, including dynamic parallelism and CUDA graphs for complex task management. It covers the use of unified memory and handling memory oversubscription, as well as leveraging CUDA streams for asynchronous execution. Additional topics include peer-to-peer memory access, inter-process communication, and multi-GPU programming. The chapter also explores the Thrust library for high-level abstractions and discusses CUDA's role in heterogeneous computing environments.

8.1 Introduction to Advanced CUDA Programming

CUDA (Compute Unified Device Architecture) programming has evolved significantly since its inception, enabling developers to harness the immense parallel processing power of NVIDIA GPUs for a wide array of applications. This chapter delves into advanced CUDA programming techniques that expand the boundaries of what can be achieved using CUDA, fostering innovations in scientific computing, machine learning, computer graphics, and various other domains.

The fundamental concepts of CUDA programming, such as kernels, threads, blocks, and the grid, form the basis of developing efficient parallel programs. Building upon these basics, advanced techniques allow for more complex and efficient management of computational tasks. Advanced CUDA programming involves optimizing resource utilization, implementing dynamic parallelism, leveraging unified memory, managing CUDA streams for asynchronous execution, and handling complex inter-device communication.

One of the key features of advanced CUDA programming is dynamic parallelism. This feature allows CUDA kernels to launch other kernels on the GPU without returning control to the CPU. Dynamic parallelism simplifies the programming model for recursive algorithms and enables more efficient use of the GPU for tasks that naturally unfold into subtasks.

Another powerful tool in the CUDA ecosystem is the CUDA graph API. CUDA graphs facilitate the creation and execution of complex task dependency workflows on the GPU. By representing a series of kernel launches, memory transfers, and synchronization points as a graph, developers can optimize execution by minimizing overhead and ensuring efficient resource utilization.

Unified memory is an essential concept in advanced CUDA programming, providing a single memory space accessible by both the CPU and GPU. Unified memory simplifies memory management, allowing developers to write more straightforward and maintainable code. Handling memory oversubscription, where the application's memory requirements exceed the physical capacity of the GPU, is possible through unified memory, streamlining resource allocation and access patterns.

CUDA streams introduce the capability for asynchronous execution and overlap of computation and memory transfers. By dividing work into multiple streams, developers can achieve higher concurrency and better resource utilization, leading to improved performance in applications with diverse workloads.

In multi-GPU systems, peer-to-peer memory access enables GPUs to directly communicate and share data, bypassing the CPU. This direct communication enhances data transfer speeds between GPUs, crucial for applications demanding high bandwidth and low latency. Interprocess communication further extends CUDA's capabilities by allowing processes on the same or different GPUs to share data, facilitating complex workflows in distributed computing environments.

Multi-GPU programming expands the computational potential by distributing workloads across multiple GPUs, each handling a portion of the overall task. Effective multi-GPU programming requires careful load balancing, synchronization, and efficient memory management to fully exploit the potential of available hardware.

Thrust, a parallel algorithms library akin to the C++ Standard Template Library (STL), provides high-level abstractions for CUDA programming. Thrust eases the development of parallel programs by offering pre-built algorithms and data structures, simplifying common operations such as sorting, reduction, and scanning. Leveraging Thrust can significantly reduce development time and foster code reusability.

CUDA's role in heterogeneous computing environments cannot be overstated. In such environments, CPUs, GPUs, FPGAs, and other accelerators work together to handle diverse workloads. CUDA programming must adapt to these scenarios, ensuring efficient collaboration between different processing units, balancing the load, and maintaining high throughput.

Each advanced technique covered in this chapter is critical for pushing the boundaries of performance and efficiency in CUDA applications. By mastering these techniques, developers can tackle increasingly complex problems, optimize computational workloads, and contribute to cutting-edge solutions leveraging CUDA-enabled GPUs.

```
// Example of a simple CUDA kernel launch
__global__ void SimpleKernel(int *data) {
    int idx = blockIdx.x * blockDim.x + threadIdx.x;
    data[idx] *= 2; // Example operation
}

int main() {
    int *d_data;
    int dataSize = 1024 * sizeof(int);
    cudaMalloc(&d_data, dataSize);

    // Launching the kernel with 256 threads per block and 4 blocks
    SimpleKernel<<<4, 256>>>(d_data);

    cudaFree(d_data);
    return 0;
}
```

The output of the above code depends on the initialized values in d_data, which are doubled by the kernel. Since d_data is not initialized, the output will reflect the initial memory values set by cudaMalloc, typically zeroed out.

8.2 Dynamic Parallelism

Dynamic parallelism is a powerful feature in CUDA that allows kernels to launch other kernels. This concept significantly enhances the flexibility of GPU programming by enabling a hierarchical execution model where kernel launches can be dynamically and adaptively managed at runtime. This ability effectively permits breaking down complex problems into smaller, more manageable tasks, which can then be executed in parallel.

Dynamic parallelism is particularly beneficial in scenarios where the workload is irregular or adaptive, making it challenging to determine the optimal parallel execution configuration during the initial host-based kernel launch. By enabling kernels to launch additional kernels, dynamic parallelism can help manage load balancing and efficiently utilize GPU resources without excessive synchronization with the CPU.

To demonstrate dynamic parallelism, let's consider a simple example where a parent kernel launches a child kernel. We'll start with a basic CUDA program where the parent kernel allocates work to the child kernel dynamically.

```
// Parent kernel
__global__ void parentKernel(int *data, int size) {
    int idx = blockIdx.x * blockDim.x + threadIdx.x;

    if (idx < size) {
        // Perform some work
        data[idx] = 2 * data[idx];

        // Launch child kernel
        childKernel<<<1, 128>>>(idx, data);
        cudaDeviceSynchronize(); // Ensure child kernel execution
    }
}

// Child kernel
__global__ void childKernel(int index, int *data) {
    int childIdx = threadIdx.x;

    if (childIdx < 128) {
        // Perform additional work
        data[index] += 1;
    }
}

int main() {
    const int dataSize = 1024;
    int *d_data;

    // Allocate memory on the device
    cudaMalloc(&d_data, dataSize * sizeof(int));
    int h_data[dataSize];
```

```
    // Initialize data and copy to device
    for(int i = 0; i < dataSize; ++i) {
        h_data[i] = i;
    }
    cudaMemcpy(d_data, h_data, dataSize * sizeof(int), cudaMemcpyHostToDevice);

    // Launch parent kernel
    parentKernel<<<8, 128>>>(d_data, dataSize);

    // Copy results back to host
    cudaMemcpy(h_data, d_data, dataSize * sizeof(int), cudaMemcpyDeviceToHost);

    // Clean up
    cudaFree(d_data);
    return 0;
}
```

In this example, the parent kernel 'parentKernel' launches a child kernel 'childKernel'. The parent kernel first performs some operations on the data and then launches the child kernel. The 'childKernel' performs further computations.

There are several important aspects to consider when using dynamic parallelism:

1. **Grid and Block Dimensions**: When launching child kernels, the grid and block dimensions should be defined carefully to match the nature of the workload. Misconfigured dimensions can lead to suboptimal performance or even failure to launch the kernel.

2. **Synchronization**: Synchronization between parent and child kernels is crucial. In the example, 'cudaDeviceSynchronize' is used to ensure that the parent kernel waits for the child kernel to complete before proceeding. This can incur additional overhead, and excessive use of synchronization should be avoided to maintain performance.

3. **Resource Management**: When a kernel launches another kernel, it uses additional resources such as registers, shared memory, and thread slots. This can lead to resource exhaustion if not managed properly. It is essential to be aware of the resource usage of both parent and child kernels to avoid exceeding the GPU's capacity.

4. **Debugging and Profiling**: Debugging and profiling dynamically launched kernels can be more challenging than for statically launched kernels. CUDA provides tools like 'cuda-gdb' and the Nsight suite to assist with debugging. Profiling might require hierarchical analysis to fully understand the performance characteristics of nested kernel launches.

5. **Legacy and Hardware Constraints**: Dynamic parallelism was introduced with the Kepler architecture (Compute Capability 3.5). Ensure

that the target hardware supports dynamic parallelism and consider hardware constraints such as maximum recursion depth and supported grid sizes.

By leveraging dynamic parallelism, CUDA applications can dynamically adapt to varying workloads and efficiently utilize the GPU. This flexibility is invaluable in applications such as adaptive mesh refinement, hierarchical algorithms, and multi-level parallel processing scenarios.

Dynamic parallelism enhances the capability of CUDA to handle complex, irregular, and hierarchical data structures by allowing recursive or nested execution of kernel functions directly on the device. This advanced feature is essential for writing more flexible, efficient, and scalable GPU applications.

8.3 CUDA Graphs

CUDA Graphs offer a flexible and efficient way to represent and execute complex sequences of GPU operations. This capability is especially beneficial for workloads that consist of multiple interdependent kernels and memory operations, taking advantage of the graph-based execution model to optimize performance and resource utilization.

CUDA Graphs are composed of nodes and edges; nodes represent actions such as kernel launches, memory copies, and host-to-device transfers, while edges define dependencies between these actions. By explicitly specifying the dependencies, CUDA can optimize the overall execution schedule, potentially overlapping operations to minimize idle periods.

Creating a CUDA Graph

The creation of a CUDA Graph involves defining a set of operations and the dependencies between them. This is done by first creating an empty graph, then adding individual nodes corresponding to the operations, and connecting these nodes with edges. The process is typically carried out through the following sequence of steps:

```
cudaGraph_t graph;
cudaGraphCreate(&graph, 0);
```

The argument 0 refers to the flag parameter, which is reserved for future use and should be set to 0.

Adding Nodes to the Graph

Nodes can be added to the graph for kernel execution, memory copy, and other operations. When adding a node, one must specify the operation details and any dependencies it has on previously defined nodes. For example, to add a kernel node:

```
cudaKernelNodeParams kernelNodeParams = {...};
cudaGraphNode_t kernelNode;
cudaGraphAddKernelNode(&kernelNode, graph, NULL, 0, &kernelNodeParams);
```

In this code, kernelNodeParams encapsulates the details of the kernel launch configuration, including the function pointer, grid dimensions, block dimensions, and any shared memory parameters. The newly created node kernelNode is then added to the graph without specifying any dependencies (indicated by NULL and 0).

Specifying Dependencies

When there are dependencies between operations, the edges in the graph must be specified accordingly. This ensures that dependent operations are executed in the correct order. For instance, if data needs to be copied from the host to the device before launching a kernel, one would create a memory copy node and establish a dependency for the kernel node:

```
cudaMemcpy3DParms memcpyParams = {...};
cudaGraphNode_t memcpyNode;
cudaGraphAddMemcpyNode(&memcpyNode, graph, NULL, 0, &memcpyParams);

cudaGraphNode_t dependencies[] = { memcpyNode };
cudaGraphAddKernelNode(&kernelNode, graph, dependencies, 1, &kernelNodeParams);
```

Here, dependencies specifies that the kernelNode has a dependency on memcpyNode and should only be executed after the memory copy operation completes.

Instantiating a CUDA Graph

Once the graph is defined with all required nodes and dependencies, it needs to be instantiated before execution. Instantiating the graph involves creating an executable CUDA graph instance which optimizes the execution plan based on the specified dependencies and operations:

```
cudaGraphExec_t graphInstance;
cudaGraphInstantiate(&graphInstance, graph, NULL, NULL, 0);
```

graphInstance is the executable version of the original graph and can now be launched on the GPU.

Launching a CUDA Graph

Launching an instantiated graph is straightforward and similar to launching traditional CUDA kernel functions but offers the benefit of executing the entire set of operations as a single workload, optimized by the CUDA runtime:

```
cudaGraphLaunch(graphInstance, stream);
```

This command schedules the entire graph for execution on the specified stream. If no stream is provided, the default stream is used.

Benefits of CUDA Graphs

Utilizing CUDA Graphs provides several benefits:

1. **Reduced Launch Overheads**: CUDA Graphs reduce the number of individual kernel and memory operation launches, which can significantly lower the launch overheads. 2. **Efficient Synchronization**: By specifying dependencies explicitly, CUDA Graphs help in efficient synchronization between kernels and memory operations. 3. **Potential for Overlapping**: CUDA can better overlap data transfers with kernel executions when the dependencies are well-defined, enhancing overall throughput. 4. **Improved Resource Utilization**: The CUDA runtime can optimize resource allocation and scheduling to make better use of computational and memory resources.

Example Use Case

Consider a scenario where multiple kernels need to be executed in a sequence, with intermediate data transfers between the host and the device. Using CUDA Graphs, this can be effectively managed as follows:

```
cudaGraph_t graph;
cudaGraphCreate(&graph, 0);

// Add memory copy node
cudaMemcpy3DParms memcpyParams1 = {...};
cudaGraphNode_t memcpyNode1;
cudaGraphAddMemcpyNode(&memcpyNode1, graph, NULL, 0, &memcpyParams1);

// Add first kernel node
cudaKernelNodeParams kernelNodeParams1 = {...};
cudaGraphNode_t kernelNode1;
cudaGraphAddKernelNode(&kernelNode1, graph, &memcpyNode1, 1, &
    kernelNodeParams1);

// Add second memory copy node
cudaMemcpy3DParms memcpyParams2 = {...};
cudaGraphNode_t memcpyNode2;
cudaGraphAddMemcpyNode(&memcpyNode2, graph, &kernelNode1, 1, &
    memcpyParams2);

// Add second kernel node
```

```
cudaKernelNodeParams kernelNodeParams2 = {...};
cudaGraphNode_t kernelNode2;
cudaGraphAddKernelNode(&kernelNode2, graph, &memcpyNode2, 1, &
    kernelNodeParams2);

// Instantiate and launch the graph
cudaGraphExec_t graphInstance;
cudaGraphInstantiate(&graphInstance, graph, NULL, NULL, 0);
cudaGraphLaunch(graphInstance, 0);
```

Through this procedure, the CUDA Graph effectively manages the sequence of operations, ensuring that each step is completed before the subsequent step begins according to the specified dependencies. This minimizes idle GPU periods and enhances execution efficiency.

8.4 Unified Memory and Memory Oversubscription

Unified Memory (UM) is a feature in CUDA that provides a single, addressable memory space accessible by both the CPU and GPU. This simplifies programming as it eliminates the need for explicit memory copies between host and device. The unified memory model allows for automatic data migration between the CPU and GPU, facilitated by the underlying CUDA runtime. This section explores the concepts of unified memory and how it helps in handling memory oversubscription.

Unified Memory is declared in a CUDA program using the cudaMallocManaged function. This allocates memory that the CUDA runtime can manage, and both the host and device can access it using the same pointer.

```
#include <cuda_runtime.h>
#include <iostream>

__global__
void add(int *a, int *b, int *c, int N) {
    int i = threadIdx.x + blockIdx.x * blockDim.x;
    if (i < N) {
        c[i] = a[i] + b[i];
    }
}

int main() {
    int N = 1<<20; // Number of elements
    size_t size = N * sizeof(int);

    int *a, *b, *c;
    cudaMallocManaged(&a, size);
    cudaMallocManaged(&b, size);
    cudaMallocManaged(&c, size);
```

```
    for (int i = 0; i < N; i++) {
        a[i] = i;
        b[i] = i;
    }

    int blockSize = 256;
    int numBlocks = (N + blockSize - 1) / blockSize;
    add<<<numBlocks, blockSize>>>(a, b, c, N);

    cudaDeviceSynchronize();

    std::cout << "Result: " << c[0] << ", " << c[N-1] << std::endl;

    cudaFree(a);
    cudaFree(b);
    cudaFree(c);

    return 0;
}
```

In this example, we allocate memory for arrays a, b, and c using cudaMallocManaged. These arrays are accessible from both the host and device. The data migration between the host and device is handled automatically by the CUDA runtime. The kernel add performs vector addition, and we synchronize the device using cudaDeviceSynchronize to ensure kernel completion before accessing results on the host side.

Memory oversubscription occurs when the logical memory usage of a program exceeds the physical memory capacity available on the GPU. Unified Memory handles oversubscription by paging data in and out of GPU memory, similar to how an operating system manages virtual memory.

Unified Memory uses page faulting to migrate data between the host and device. When a memory page required by the GPU is not resident in GPU memory, a page fault occurs. The CUDA runtime then copies the required memory page from the host to the GPU, allowing the kernel to proceed. This mechanism can cause performance overhead due to frequent page migrations; however, it allows the execution of applications that require more memory than the GPU's physical memory.

To better manage memory usage and reduce the overhead associated with page migrations, CUDA developers can use cudaMemAdvise. This function provides hints to the CUDA runtime about the intended usage patterns of managed memory. This can help optimize the data placement in host or device memory.

```
cudaMemAdvise(a, size, cudaMemAdviseSetPreferredLocation, cudaCpuDeviceId);
cudaMemAdvise(b, size, cudaMemAdviseSetPreferredLocation, cudaCpuDeviceId);
cudaMemAdvise(c, size, cudaMemAdviseSetPreferredLocation, cudaCpuDeviceId);
```

This example sets the preferred location of arrays a, b, and c to the CPU, which means the CUDA runtime will keep these arrays in CPU memory unless the GPU accesses the data. Proper utilization of cudaMemAdvise can lead to performance improvements by reducing unnecessary data migrations and keeping data closer to where it is used most.

Another useful function is cudaMemPrefetchAsync, allowing explicit prefetching of managed memory to the desired location, either the CPU or GPU. This function can be useful to preload data to the GPU before kernel execution.

```
cudaMemPrefetchAsync(a, size, 0, 0); // Prefetch to GPU
```

Using cudaMemPrefetchAsync ensures that the array a is preloaded into the GPU memory, reducing the likelihood of page faults during the kernel execution. By managing memory access patterns and prefetching data, developers can minimize the performance impact of memory oversubscription.

Unified Memory provides a simplified model for memory management in CUDA programs, but developers must be aware of the potential performance implications due to automatic data migration and memory oversubscription. By leveraging functions like cudaMemAdvise and cudaMemPrefetchAsync, developers can optimize data placement and access patterns, enhancing the overall performance of their CUDA applications.

8.5 CUDA Streams and Asynchronous Execution

CUDA streams provide a mechanism to manage concurrent operations on the GPU, allowing for more efficient utilization of hardware resources and potential reductions in execution time. By default, CUDA operations are performed in the *default stream*, which executes sequentially. However, by leveraging additional streams, developers can initiate kernels and memory operations in parallel, leading to increased performance for tasks that can be decomposed into independent parts.

Creating and Managing Streams

Streams are created and destroyed using the cudaStreamCreate and cudaStreamDestroy functions, respectively. Each stream represents a sequence of operations that are ordered within the stream but can execute concurrently with operations in other streams.

```
cudaStream_t stream1, stream2;
cudaStreamCreate(&stream1);
cudaStreamCreate(&stream2);

// Perform operations on stream1
someKernel<<<blocks, threads, 0, stream1>>>();
cudaMemcpyAsync(destination1, source1, size, cudaMemcpyDeviceToHost, stream1);

// Perform operations on stream2
someOtherKernel<<<blocks, threads, 0, stream2>>>();
cudaMemcpyAsync(destination2, source2, size, cudaMemcpyDeviceToHost, stream2);

// Clean up
cudaStreamDestroy(stream1);
cudaStreamDestroy(stream2);
```

In this example, two streams are created, and separate sets of operations are issued to each stream. The kernels someKernel and someOtherKernel can execute concurrently, as can the asynchronous memory copies.

Synchronization and Stream Dependencies

While streams allow for parallel execution, it may be necessary to synchronize streams to ensure correct operation order. CUDA provides several functions for synchronizing streams, including cudaStreamSynchronize and cudaEvent_t.

Events are used to establish synchronization points in streams. They record timestamps of the successful completion of operations and 'tie' dependent operations across different streams. Below is an example illustrating event usage:

```
cudaStream_t stream1, stream2;
cudaStreamCreate(&stream1);
cudaStreamCreate(&stream2);

cudaEvent_t event;
cudaEventCreate(&event);

// Launch a kernel in stream1
someKernel<<<blocks, threads, 0, stream1>>>();

// Record an event after the kernel in stream1
cudaEventRecord(event, stream1);

// Make stream2 wait on the event recorded in stream1
cudaStreamWaitEvent(stream2, event, 0);

// Launch another kernel in stream2
someOtherKernel<<<blocks, threads, 0, stream2>>>();

// Clean up
cudaEventDestroy(event);
cudaStreamDestroy(stream1);
```

```
cudaStreamDestroy(stream2);
```

In this example, someOtherKernel in stream2 is forced to wait until someKernel in stream1 completes, ensuring proper synchronization.

Asynchronous Memory Operations

CUDA supports several types of asynchronous memory operations, crucial for maximizing computational overlap and data transfer. Functions such as cudaMemcpyAsync allow for memory copying operations to overlap with kernel execution. They require the destination stream as an argument, permitting seamless integration with ongoing stream activities. Here is an example:

```
cudaStream_t stream1;
cudaStreamCreate(&stream1);

float *deviceData, *hostData;
// Assume memory allocations and initializations are done

// Initiate memory copy asynchronously
cudaMemcpyAsync(deviceData, hostData, size, cudaMemcpyHostToDevice, stream1);

// Launch kernel that uses deviceData
someKernel<<<blocks, threads, 0, stream1>>>();

// Another memory copy after kernel execution
cudaMemcpyAsync(hostData, deviceData, size, cudaMemcpyDeviceToHost, stream1);

// Synchronize stream to ensure all operations are complete
cudaStreamSynchronize(stream1);

// Clean up
cudaStreamDestroy(stream1);
```

In this case, memory transfers and kernel executions are dynamically managed within stream1, optimizing their concurrent execution.

Stream Priorities

To enforce an order of importance among streams, CUDA supports stream priorities. Higher priority streams can preempt lower priority streams, giving developers finer control over execution ordering. Stream priority is assigned during stream creation:

```
int leastPriority;
int greatestPriority;
cudaDeviceGetStreamPriorityRange(&leastPriority, &greatestPriority);

cudaStream_t highPriorityStream, lowPriorityStream;
cudaStreamCreateWithPriority(&highPriorityStream, cudaStreamDefault,
      greatestPriority);
cudaStreamCreateWithPriority(&lowPriorityStream, cudaStreamDefault, leastPriority);

// High-priority operation
```

```
someKernel<<<blocks, threads, 0, highPriorityStream>>>();

// Low-priority operation
someOtherKernel<<<blocks, threads, 0, lowPriorityStream>>>();

// Clean up
cudaStreamDestroy(highPriorityStream);
cudaStreamDestroy(lowPriorityStream);
```

This mechanism is beneficial in scenarios requiring differentiated service levels among multiple workloads.

Concurrent Kernel Execution

When multiple kernels are launched in different streams, CUDA-capable GPUs that support *Concurrent Kernel Execution* can run multiple kernels simultaneously. This feature, combined with stream utilization, allows for efficient multitasking on the GPU.

Consider the following:

```
cudaStream_t stream1, stream2;
cudaStreamCreate(&stream1);
cudaStreamCreate(&stream2);

someKernel<<<blocks, threads, 0, stream1>>>();
someOtherKernel<<<blocks, threads, 0, stream2>>>();

cudaStreamSynchronize(stream1);
cudaStreamSynchronize(stream2);

cudaStreamDestroy(stream1);
cudaStreamDestroy(stream2);
```

Here, someKernel and someOtherKernel can execute concurrently, assuming the GPU supports this feature. This level of parallelism significantly boosts throughput for independent kernels.

Caveats and Considerations

Despite their advantages, streams must be used judiciously to avert potential pitfalls. Resource contention, such as shared memory or register file saturation, can arise. Ensuring data consistency across streams is crucial since race conditions could lead to erroneous results.

Memory allocation and deallocation should be handled with care within streams, avoiding synchronous calls that might negate the benefits of asynchronous execution.

Awareness of hardware capabilities—such as the number of concurrent streams supported and the device's compute capability—is paramount for effective stream management and occurrence avoidance of oversubscription.

Leveraging streams' full potential requires mindful design and empirical performance tuning. By strategically partitioning workloads and synchronizing operations prudently, significant computational savings and efficiency improvements are achievable.

8.6 Peer-to-Peer Memory Access

Peer-to-peer (P2P) memory access in CUDA facilitates direct memory transfer between GPUs without the need for the host CPU to mediate the transfer. This technique is particularly valuable in multi-GPU systems as it significantly enhances data transfer efficiency and reduces latency. The capability for GPUs to directly access each other's memory is subject to the architecture of the system and the specific GPUs in use. NVIDIA's NVLink and PCI Express provide the physical infrastructure enabling this functionality.

To utilize peer-to-peer memory access, certain prerequisite conditions must be met: both GPUs need to support P2P access, and they must be interconnected via NVLink or be on the same PCIe bus. The following steps outline the key processes involved in setting up and utilizing P2P memory access in CUDA.

First, it is necessary to enable P2P access between two GPUs. The 'cudaDeviceCanAccessPeer' function is used to check if a device has access to the peer device's memory. Following a successful check, the 'cudaDeviceEnablePeerAccess' function is employed to enable access. The subsequent code snippet demonstrates this setup.

```
int devID0 = 0, devID1 = 1;
cudaSetDevice(devID0);

// Check P2P capability
int canAccessPeer = 0;
cudaDeviceCanAccessPeer(&canAccessPeer, devID0, devID1);
if (canAccessPeer) {
    cudaDeviceEnablePeerAccess(devID1, 0);
} else {
    std::cerr << "Device 0 cannot access device 1" << std::endl;
}

// Repeat for the other direction
cudaSetDevice(devID1);
cudaDeviceCanAccessPeer(&canAccessPeer, devID1, devID0);
if (canAccessPeer) {
    cudaDeviceEnablePeerAccess(devID0, 0);
} else {
    std::cerr << "Device 1 cannot access device 0" << std::endl;
}
```

With P2P access enabled, memory transfers can be performed directly between two GPUs using the 'cudaMemcpyPeer' function. This circumvents the CPU, leading to improved performance. The following code illustrates transferring data from GPU 0 to GPU 1.

```
cudaSetDevice(devID0);
float *d_A;
cudaMalloc(&d_A, size);
initializeData<<<blocks, threads>>>(d_A, size);

// Allocate memory on the peer device
cudaSetDevice(devID1);
float *d_B;
cudaMalloc(&d_B, size);

// Perform peer memory copy
cudaMemcpyPeer(d_B, devID1, d_A, devID0, size);
```

The above steps are essential for direct P2P memory access. Enabling P2P transfers between devices can significantly improve data throughput in scenarios requiring frequent inter-GPU communication. However, it is crucial to manage P2P connections properly. CUDA offers the 'cudaDeviceDisablePeerAccess' function to disable peer-to-peer access when it is no longer needed, helping to release resources:

```
cudaSetDevice(devID0);
cudaDeviceDisablePeerAccess(devID1);

cudaSetDevice(devID1);
cudaDeviceDisablePeerAccess(devID0);
```

Performance gains from P2P memory access can be substantial depending on the workload and data transfer patterns. The physical interconnect, such as NVLink, often determines the maximum achievable bandwidth. It is advisably optimal to benchmark typical workloads to ascertain the performance benefits.

Achieving optimal performance also necessitates an understanding of the system topology. Utilizing tools like 'nvidia-smi topo -m' provides a detailed mapping of the GPU interconnections, assisting in identifying compatible P2P pairs.

For instance, consider the following hypothetical output from 'nvidia-smi topo -m':

	GPU0	GPU1	GPU2	GPU3	CPU Affinity
GPU0	X	PIX	PHB	PHB	0-11
GPU1	PIX	X	PHB	PHB	0-11
GPU2	PHB	PHB	X	PIX	12-23
GPU3	PHB	PHB	PIX	X	12-23

In this context, 'PIX' indicates that the GPUs share the same PCIe switch, providing lower latency connections compared to 'PHB', which indicates communication through the PCIe root complex. Maximizing P2P performance involves strategically placing data to exploit these faster paths.

Conclusively, direct peer-to-peer memory access in CUDA delivers a valuable mechanism for inter-GPU data transfer, minimizing the involvement of the host CPU. Understanding system topology and correctly configuring devices are pivotal to leveraging this capability effectively. Through careful implementation, P2P access can significantly enhance both performance scalability and resource utilization in multi-GPU applications.

8.7 Inter-Process Communication

Inter-Process Communication (IPC) in CUDA programming allows separate processes to share data and synchronize their operations. This is essential for applications that require collaboration across different processes running on the same or different GPUs. IPC can be leveraged to improve performance by minimizing data transfers between host and device, or between devices.

Utilizing IPC in CUDA involves several steps, including the sharing of CUDA memory objects and the synchronization of processes. The following subsections detail these steps, providing sample code where necessary.

1. Creation and Export of CUDA Memory Objects

The IPC feature in CUDA starts by creating memory objects that one process can share with another. This is typically done using CUDA APIs such as 'cudaMalloc' to allocate device memory, followed by 'cudaIpcGetMemHandle' to get a handle that can be shared.

```
#include <cuda_runtime.h>
#include <iostream>

__global__ void kernel(int *data) {
    int idx = threadIdx.x + blockIdx.x * blockDim.x;
    data[idx] += 1;
}

int main() {
    int *d_data;
    cudaIpcMemHandle_t memHandle;

    cudaMalloc(&d_data, sizeof(int) * 256);
```

```
    // Launch a kernel to modify the memory
    kernel<<<1, 256>>>(d_data);
    cudaDeviceSynchronize();

    // Generate an IPC memory handle for the allocated memory
    cudaIpcGetMemHandle(&memHandle, d_data);

    // Pass the handle to another process
    // (Not shown here: Use IPC mechanism like pipes, sockets, or shared files to pass
        the handle)

    // Clean up
    cudaFree(d_data);
    return 0;
}
```

2. Importing and Using CUDA IPC Memory Handles

The receiving process must import the shared memory handle using 'cudaIpcOpenMemHandle'. Once imported, it can access and manipulate the memory just like any other device memory.

```
#include <cuda_runtime.h>
#include <iostream>

__global__ void kernel_add(int *data) {
    int idx = threadIdx.x + blockIdx.x * blockDim.x;
    data[idx] += 2;
}

int main() {
    int *d_data;
    cudaIpcMemHandle_t memHandle;

    // Assume memHandle is received from another process

    // Open the IPC memory handle
    cudaIpcOpenMemHandle((void**)&d_data, memHandle,
        cudaIpcMemLazyEnablePeerAccess);

    // Launch a kernel to modify the shared memory
    kernel_add<<<1, 256>>>(d_data);
    cudaDeviceSynchronize();

    // Clean up
    cudaIpcCloseMemHandle(d_data);
    return 0;
}
```

3. Synchronizing Processes

Synchronization is crucial for ensuring that one process does not modify memory while another is using it, which could lead to data corruption. CUDA provides events for this purpose. Events can be shared across processes using 'cudaIpcGetEventHandle' and 'cudaIpcOpenEventHandle'.

```
#include <cuda_runtime.h>
#include <iostream>

int main() {
    cudaEvent_t event;
    cudaIpcEventHandle_t eventHandle;

    // Create an event and get the event handle
    cudaEventCreate(&event);
    cudaEventRecord(event);
    cudaIpcGetEventHandle(&eventHandle, event);

    // Pass the event handle to another process
    // (Not shown here: Use IPC mechanism to pass the event handle)

    // Use the event handle to synchronize
    cudaEventSynchronize(event);

    // Clean up
    cudaEventDestroy(event);
    return 0;
}
```

In the receiving process, the event handle is imported and used to synchronize operations.

```
#include <cuda_runtime.h>
#include <iostream>

int main() {
    cudaEvent_t event;
    cudaIpcEventHandle_t eventHandle;

    // Assume eventHandle is received from another process

    // Open the IPC event handle
    cudaIpcOpenEventHandle(&event, eventHandle);

    // Synchronize using the received event
    cudaEventSynchronize(event);

    // Clean up
    cudaEventDestroy(event);
    return 0;
}
```

These examples highlight the key aspects of IPC in CUDA. Using shared memory handles and event synchronization allows multiple processes to efficiently collaborate, leveraging GPU resources effectively.

8.8 CUDA and Multi-GPU Programming

The scalability of CUDA extends beyond a single GPU, enabling the harnessing of multiple GPUs within a single system to tackle large-scale computational problems. This section discusses the fundamentals and advanced aspects of multi-GPU programming in CUDA, focusing on device selection, memory management, synchronization, and data transfer methods between GPUs.

CUDA applications can leverage multiple GPUs by selecting specific devices via the cudaSetDevice() function. It is crucial to check for the number of GPUs available in the system using the cudaGetDeviceCount() function. The choice of device selection strategies often depends on the problem being solved and the desired parallelization level. Example code for querying and setting devices is provided below:

```
int deviceCount = 0;
cudaError_t err = cudaGetDeviceCount(&deviceCount);
if (err != cudaSuccess) {
    // Handle error
}

for (int dev = 0; dev < deviceCount; ++dev) {
    cudaDeviceProp deviceProp;
    cudaGetDeviceProperties(&deviceProp, dev);
    printf("Device %d: %s\n", dev, deviceProp.name);
}

// Set device 0 as the active device
cudaSetDevice(0);
```

Multi-GPU programming necessitates careful memory management to ensure efficient data distribution and minimize latency. Each GPU has its memory space, leading to challenges in data sharing and coherence. Two primary approaches are employed: copying data between GPUs and utilizing Unified Memory. Direct memory allocation and copying can be achieved using cudaMalloc() and cudaMemcpy(). For example:

```
// Allocate memory on device 0
cudaSetDevice(0);
float *d_A;
cudaMalloc((void**)&d_A, size);

// Allocate memory on device 1
cudaSetDevice(1);
float *d_B;
cudaMalloc((void**)&d_B, size);

// Copy data from host to device 0
cudaMemcpy(d_A, h_A, size, cudaMemcpyHostToDevice);

// Copy data between devices
cudaMemcpyPeer(d_B, 1, d_A, 0, size);
```

Unified Memory simplifies multi-GPU programming by providing a shared memory address space accessible by all GPUs. It uses on-demand paging to manage memory oversubscription scenarios, transparently migrating data between host and GPU memory as needed. Its usage involves allocating memory with cudaMallocManaged():

```
float *A;
cudaMallocManaged(&A, size);

// Perform operations on A, accessible by any GPU
cudaMemPrefetchAsync(A, size, 0);
cudaMemPrefetchAsync(A, size, 1);
```

Efficient data transfer and synchronization are critical in multi-GPU programming to maintain coherence and optimize performance. Asynchronous memory copy operations using CUDA streams allow overlapping data transfers with computation, reducing idle times. For example:

```
cudaStream_t stream0, stream1;
cudaStreamCreate(&stream0);
cudaStreamCreate(&stream1);

// Initiate asynchronous copies
cudaMemcpyAsync(d_A, h_A, size, cudaMemcpyHostToDevice, stream0);
cudaMemcpyAsync(d_B, d_A, size, cudaMemcpyDeviceToDevice, stream1);
```

Synchronization mechanisms ensure that operations dependent on specific data completion order maintain correctness. calls like cudaDeviceSynchronize() or cudaStreamSynchronize() are employed:

```
cudaDeviceSynchronize(); // Synchronize all operations on the current device
cudaStreamSynchronize(stream0); // Synchronize all operations in stream0
```

Peer-to-peer memory access further enhances inter-GPU data transfer by allowing one GPU to directly access the memory of another, thereby reducing latency. This requires enabling peer access, as shown in the following example:

```
// Enable peer access
cudaSetDevice(0);
cudaDeviceEnablePeerAccess(1, 0);

cudaSetDevice(1);
cudaDeviceEnablePeerAccess(0, 0);

// Now GPU 0 and GPU 1 can directly access each other's memory
cudaMemcpyPeer(d_B, 1, d_A, 0, size);
```

Handling large-scale computations across multiple GPUs also necessitates efficient workload distribution. Considerations include balancing load across GPUs and minimizing inter-GPU communication. Strategies like domain decomposition, pipelining, and workload replication are commonly used to achieve these goals.

The Host API provides facilities for dynamically launching work across multiple devices, considering factors such as GPU capabilities, current load, and availability of resources. Flexible task partitioning and aggregation schemes play a pivotal role in achieving optimal performance in multi-GPU configurations.

The integration of these techniques establishes a robust framework for exploiting multiple GPUs, extending the capabilities of CUDA applications to solve highly complex and data-intensive problems efficiently. The balance between computation, data transfer, and synchronization is vital for optimizing performance in such environments.

8.9 Using Thrust Library for High-Level Abstractions

Thrust is a parallel algorithms library that resembles the C++ Standard Template Library (STL). By providing a collection of data parallel primitives, Thrust facilitates the development of high-performance CUDA applications with a focus on productivity and ease of use. Thrust enables developers to express complex parallel algorithms at a high level of abstraction, consequently improving code readability and maintainability.

To utilize Thrust, it is essential to understand its two core components: thrust::device and thrust::host vectors, and its algorithm library which includes operations such as sorting, scanning, and transforming. The library abstracts GPU programming complexities by providing a high-level interface for performing common parallel operations.

```
#include <thrust/host_vector.h>
#include <thrust/device_vector.h>
#include <thrust/sort.h>
#include <thrust/reduce.h>
```

We begin by including the necessary header files. The thrust::host_vector.h and thrust::device_vector.h headers are required for defining host and device vectors, respectively. The thrust/sort.h and thrust/reduce.h headers provide access to the algorithms for sorting and reduction.

For illustrative purposes, consider a simple example where we sort an array of integers and compute the sum of its elements. The following code demonstrates the use of thrust::host_vector and thrust::device_vector, as well as the thrust::sort and thrust::reduce algorithms.

```
int main(void)
{
    // Initialize host array
    int host_data[6] = {1, 3, 5, 7, 9, 2};

    // Transfer to device
    thrust::device_vector<int> d_data(host_data, host_data + 6);

    // Sort data on the device
    thrust::sort(d_data.begin(), d_data.end());

    // Compute the sum of sorted elements
    int total = thrust::reduce(d_data.begin(), d_data.end(), 0, thrust::plus<int>());

    // Transfer data back to host
    thrust::copy(d_data.begin(), d_data.end(), host_data);

    // Output the results
    for (int i = 0; i < 6; i++)
        std::cout << "Sorted data: " << host_data[i] << std::endl;

    std::cout << "Total sum: " << total << std::endl;

    return 0;
}
```

The key steps in this example include initializing a host array, transferring the array to the device using thrust::device_vector, sorting the array on the device using thrust::sort, reducing the sorted array elements to a single sum using thrust::reduce, and then copying the data back to the host for output.

The Thrust library's design principles ensure that algorithms operate on both host and device vectors seamlessly. Additionally, it supports custom data types and operations. For custom operations, we can use functors or lambda expressions. For example, if we want to square the elements of the vector before sorting, we can utilize thrust::transform as follows:

```
struct square
{
    __host__ __device__
    int operator()(const int& x) const
    {
        return x * x;
    }
};

int main(void)
{
    int host_data[6] = {1, 3, 5, 7, 9, 2};
    thrust::device_vector<int> d_data(host_data, host_data + 6);

    // Apply the square transformation
    thrust::transform(d_data.begin(), d_data.end(), d_data.begin(), square());

    // Sort the squared values
```

```
    thrust::sort(d_data.begin(), d_data.end());

    // Compute the sum of the sorted squared elements
    int total = thrust::reduce(d_data.begin(), d_data.end(), 0, thrust::plus<int>());

    thrust::copy(d_data.begin(), d_data.end(), host_data);

    for (int i = 0; i < 6; i++)
        std::cout << "Sorted squared data: " << host_data[i] << std::endl;

    std::cout << "Total sum of squares: " << total << std::endl;

    return 0;
}
```

In this example, we define a functor square that squares an integer value. We use thrust::transform to apply this functor to the device_-vector elements before performing the sort and reduction operations.

The Thrust library also supports more advanced operations such as stencil-based algorithms and user-defined reductions. For instance, when working with non-integer data or performing operations conditioned on other arrays, Thrust can significantly simplify implementation.

It is critical to note that Thrust leverages stream-based execution for non-blocking operations. This enables overlap of computation and memory transfers, thereby improving performance.

```
int main(void)
{
    int N = 1<<20;
    thrust::host_vector<int> h_vec(N);
    thrust::generate(h_vec.begin(), h_vec.end(), rand);

    // Transfer to device
    thrust::device_vector<int> d_vec = h_vec;

    // Create CUDA stream
    cudaStream_t stream;
    cudaStreamCreate(&stream);

    // Attach stream to Thrust execution policy
    thrust::sort(thrust::cuda::par.on(stream), d_vec.begin(), d_vec.end());

    // Synchronize and destroy stream
    cudaStreamSynchronize(stream);
    cudaStreamDestroy(stream);

    thrust::copy(d_vec.begin(), d_vec.end(), h_vec.begin());

    return 0;
}
```

In this example, a CUDA stream is created using cudaStreamCreate, and the stream-based execution is facilitated by thrust::cuda::par.on(stream). Sorting the vector on the specified stream enables non-blocking execution, enhancing performance especially when concurrent streams are utilized.

Thrust's powerful abstractions allow expert users to focus on the algorithmic aspects of their applications, thereby accelerating development cycles and optimizing performance. By mastering the Thrust library, CUDA developers can achieve greater flexibility and productivity, effectively addressing complex parallel computing challenges.

8.10 CUDA in Heterogeneous Computing Environments

Heterogeneous computing environments integrate multiple computing resources, including GPUs (Graphics Processing Units) and CPUs (Central Processing Units), to exploit the full computational potential of a system. In such environments, CUDA facilitates the leveraging of GPU capabilities alongside traditional CPU functions, effectively enabling high-performance computing tasks. This section examines several key aspects and best practices for utilizing CUDA within heterogeneous computing environments.

To effectively harness both CPU and GPU resources, one must understand the respective roles of each in a computational task. CPUs are optimized for latency-sensitive, sequential tasks, whereas GPUs excel at throughput-oriented, parallel workloads. Efficient heterogeneous computing involves appropriately partitioning the workload to balance the strengths of each processor type.

Hybrid Execution Models One fundamental strategy in heterogeneous computing is the hybrid execution model. This model allocates computation simultaneously across CPU and GPU. The concurrent execution maximizes resource utilization and improves performance. An illustrative example follows:

```
#include <cuda_runtime.h>
#include <iostream>

// Kernel function for GPU computation
__global__ void gpuComputation(float* a, int N) {
    int idx = blockIdx.x * blockDim.x + threadIdx.x;
    if (idx < N) {
        a[idx] = a[idx] * a[idx];
    }
}
```

```
// Function for CPU computation
void cpuComputation(float* a, int N) {
    for (int i = 0; i < N; ++i) {
        a[i] = a[i] * a[i];
    }
}

int main() {
    const int N = 1 << 20;
    float* h_a = new float[N];
    float* d_a;

    // Allocate memory on GPU
    cudaMalloc(&d_a, N * sizeof(float));

    // Initialize data
    for (int i = 0; i < N; ++i) {
        h_a[i] = static_cast<float>(i);
    }

    // Copy data to GPU
    cudaMemcpy(d_a, h_a, N * sizeof(float), cudaMemcpyHostToDevice);

    // Launch GPU kernel
    gpuComputation<<<(N + 255) / 256, 256>>>(d_a, N);

    // Perform CPU computation in parallel
    cpuComputation(h_a, N);

    // Copy results back to Host
    cudaMemcpy(h_a, d_a, N * sizeof(float), cudaMemcpyDeviceToHost);

    // Cleanup
    cudaFree(d_a);
    delete[] h_a;

    std::cout << "Hybrid computation completed." << std::endl;
    return 0;
}
```

In this example, ‘gpuComputation‘ executes on the GPU, while ‘cpuComputation‘ runs on the CPU. By overlapping these operations, the system’s computational throughput increases.

Data Management Strategies Efficient data movement between CPU and GPU is crucial. CUDA provides several methods to facilitate optimal data transfers. The following strategies are essential:

1. **Pinned Memory:** Using pinned (page-locked) memory can significantly reduce the overhead of data transfers between the host and device. Pinned memory remains in a fixed physical location, enhancing transfer rates.

```
cudaHostAlloc((void**)&h_a, N * sizeof(float), cudaHostAllocDefault);
```

2. **Unified Memory:** Unified Memory provides a single memory space accessible from any processor in a system. This simplifies memory management but may introduce inconsistencies in performance due to implicit data migration.

```
cudaMallocManaged(&d_a, N * sizeof(float));
```

3. **Streams and Concurrency:** Using CUDA streams allows overlapping data transfers with computation. Each stream operates independently, enabling concurrent execution of kernel launches and memory operations.

```
cudaStream_t stream1, stream2;
cudaStreamCreate(&stream1);
cudaStreamCreate(&stream2);

// Asynchronous data transfer
cudaMemcpyAsync(d_a, h_a, N * sizeof(float), cudaMemcpyHostToDevice, stream1);

// Kernel launch in another stream
gpuComputation<<<(N + 255) / 256, 256, 0, stream2>>>(d_a, N);

// Synchronize streams
cudaStreamSynchronize(stream1);
cudaStreamSynchronize(stream2);
```

Task Orchestration and Libraries Task orchestration in a heterogeneous environment often involves third-party libraries and frameworks to manage and schedule work efficiently. Libraries such as Thrust, cuBLAS, and cuDNN provide high-level abstractions for common tasks like vector operations, linear algebra, and deep learning.

Performance Considerations CPU-GPU synchronization is a critical performance consideration. Avoid frequent synchronization, as this can degrade overall performance. Instead, batching tasks and overlapping computation with data transfers yield better results.

Moreover, profiling tools such as NVIDIA Nsight Systems and Nsight Compute are invaluable. These tools provide detailed insights into performance bottlenecks and optimization opportunities within heterogeneous workloads.

Here is an example of using Nsight Systems for profiling:

```
nsys profile ./a.out
```

```
Generating trace1254.qdrep trace file...
Profiling completed.
```

By opening the generated '.qdrep' file in Nsight Systems, one can visualize the execution timeline and identify potential inefficiencies.

Understanding and applying these principles enable effectively leveraging CUDA in heterogeneous environments, boosting computational performance across various applications.

Chapter 9

Debugging and Profiling CUDA Applications

This chapter provides a detailed guide to debugging and profiling CUDA applications, starting with common CUDA errors and their resolutions. It covers the use of NVIDIA Nsight and CUDA-GDB for debugging and discusses manual debugging techniques. The chapter also explores tools like NVIDIA Visual Profiler for analyzing kernel performance and profiling CPU-GPU interactions. It offers insights into interpreting profiling results, optimizing code based on profiling data, and presents best practices for efficient debugging and profiling.

9.1 Introduction to Debugging and Profiling

Debugging and profiling are integral components of the software development lifecycle, particularly in High-Performance Computing (HPC) environments such as CUDA programming. Effective debugging ensures that your application functions correctly, while profiling helps you understand and optimize the performance characteristics of your application. Mastery of these topics is essential for developing efficient and robust CUDA applications.

In the context of CUDA programming, debugging refers to the process of identifying and resolving errors or bugs within your CUDA code.

These could be syntax errors, runtime errors, or logical errors that prevent the program from producing the correct output or functioning as expected. Debugging CUDA applications can be more complex than debugging traditional CPU-based applications due to the concurrent and parallel nature of GPU execution. Different techniques and tools are necessary to address these unique challenges.

Profiling, on the other hand, involves monitoring the performance of your CUDA application to identify bottlenecks, inefficient code paths, and resource utilization issues. The goal of profiling is to gain insights into how your code interacts with the hardware, allowing you to make informed optimizations that enhance performance. Profiling tools provide detailed metrics on various aspects of CUDA programs, such as execution time, memory usage, and the efficiency of kernel executions.

One of the fundamental concepts in CUDA programming is understanding the hardware architecture. CUDA-enabled GPUs consist of multiple Streaming Multiprocessors (SMs), each containing numerous cores capable of executing threads simultaneously. The hierarchical memory model, including global, shared, and local memory, further complicates the performance dynamics. As such, debugging and profiling require a thorough understanding of how these hardware components work and interact with your code.

Consider the following simple CUDA kernel that adds two vectors:

```
// Kernel function to add the elements of two arrays
__global__
void add(int n, float *x, float *y) {
    int index = threadIdx.x + blockIdx.x * blockDim.x;
    int stride = blockDim.x * gridDim.x;
    for (int i = index; i < n; i += stride) {
        y[i] = x[i] + y[i];
    }
}
```

When debugging this CUDA kernel, some common errors might include:

1. **Out-of-bounds Memory Access:** Accessing elements beyond the allocated memory limits. 2. **Race Conditions:** Multiple threads simultaneously writing to shared memory without proper synchronization. 3. **Incorrect Index Calculation:** Errors in calculating thread and block indices leading to incorrect results.

Each of these errors requires different debugging techniques to resolve. For instance, out-of-bounds memory access can be detected using tools like CUDA-MEMCHECK:

```
$ cuda-memcheck ./your_cuda_application
```

Profiling this simple kernel to understand its performance implications involves several detailed steps. Tools such as NVIDIA Visual Profiler offer visual insights into kernel execution, memory transfer, and GPU utilization. To profile the kernel, you can launch the profiler with your application:

```
$ nvprof --analysis-metrics -o profile_output.nvprof ./your_cuda_application
```

This command generates a detailed report providing metrics such as kernel execution time, achieved occupancy, and memory throughput. Such profiling data is pivotal when optimizing the kernel. For example, if the profiler indicates low occupancy, you might consider adjusting the grid and block dimensions to better utilize the GPU resources.

Understanding how to interpret the profiling data is crucial. High memory transfer times between CPU and GPU might suggest an opportunity to optimize data transfer strategies. Kernel execution metrics can highlight bottlenecks, enabling targeted optimizations such as loop unrolling, memory coalescing, or minimizing divergent branches within your kernels.

In this chapter, we will delve deeper into the strategies and tools essential for effective debugging and profiling. The goal is to equip you with the practical knowledge required to develop optimized CUDA applications that leverage the full potential of GPU computing.

9.2 Common CUDA Errors and How to Fix Them

The development of CUDA applications can sometimes lead to errors that are specific to the CUDA environment. This section outlines some of the most common CUDA errors, as well as strategies for identifying and resolving these issues.

1. CUDA Memory Allocation Errors

CUDA memory allocation errors often arise when there is insufficient device memory available to allocate new memory segments. The cudaMalloc function is typically where such errors manifest. A common symptom of this problem is encountering cudaErrorMemoryAllocation.

To diagnose and resolve memory allocation errors:

- **Check Available Memory:** Use cudaMemGetInfo to check the available memory on the device before attempting to allocate more memory. This function provides the total and free memory available on the device.

```
size_t freeMem, totalMem;
cudaError_t err = cudaMemGetInfo(&freeMem, &totalMem);
if (err != cudaSuccess) {
    fprintf(stderr, "cudaMemGetInfo failed: %s\n", cudaGetErrorString(err));

    // handle error
}
printf("Free memory: %zu bytes, Total memory: %zu bytes\n", freeMem,
      totalMem);
```

- **Optimize Memory Usage:** Ensure that you are efficiently using device memory. This can be done by reusing memory allocations and deallocating memory that is no longer needed using cudaFree.

```
cudaFree(devPtr);
```

- **Adjust Data Structures:** Sometimes, optimizing the data structures to make them more memory-efficient can prevent allocation failures. Use compact data types and structures when possible.

- **Increase Device Memory:** If available, consider using a GPU with more memory.

2. Kernel Launch Failures

Kernel launch failures are indicated by the error cudaErrorLaunchFailure, often caused by illegal memory access, misconfigured shared memory, or exceeding the limits of the kernel parameters.

To address kernel launch failures:

- **Check for Illegal Memory Accesses:** Use the cuda-memcheck tool, which can detect out-of-bounds memory accesses and misaligned memory accesses.

```
cuda-memcheck ./myCudaApp
```

  Review the resulting report to locate the problematic areas in the code.

- **Verify Kernel Parameters:** Ensure that the number of threads, blocks, and the amount of shared memory specified during the kernel launch do not exceed the limits of the GPU. Verify these parameters using functions like cudaDeviceProp.

```
cudaDeviceProp deviceProp;
cudaGetDeviceProperties(&deviceProp, 0);
printf("Max threads per block: %d\n", deviceProp.maxThreadsPerBlock);
printf("Max blocks in grid: (%d, %d, %d)\n", deviceProp.maxGridSize[0],
       deviceProp.maxGridSize[1], deviceProp.maxGridSize[2]);
printf("Shared memory per block: %zu\n", deviceProp.sharedMemPerBlock);
```

- **Debug Shared Memory Usage:** Excessive use of shared memory beyond the GPU's capabilities can cause launch failures. Carefully compute the shared memory requirements and ensure they fit within the device limits.

3. Synchronization Errors

Synchronization errors occur when there is improper coordination between host and device code, leading to partial completion of tasks or data inconsistencies. The error cudaErrorSyncFailure typically indicates such issues.

Fixing synchronization errors involves:

- **Ensure Proper Synchronization:** Use synchronization functions such as cudaDeviceSynchronize, cudaStreamSynchronize, and __syncthreads() to ensure proper coordination between host and device, and among threads in a block.

```
cudaError_t err = cudaDeviceSynchronize();
if (err != cudaSuccess) {
    fprintf(stderr, "cudaDeviceSynchronize returned error code %d: %s\n",
            err, cudaGetErrorString(err));
    // handle error
}
```

- **Verify Stream Usage:** When using CUDA streams, ensure that operations intended to occur in sequence are properly enqueued in the correct stream and that sequential dependencies are maintained with stream synchronization functions.

```
cudaStream_t stream;
cudaStreamCreate(&stream);
kernelA<<<blocks, threads, 0, stream>>>(...);
cudaStreamSynchronize(stream);
kernelB<<<blocks, threads, 0, stream>>>(...);
cudaStreamDestroy(stream);
```

4. Out-of-Bounds and Illegal Memory Access

Accessing memory out of the allocated bounds or in an illegal manner can lead to unpredictable behavior and crashes, often flagging cudaErrorInvalidDevicePointer or cudaErrorInvalidValue.

To prevent illegal memory access:

- **Bounds Checking:** Ensure that all memory accesses within kernels are within the appropriate bounds. Utilize consistent indexing and boundary checks.

```
__global__ void myKernel(int *data, int size) {
    int idx = blockIdx.x * blockDim.x + threadIdx.x;
    if (idx < size) {
        data[idx] = ...; // valid array access
    }
}
```

- **Use Unified Memory:** CUDA Unified Memory can simplify memory management and reduce instances of illegal access by providing a single memory space accessible by both CPU and GPU.

```
cudaMallocManaged(&data, size * sizeof(int));
```

- **Debugging Tools:** Leverage CUDA's debugging tools such as cuda-memcheck to identify illegal memory access patterns during runtime.

5. Uninitialized Memory

Uninitialized memory can lead to undefined behavior and obscure bugs in CUDA applications.

To manage uninitialized memory:

- **Initialize Memory:** Always initialize memory after allocation. Use functions like cudaMemset for device memory initialization.

```
cudaError_t err = cudaMemset(devPtr, 0, size);
if (err != cudaSuccess) {
    fprintf(stderr, "cudaMemset failed: %s\n", cudaGetErrorString(err));
    // handle error
}
```

- **Valgrind and cuda-memcheck:** Utilize tools like Valgrind (with host code) and cuda-memcheck (with device code) to track usage of uninitialized memory locations.

These common errors provide critical learning opportunities for CUDA developers. Methods to diagnose and address these errors can enhance understanding and lead to more efficient CUDA code. By rigorously checking and managing memory, verifying kernel launches, ensuring synchronization, and debugging thoroughly, developers can significantly reduce the incidence of these typical CUDA pitfalls.

9.3 Using NVIDIA Nsight for Debugging

NVIDIA Nsight is an advanced tool designed to facilitate the debugging and analysis of CUDA applications. It provides an integrated development environment (IDE) for inspecting code execution on both the CPU and GPU, making it significantly easier to detect and resolve issues.

To begin utilizing NVIDIA Nsight for debugging, it is essential to install the tool and configure your development environment correctly. Nsight is part of the NVIDIA Nsight suite of tools, and the specific component for debugging CUDA applications is NVIDIA Nsight Compute.

Installation and Setup:

NVIDIA Nsight requires certain prerequisites to be installed on your system. These include:

- An NVIDIA GPU with CUDA capability.
- The CUDA Toolkit corresponding to your GPU's compute capability.
- An appropriate driver version compatible with both Nsight and the CUDA Toolkit.

Once the prerequisites are in place, Nsight can be downloaded from the NVIDIA website and installed following the provided instructions. After installation, the environment variables should be verified to ensure that the Nsight executables are accessible from the command line.

Launching Nsight:

Nsight can be launched from within an Integrated Development Environment such as Visual Studio, or as a standalone application. To launch Nsight within Visual Studio, follow these steps:

- Open your CUDA project in Visual Studio.

- Navigate to the "Nsight" menu item in the top toolbar.
- Select "Start CUDA Debugging" to initiate Nsight.

If running Nsight as a standalone application, execute the following command in your terminal:

```
nsight
```

Setting Breakpoints:

Breakpoints are crucial for debugging complex CUDA applications. They allow the developer to pause execution at specific points, enabling detailed inspection of program state. To set a breakpoint in Nsight:

- Open the source file in the editor.
- Click in the left margin next to the line number where you want to set the breakpoint.
- A red dot should appear, indicating that a breakpoint has been set.

When execution reaches this line, Nsight will pause, allowing you to examine variables, memory, and call stacks.

Inspecting Variables and Memory:

During a paused execution state, Nsight provides extensive tools for inspecting the status of variables and memory:

- **Locals and Watch Windows:** You can view local variables and watch specific expressions to track their values.
- **Memory View:** The memory view displays the contents of memory regions, helpful for inspecting arrays and pointers.
- **Registers View:** This shows the contents of the GPU registers, useful for low-level debugging.

Stepping Through Code:

Nsight provides several options for stepping through your code:

- **Step Over (F10):** Executes the next line of code, stepping over function calls.

- **Step Into (F11):** Steps into the next function call for detailed debugging within functions.
- **Step Out (Shift+F11):** Completes the current function execution and steps out to the calling function.

Each of these options allows for a different granularity of control over the debugging process, enabling a comprehensive understanding of code flow and behavior.

Analyzing Call Stacks:

The call stack window in Nsight is instrumental for tracing the sequence of function calls that led to a specific point in code execution. This is particularly useful in CUDA applications that often involve deep call stacks with multiple nested kernel invocations.

Examining Thread and Warps:

CUDA applications execute on the GPU using threads grouped into warps. Nsight provides tools to examine the state of individual threads and warps:

- **Thread View:** Displays all active threads and their statuses.
- **Warp View:** Shows the distribution of threads within warps and their execution divergence.

This detailed insight is critical for identifying issues such as warp divergence and synchronization problems.

Debugging Multiple Kernels:

In complex applications with multiple kernel calls, Nsight can be configured to handle multiple kernels within a single debugging session. This is done through:

- **Kernel Grid View:** Shows all launched kernels and their statuses.
- **Break on Kernel Launch:** Option to break the debugger when a new kernel is launched.

When a breakpoint is hit within a kernel, you can switch between different kernel contexts to debug specific issues within each kernel.

Advanced Debugging Features:

Nsight also offers advanced debugging features such as:

- **Conditional Breakpoints:** Breakpoints that trigger based on specific conditions or expressions.
- **Data Breakpoints:** Trigger when a particular variable or memory location changes.
- **GPU Performance Metrics:** Access performance metrics directly within the debugger for performance analysis alongside functional debugging.

Common Issues and Resolutions:

While using Nsight for debugging, common issues may arise such as:

- **Kernel launch failures:** Ensure that the kernel launch parameters are correctly set.
- **Memory allocation errors:** Use Nsight's memory inspection tools to verify correct memory allocation and usage.
- **Synchronization issues:** Examine thread and warp views to detect synchronization problems.

Each of these issues requires specific tools and techniques provided by Nsight to resolve effectively.

9.4 Manual Debugging Techniques

Ensuring the reliability and correctness of CUDA programs involves a thorough understanding of manual debugging techniques. These techniques are essential for scenarios where automated tools may fall short and offer deeper insights into the underlying issues. This section delves into methods such as the use of printf, error code checking, and memory access validation.

Using printf for Debugging

The printf function in CUDA kernels, just as in standard C++, is a useful debugging tool. To effectively utilize printf within a CUDA kernel, it is necessary to ensure the proper inclusion of the cuda_device_runtime_api.h header and confirm kernel output is correctly synchronized and checked after kernel execution.

```
#include <cstdio>
#include <cuda_runtime.h>

__global__ void kernelDebug(int *d_array) {
    int idx = threadIdx.x + blockDim.x * blockIdx.x;
    if (idx < 10) {
        printf("Thread %d: %d\n", idx, d_array[idx]);
    }
}

int main() {
    int numElements = 10;
    size_t size = numElements * sizeof(int);
    int h_array[numElements] = {0, 1, 2, 3, 4, 5, 6, 7, 8, 9};
    int *d_array = nullptr;
    cudaMalloc((void **)&d_array, size);
    cudaMemcpy(d_array, h_array, size, cudaMemcpyHostToDevice);

    kernelDebug<<<1, numElements>>>(d_array);
    cudaDeviceSynchronize();

    cudaFree(d_array);
    return 0;
}
```

Supporting printf in device code may require setting the –generate-code arch=compute_X.X,code=sm_X.X flags to ensure compatibility with the device architecture. Adequate comprehension of thread behavior and proper placement of printf statements guide the evaluation of intermediate values and parallel execution flow, minimizing the need for more intrusive debugging methods.

Error Code Checking

CUDA API functions return error codes which should be explicitly checked to ascertain the correctness of operations. Implementing a utility function to wrap these calls enhances readability and ensures errors are not overlooked.

```
#define gpuErrchk(ans) { gpuAssert((ans), __FILE__, __LINE__); }
inline void gpuAssert(cudaError_t code, const char *file, int line, bool abort=true) {
    if (code != cudaSuccess) {
        fprintf(stderr, "GPUassert: %s %s %d\n", cudaGetErrorString(code), file, line);
        if (abort) exit(code);
    }
}

int main() {
    int *d_array;
    gpuErrchk(cudaMalloc((void **)&d_array, 10 * sizeof(int)));

    // Various CUDA API calls
```

```
    gpuErrchk(cudaFree(d_array));
    return 0;
}
```

This macro, gpuErrchk, captures the file name and line number in case of errors, facilitating quicker issue identification and resolution. An error message indicative of a specific issue can often be correlated with certain known problem areas such as memory corruption, illegal memory access, or resource exhaustion.

Memory Access Validation

Validating memory accesses is critical, particularly in kernels operating at large data scales. Such kernels may inadvertently access out-of-bound memory locations leading to undefined behaviors. By leveraging bounds checking and detecting access patterns at runtime, many issues are preempted.

```
__global__ void kernelMemoryCheck(int *d_array, int numElements) {
    int idx = threadIdx.x + blockDim.x * blockIdx.x;
    if (idx < numElements) {
        printf("Accessing element %d: %d\n", idx, d_array[idx]);
    } else {
        printf("Out of bounds access at thread %d\n", idx);
    }
}

int main() {
    int numElements = 10;
    size_t size = numElements * sizeof(int);
    int h_array[numElements] = {0, 1, 2, 3, 4, 5, 6, 7, 8, 9};
    int *d_array = nullptr;
    cudaMalloc((void **)&d_array, size);
    cudaMemcpy(d_array, h_array, size, cudaMemcpyHostToDevice);

    kernelMemoryCheck<<<1, 20>>>(d_array, numElements);
    cudaDeviceSynchronize();

    cudaFree(d_array);
    return 0;
}
```

In scenarios where kernels are executed with higher thread counts than necessary, it becomes imperative to bound thread operations, ensuring they remain within the valid data range. Providing real-time feedback through conditional printf statements forestalls the inadvertent processing of unintended memory regions.

Common Pitfalls and Considerations

While manual debugging techniques serve as powerful tools, it is essential to be aware of potential pitfalls such as excessive printf calls leading to performance degradation and cluttered output. Additionally, initializing device memory thoroughly before kernel execution and ensuring kernels complete successfully enhance stability. Adhering to best practices minimizes the intrusiveness of these techniques while maintaining application reliability.

Incorporating these manual debugging methods reveals a more nuanced understanding of CUDA programs, equipping developers with robust strategies for diagnosing and resolving diverse issues encountered during development and testing.

9.5 Using CUDA-GDB Debugger

The CUDA-GDB debugger is a powerful tool provided by NVIDIA, enabling developers to perform CUDA-specific debugging tasks. It is an extension of GDB (GNU Debugger), tailored to address discrepancies that arise from the concurrent execution models and memory hierarchy unique to GPU architectures. Utilizing CUDA-GDB involves understanding the core principles of debugging within the GPU environment, setting up the proper environment, and executing debugging commands effectively.

Core Principles of Debugging with CUDA-GDB CUDA-GDB supports debugging on CUDA devices, ensuring that developers can inspect and control the execution of CUDA kernels running on GPU hardware. Unlike traditional CPU debugging, debugging on the GPU involves considerations for thread hierarchies, memory spaces (global, shared, and local), and synchronization issues. Some essential principles include:

- *Thread and Block Management*: Understanding how to target specific warps, threads, and blocks when setting breakpoints or inspecting variables.
- *Device Memory Inspection*: Examining the content of different CUDA memory spaces.
- *Kernel Launch Control*: Managing kernel launches, including setting breakpoints before or after specific launches.
- *Synchronization Handling*: Handling synchronization primitives, such as barriers, to uncover race conditions and deadlocks.

Setting Up the Debugging Environment Before initiating debugging tasks, ensure that the CUDA environment and the CUDA-GDB debugger are appropriately configured. The following command sequence demonstrates the setup and initialization:

```
# Update package lists
sudo apt-get update

# Install CUDA-GDB with the CUDA toolkit
sudo apt-get install cuda-toolkit-X.Y

# Verify the installation
cuda-gdb --version
```

Replace $X.Y$ with the appropriate version number of the installed CUDA toolkit.

Starting CUDA-GDB To commence a debugging session using CUDA-GDB, load your compiled CUDA application into the debugger using the following command:

```
cuda-gdb ./my_cuda_application
```

Upon execution, the CUDA-GDB interface appears, awaiting further instructions.

Setting Breakpoints Breakpoints allow developers to pause program execution at specific points to inspect the state. In CUDA-GDB, breakpoints can be set at various code locations, including kernel launches. For instance:

```
# Set a breakpoint at the beginning of the main function
(cuda-gdb) break main

# Set a breakpoint at a specific line number within a kernel
(cuda-gdb) break my_kernel.cu:42
```

Breakpoints can also be conditional, triggered only when specific criteria are met:

```
# Set a conditional breakpoint
(cuda-gdb) break my_kernel.cu:42 if threadIdx.x == 0
```

Inspecting Variables and Memory Inspecting variables, arrays, and memory spaces is crucial in CUDA debugging. Use the following commands to examine different memory locations:

```
# Print the value of a variable
(cuda-gdb) print my_variable

# Print the contents of an array
(cuda-gdb) print my_array
```

```
# Examine global memory
(cuda-gdb) info cuda global

# Examine shared memory
(cuda-gdb) info cuda shared

# Examine local memory for a specific thread
(cuda-gdb) cuda thread 3
(cuda-gdb) info cuda local
```

These commands provide detailed insights into the state of variables and memory across different threads and blocks.

Managing Kernel Launches Controlling kernel launches is pivotal during GPU debugging. The cuda kernel command provides mechanisms to list and control kernel executions:

```
# List all kernels that have been launched
(cuda-gdb) info cuda kernels

# Set a breakpoint on a kernel function
(cuda-gdb) break myKernel

# Continue execution until the next kernel launch
(cuda-gdb) cuda continue
```

Use these controls to break execution before or after specific kernel launches, enabling finer control over debugging sessions.

Monitoring Execution Flow Handling the concurrent execution of threads requires monitoring active threads and blocks. The following commands help manage execution flow:

```
# List all threads
(cuda-gdb) info threads

# Switch to a specific thread
(cuda-gdb) thread <thread_id>

# List all blocks and corresponding threads within the current kernel
(cuda-gdb) info cuda blocks
```

Handling Synchronization Issues Synchronization primitives, such as __syncthreads() and other barrier functions, can cause race conditions and deadlocks. Use CUDA-GDB to step through synchronization points:

```
# Step through a barrier function call
(cuda-gdb) next

# Check the state of threads at a barrier
(cuda-gdb) info cuda barrier
```

Running and Stopping the Program The common commands for running and managing the program's execution within CUDA-GDB are as follows:

```
# Start or continue execution
(cuda-gdb) run
(cuda-gdb) continue

# Pause execution
(cuda-gdb) interrupt

# Step by line or instruction
(cuda-gdb) step
(cuda-gdb) next
(cuda-gdb) stepi

# Exit CUDA-GDB
(cuda-gdb) quit
```

Example Debugging Session Consider a simple CUDA kernel that adds two arrays. The debugging session involves setting breakpoints, inspecting variables, and stepping through the kernel execution:

```
#include <cuda_runtime.h>
#include <iostream>

__global__ void add(int *a, int *b, int *c) {
    int index = threadIdx.x + blockIdx.x * blockDim.x;
    c[index] = a[index] + b[index];
}

int main() {
    const int arraySize = 5;
    int a[arraySize] = {1, 2, 3, 4, 5};
    int b[arraySize] = {10, 20, 30, 40, 50};
    int c[arraySize] = {0};

    int *d_a, *d_b, *d_c;
    cudaMalloc(&d_a, arraySize * sizeof(int));
    cudaMalloc(&d_b, arraySize * sizeof(int));
    cudaMalloc(&d_c, arraySize * sizeof(int));

    cudaMemcpy(d_a, a, arraySize * sizeof(int), cudaMemcpyHostToDevice);
    cudaMemcpy(d_b, b, arraySize * sizeof(int), cudaMemcpyHostToDevice);

    add<<<1, arraySize>>>(d_a, d_b, d_c);

    cudaMemcpy(c, d_c, arraySize * sizeof(int), cudaMemcpyDeviceToHost);

    std::cout << "Result: ";
    for (int i = 0; i < arraySize; ++i) {
        std::cout << c[i] << " ";
    }
    std::cout << std::endl;

    cudaFree(d_a);
    cudaFree(d_b);
    cudaFree(d_c);
    return 0;
}
```

Launch the debugging session:

```
cuda-gdb ./my_cuda_application
(cuda-gdb) break add
(cuda-gdb) run
(cuda-gdb) print a
(cuda-gdb) print threadIdx.x
(cuda-gdb) step
(cuda-gdb) continue
(cuda-gdb) quit
```

The CUDA-GDB debugger is an intricate tool that, when wielded effectively, can significantly enhance the debugging process of CUDA applications. It demands familiarity with GPU architectures and thoughtful application of debugging commands tailored for heterogeneous computing environments.

9.6 Analyzing Kernel Performance with NVIDIA Visual Profiler

NVIDIA Visual Profiler, also known as nvvp, is a comprehensive performance analysis tool for CUDA applications. It provides detailed insights into the performance characteristics of CUDA kernels, helping to identify bottlenecks and optimize code for better performance. This section outlines the procedure for using NVIDIA Visual Profiler to analyze kernel performance, interpret key metrics, and gain actionable insights.

To begin with, ensure that your CUDA application is compiled with the appropriate flags to enable profiling. Use the -lineinfo flag for generating line information, which is invaluable for associating performance metrics with source code lines. An example compilation command is shown below:

```
nvcc -g -G -lineinfo -o my_cuda_app my_cuda_app.cu
```

Launch NVIDIA Visual Profiler either from the terminal by typing nvvp, or through an integrated development environment that supports it. Once the profiler is open, load your application by selecting File > Import Application....

Upon executing your CUDA application within the profiler, various performance metrics and timeline views will be displayed. Key components to focus on are:

- **Timeline View**: Displays a graphical representation of kernel execution, memory copies, and CPU activities. This view helps to visualize the concurrency and overlap between CPU and GPU operations.
- **Summary View**: Provides aggregated performance metrics such as kernel execution times, memory transfer rates, and occupancy.
- **Kernel Profiling Details**: Offers deep insights into each kernel's performance characteristics, including memory access patterns, instruction throughput, and execution efficiency.

The Timeline View is beneficial for understanding the execution flow of your application. It helps identify periods where the GPU is idle, indicating potential inefficiencies. Analyzing the overlap between data transfers and kernel execution can reveal opportunities to optimize data movement or kernel concurrency.

Delving into the Summary View provides a comprehensive overview of your application's performance. Key metrics in this view include:

- **Execution Time**: The total time taken by each kernel. Long execution times may indicate areas worth optimizing.
- **Memory Throughput**: The rate of data transfer between global memory and the GPU. Suboptimal throughput could suggest memory-bound kernels.
- **Occupancy**: The ratio of active warps to the maximum number of warps supported on a multiprocessor. Low occupancy might hint at either computational inefficiency or divergence.

For in-depth kernel analysis, examine the Kernel Profiling Details. Key performance metrics include:

- **Instruction Throughput**: The rate of instruction execution within a kernel. High instruction throughput generally correlates with efficient use of GPU resources.
- **Memory Access Patterns**: Metrics such as global memory load-/store efficiency, shared memory throughput, and L2 cache utilization. Inefficient memory access can drastically affect performance and needs to be optimized.

- **Execution Efficiency**: The ratio of the number of instructions executed to the theoretical maximum. This metric helps determine whether the kernel fully utilizes the available computational resources.

To illustrate, consider a scenario where the Visual Profiler reports low global memory load efficiency for a kernel. This inefficiency might be caused by non-coalesced memory accesses. Coalescing memory accesses can be achieved by ensuring that threads access contiguous memory locations, which enables the GPU to group these accesses into fewer transactions. This optimization can be implemented as follows:

```
__global__ void MyKernel(float *d_data) {
    int idx = threadIdx.x + blockIdx.x * blockDim.x;
    float value = d_data[idx]; // Ensure that d_data is aligned and accessible
          contiguously
    // Kernel computation
}
```

Further, if the profiler indicates low shared memory utilization, integrating shared memory can enhance performance. Shared memory provides faster data access compared to global memory. The following snippet demonstrates the usage of shared memory:

```
__global__ void MyOptimizedKernel(float *d_data) {
    extern __shared__ float s_data[];
    int idx = threadIdx.x + blockIdx.x * blockDim.x;
    s_data[threadIdx.x] = d_data[idx];
    __syncthreads();
    // Use s_data for computation
}
```

Moreover, if kernel occupancy is reported to be low, consider optimizing the kernel configuration parameters such as block size and grid size. Tools like the NVIDIA Occupancy Calculator can assist in determining optimal configurations. For example:

```
cudaOccupancyMaxPotentialBlockSize(&minGridSize, &blockSize, MyKernel, 0, 0);
dim3 grid(minGridSize);
dim3 block(blockSize);
MyKernel<<<grid, block>>>(d_data);
```

By systematically leveraging the insights provided by NVIDIA Visual Profiler, common performance bottlenecks can be identified, analyzed, and resolved. Optimal kernel performance hinges on fine-tuning memory access patterns, maximizing instruction throughput, and achieving high occupancy.

Program execution results should be constantly checked to ensure that the optimized kernels perform as expected. Here is an example of expected output post-optimization:

```
Kernel Execution Time: Reduced by 30%
Memory Throughput: Improved to 85% utilization
Occupancy: Improved to 70%
```

Regularly profiling CUDA applications with NVIDIA Visual Profiler and making iterative optimizations based on profiling data are key practices in developing high-performance GPU-accelerated software.

9.7 Profiling CPU-GPU Interactions

Profiling CPU-GPU interactions is critical for understanding and optimizing the performance of CUDA applications. Effective profiling allows developers to identify bottlenecks and performance issues that arise from the communication and coordination between the CPU and GPU. This section will delve into the techniques and tools for profiling these interactions, focusing primarily on how to utilize the NVIDIA Visual Profiler and other relevant tools.

Profiling these interactions involves several key metrics such as memory transfers, kernel launches, and synchronization points. By examining these metrics, we can gain insights into the efficiency of our application and identify areas for improvement.

Memory Transfer Analysis

Memory transfer between the CPU and GPU is a common source of bottlenecks in CUDA applications due to the relatively slow PCIe bus compared to the high speed of on-chip operations. Profiling these memory transfers helps us understand the volume and cost associated with such operations.

To profile memory transfers, employ the NVIDIA Visual Profiler to visualize and measure the time spent on these operations. The profiler provides a timeline that highlights the various stages of memory transfer, depicted using different color codes which help distinguish between Host-to-Device (HtoD) and Device-to-Host (DtoH) transfers.

The following code example demonstrates how to use CUDA API calls for timing memory transfers:

```
cudaEvent_t start, stop;
float elapsedTime;
```

```
cudaEventCreate(&start);
cudaEventCreate(&stop);
cudaEventRecord(start, 0);

cudaMemcpy(d_ptr, h_ptr, size, cudaMemcpyHostToDevice);

cudaEventRecord(stop, 0);
cudaEventSynchronize(stop);
cudaEventElapsedTime(&elapsedTime, start, stop);

printf("Memory transfer time from Host to Device: %f ms\n", elapsedTime);

cudaEventDestroy(start);
cudaEventDestroy(stop);
```

Using this code, we can measure and display the time taken to transfer data from the host (CPU) to the device (GPU). By recording distinct events before and after the cudaMemcpy call, we compute the elapsed time to understand transfer latency.

Kernel Launch Analysis

Kernel launches represent another crucial aspect of CPU-GPU interaction. Each kernel launch involves setting up execution configurations and initiating the actual kernel on the GPU. Profiling these launches helps us recognize overheads due to repeated kernel launches or inefficient configurations.

The NVIDIA Visual Profiler offers detailed insights into kernel launches, including launch time, configuration details (grid size, block size), and kernel execution performance. The profiler's timeline provides a precise view of when kernels are launched and completed.

To examine the efficiency of kernel launches, we can use CUDA events similar to memory transfer profiling. Here's an example:

```
__global__ void myKernel() {
    // Kernel code
}

int main() {
    cudaEvent_t start, stop;
    float elapsedTime;

    cudaEventCreate(&start);
    cudaEventCreate(&stop);
    cudaEventRecord(start, 0);

    myKernel<<<dim3(gridSize), dim3(blockSize)>>>();

    cudaEventRecord(stop, 0);
    cudaEventSynchronize(stop);
    cudaEventElapsedTime(&elapsedTime, start, stop);

    printf("Kernel execution time: %f ms\n", elapsedTime);
```

```
    cudaEventDestroy(start);
    cudaEventDestroy(stop);

    return 0;
}
```

This code records the time taken by a single kernel launch, providing insights into the kernel's execution performance.

Synchronization Points

Synchronization between the CPU and GPU is necessary when ensuring that all GPU tasks are complete before accessing their results on the CPU or initiating another task. Profiling synchronization points reveals potential delays due to synchronization, which can indicate performance bottlenecks.

The CUDA API provides several synchronization functions such as cudaDeviceSynchronize() and cudaStreamSynchronize(). Profiling the usage of these functions can indicate how much time the CPU waits for the GPU.

Example usage of synchronization in code:

```
cudaEvent_t start, stop;
float elapsedTime;

cudaEventCreate(&start);
cudaEventCreate(&stop);
cudaEventRecord(start, 0);

myKernel<<<dim3(gridSize), dim3(blockSize)>>>();

cudaEventRecord(stop, 0);
cudaEventSynchronize(stop);
cudaEventElapsedTime(&elapsedTime, start, stop);

printf("Time with synchronization: %f ms\n", elapsedTime);

cudaDeviceSynchronize();
```

The time recorded here will include both kernel execution and the synchronization overhead, reflecting any delays incurred due to waiting for the GPU tasks to complete.

Using NVIDIA Visual Profiler for Detailed Analysis

The NVIDIA Visual Profiler is a powerful tool that provides a graphical interface for detailed analysis of CPU-GPU interactions. By running the profiler on a CUDA application, we can obtain a comprehensive timeline of memory transfers, kernel launches, and synchronization points.

To launch the Visual Profiler, use the following command:

nvvp

Load your application's execution session, and the profiler will display a detailed timeline. The timeline includes different views:

- **Memory Transfer View:** Highlights the periods during which data is being transferred between CPU and GPU.
- **Kernel Execution View:** Shows when and how long kernels are executed.
- **Synchronization View:** Displays synchronization points and their durations.

By analyzing these views, we can identify inefficiencies and areas requiring optimization.

Optimizing CPU-GPU interaction involves minimizing memory transfer times, optimizing kernel launches, and reducing synchronization overhead. The insights obtained from the NVIDIA Visual Profiler guide the necessary changes in the application code to achieve these optimizations, ultimately leading to improved performance of CUDA programs.

9.8 Interpreting Profiling Results

Profiling offers a comprehensive breakdown of your CUDA application's performance characteristics. The results of profiling runs are typically presented in the form of datasets that reflect various metrics obtained during the execution of your application. Understanding these results requires familiarity with the metrics themselves and how they relate to the performance and efficiency of your CUDA kernels and overall application.

Key Metrics and Their Significance

When you profile a CUDA application using tools such as the NVIDIA Visual Profiler or Nsight Compute, several key metrics are generated, each offering insights into different aspects of the performance. The following are some of the most critical metrics and their interpretations:

- **Kernel Execution Time**: This metric indicates the amount of time each kernel takes to execute. It is fundamental for identifying bottlenecks; longer execution times suggest areas where optimization may be necessary.

- **Occupancy**: Occupancy is the ratio of active warps per multiprocessor to the maximum number of warps that the multiprocessor can support. Higher occupancy usually correlates with better performance but is not the sole determinant. It helps in understanding resource utilization.
- **Global Memory Throughput**: Measures the rate of data transfer between global memory and the GPU. Low throughput may indicate issues like uncoalesced memory accesses or excessive memory transactions, suggesting optimizations in memory usage are needed.
- **Shared Memory Usage**: Provides insights into how shared memory is being utilized. Excessive usage can lead to bank conflicts, which degrade performance. Optimizing shared memory usage can significantly improve kernel performance.
- **Warp Serialization**: Indicates the degree to which warps are forced to serialize due to dependencies. High levels of warp serialization often suggest opportunities for improving instruction-level parallelism within your kernels.
- **Branch Divergence**: Quantifies the impact of divergent branching within warps. Minimizing branch divergence by restructuring code can lead to better performance.

Visualizing Performance With NVIDIA Visual Profiler

The NVIDIA Visual Profiler provides various visual tools to help interpret profiling data effectively. Below are important visual aids and how to read them:

- **Timeline View**: Displays a sequential overview of kernel executions and memory transfers. It helps in identifying periods of GPU idleness, overlapping of data transfers with kernel execution, and opportunities for concurrency.
- **Memory Chart**: Illustrates memory usage patterns, showing read and write operations over time. Analyzing these patterns can highlight inefficiencies in memory access and guide optimization of memory transactions.
- **Source Code View**: Highlights performance-critical code sections by linking back to the source code, making it easier to pinpoint which lines of code correspond to hotspots.

Advanced Metrics for Optimization

Advanced users might delve into more granular metrics for finer optimizations:

- **Instruction Throughput**: Measures the rate at which instructions are executed. Bottlenecks in this metric may suggest a need for improved instruction-level parallelism.
- **SM (Streaming Multiprocessor) Efficiency**: Reflects how efficiently the SMs are being utilized. Low efficiency often indicates that workloads could be balanced more effectively across the SMs.
- **L2 Cache Utilization**: Indicates how effectively the L2 cache is being used. Poor utilization suggests the need to optimize data access patterns to reduce memory latency.
- **PCIe Bandwidth Utilization**: Measures data transfer rates between the CPU and GPU. This metric is crucial for applications that involve significant data movement and may indicate possible optimizations in data transfer patterns.

Case Study: Interpreting Profiling Data

Consider a scenario where an application is profiled, revealing that certain kernels exhibit unexpectedly high execution times. Further examination through the NVIDIA Visual Profiler might show:

```
Kernel-1: Execution Time = 150 ms, Occupancy = 75%
Kernel-2: Execution Time = 300 ms, Occupancy = 35%
```

The high execution time and low occupancy of Kernel-2 suggest that resource allocation within the kernel might be suboptimal. Breaking down the profiling results might reveal:

```
Memory Transactions: High, with several uncoalesced accesses
Shared Memory Conflicts: Moderate
Branch Divergence: High
```

Based on this data, optimizing Kernel-2 could involve:

- Reorganizing data structures to ensure coalesced memory accesses.
- Reducing shared memory bank conflicts by spreading data across banks more evenly.

- Refining the branching logic to minimize divergence within warps.

By systematically interpreting and acting upon profiling results, significant performance gains can be achieved, optimizing the utilization of the GPU's computational and memory resources.

9.9 Optimizing Code Based on Profiling Data

Optimizing code based on profiling data is a multi-faceted process that requires both a detailed understanding of the profiling results and a methodical approach to refining the CUDA code. Profiling tools like the NVIDIA Visual Profiler provide a rich set of metrics that reveal various aspects of the application's performance. These metrics include memory throughput, kernel execution times, and occupancy, among others.

The first step in optimization is to interpret the profiling data correctly. Start by identifying the kernels that consume the most time. Focus on these kernels, as optimizing the most time-consuming parts of your code will yield the most significant performance improvements. Profiling data typically includes graphical representations and tables; pay attention to both for a comprehensive understanding.

```
__global__ void exampleKernel(float *data, int size) {
    int idx = blockIdx.x * blockDim.x + threadIdx.x;
    if (idx < size) {
        data[idx] = sqrt(data[idx]);
    }
}
```

The above kernel may show poor performance due to several factors: low occupancy, inefficient memory access patterns, or insufficient instruction-level parallelism.

Memory Access Patterns: Efficient memory usage is crucial for GPU performance. The memory hierarchy in CUDA comprises global, shared, and local memory, among other types. Accessing global memory is particularly slow compared to shared memory. One common optimization involves coalescing global memory accesses to ensure that memory transactions are efficient.

```
__global__ void optimizedKernel(float *data, int size) {
    int idx = blockIdx.x * blockDim.x + threadIdx.x;
    if (idx < size) {
        float value = data[idx];
        data[idx] = sqrt(value);
    }
}
```

In this example, reading data into a temporary register (value) helps improve memory coalescing.

Occupancy: Occupancy refers to the ratio of active warps per multiprocessor to the maximum number of warps that can be active. High occupancy does not guarantee high performance, but low occupancy often indicates inefficient use of resources. Adjusting the block size is one way to influence occupancy. It is essential to balance the block size to maximize occupancy without causing excessive register pressure.

```
__global__ void occupancyOptimizedKernel(float *data, int size) {
    int idx = blockIdx.x * blockDim.x + threadIdx.x;
    if (idx < size) {
        data[idx] = sqrt(data[idx]);
    }
}

// Kernel launch with optimized block size
int blockSize = 256; // optimal block size found through profiling
int gridSize = (size + blockSize - 1) / blockSize;
occupancyOptimizedKernel<<<gridSize, blockSize>>>(data, size);
```

Instruction-Level Parallelism: Increasing instruction-level parallelism (ILP) can also boost performance. A simple yet effective way to achieve this is through loop unrolling. Loop unrolling expands the loop's body, reducing the overhead of branch instructions and increasing ILP by allowing more instructions to be parallelized.

```
__global__ void ilpOptimizedKernel(float *data, int size) {
    int idx = blockIdx.x * blockDim.x + threadIdx.x * 4; // unroll factor of 4
    if (idx < size) {
        data[idx] = sqrt(data[idx]);
        if (idx + 1 < size) data[idx + 1] = sqrt(data[idx + 1]);
        if (idx + 2 < size) data[idx + 2] = sqrt(data[idx + 2]);
        if (idx + 3 < size) data[idx + 3] = sqrt(data[idx + 3]);
    }
}
```

Shared Memory Usage: Shared memory provides a significant performance boost when used correctly. It is much faster than global memory but is limited in size. The following example demonstrates how to use shared memory effectively:

```
__global__ void sharedMemoryKernel(float *data, int size) {
    __shared__ float sharedData[256];
    int idx = blockIdx.x * blockDim.x + threadIdx.x;

    if (idx < size) {
        sharedData[threadIdx.x] = data[idx];
        __syncthreads();

        sharedData[threadIdx.x] = sqrt(sharedData[threadIdx.x]);
        __syncthreads();
```

```
        data[idx] = sharedData[threadIdx.x];
    }
}
```

In the shared memory example, data is first loaded into the shared memory, computations are performed, and results are then written back to global memory. This method minimizes global memory access and leverages the high speed of shared memory.

Performance Tuning with Compiler Flags: Sometimes, fine-tuning compiler options can yield performance benefits. The nvcc compiler offers several options that control the optimization level. For example, the flag -O3 provides a high level of optimization. Additionally, the -use_fast_math flag enables faster but less accurate mathematical functions.

```
nvcc -O3 -use_fast_math optimized_kernel.cu -o optimized_kernel
```

Execution Results and Analysis: After making optimizations, reprofile the application to measure the impact of your changes. Use the NVIDIA Visual Profiler to compare the new performance metrics against the baseline. Look for improvements in kernel execution time, memory throughput, and occupancy.

```
Grid size: 32, Block size: 256

Initial Kernel Execution Time: 200ms
Optimized Kernel Execution Time: 120ms
```

By iteratively profiling and optimizing, significant performance improvements can be achieved. Focus on one aspect at a time, verify the impact of your changes, and ensure that you are systematically improving the most performance-critical sections of your code.

9.10 Best Practices for Efficient Debugging and Profiling

Efficient debugging and profiling are critical skills in CUDA programming to ensure high performance and correctness. By adhering to essential best practices, developers can streamline the process, reduce development time, and enhance application efficiency. The following practices provide a structured approach to debugging and profiling CUDA applications.

Understand the Architecture: Gaining a comprehensive understanding of GPU architectures, including differences across various NVIDIA families, is a fundamental step. This knowledge helps in predicting potential bottlenecks and optimizing memory usage effectively.

Code Organization: Proper code organization is paramount. Use clear, consistent naming conventions and modularize code to separate concerns. Encapsulating kernel functions in separate files can make debugging more manageable and allow for easier updates and testing of individual components.

Error Checking: Always perform error checking after kernel launches and memory operations using CUDA error handling functions. For instance:

```
cudaError_t err = cudaGetLastError();
if (err != cudaSuccess) {
    printf("CUDA Error: %s\n", cudaGetErrorString(err));
}
```

This practice ensures that errors are caught early and debugging is simplified by pinpointing the source.

Use Assertions: Employing assertions in the codebase can help catch logical errors and invalid assumptions during the development phase. For instance:

```
assert(threadIdx.x >= 0 && threadIdx.x < blockDim.x);
```

Assertions serve as a form of documentation and a means to verify conditions that should always be true.

Leverage CUDA-MEMCHECK: Utilize tools like cuda-memcheck to identify and debug memory errors. This tool can detect out-of-bounds accesses, misalignments, and illegal memory accesses. For example, running cuda-memcheck on an application can be done as follows:

```
cuda-memcheck ./your_cuda_application
```

Profiling Early and Often: Integrate profiling into the development workflow from early stages. Profiling intermittently during development helps in understanding performance characteristics and making incremental optimizations rather than waiting until the end of the project.

Minimize Data Transfer Overheads: As data transfers between host and device are costly, keep them to a minimum. Use asynchronous memory transfers and overlap computation with data transfer where possible. An example of CUDA streams to overlap data transfer and computation is:

```
cudaStream_t stream;
cudaStreamCreate(&stream);
cudaMemcpyAsync(d_a, h_a, size, cudaMemcpyHostToDevice, stream);
kernel<<<blocks, threads, 0, stream>>>(d_a);
cudaStreamSynchronize(stream);
cudaStreamDestroy(stream);
```

Analyze Compute and Memory Bottlenecks: Profiling tools like NVIDIA Nsight and Visual Profiler provide insights into bottlenecks related to compute or memory operations. Understanding whether the application is compute-bound or memory-bound guides targeted optimizations, such as optimizing shared memory and using coalesced memory accesses.

Consider Precision: Use the appropriate precision for computations. Single precision can offer performance benefits over double precision, but precision loss must be acceptable for the application. Choose the data types judiciously and test thoroughly to ensure numerical stability.

Apply Loop Tiling and Unrolling: Techniques like loop tiling and unrolling can expose more parallelism and improve cache efficiency. These techniques, when applied correctly, can significantly enhance performance.

```
#pragma unroll
for (int i = 0; i < N; i++) {
    // Loop body
}
```

Thread Divergence Reduction: To mitigate the impact of thread divergence, ensure threads within the same warp follow similar execution paths. This can be achieved by restructuring code to minimize conditional branches within warps.

```
// Avoid
if (threadIdx.x % 2 == 0) {
    // Do something
} else {
    // Do something else
}

// Use
int condition = (threadIdx.x % 2 == 0);
if (condition) {
    // Do something
}
// Ensure similar execution paths
```

Take Advantage of Unified Memory: Unified memory simplifies memory management and can reduce programming complexity. However, performance impact depends on the specific use case. Profiling tools can help determine if the trade-off is beneficial.

Incorporating these best practices fosters a structured and effective approach to developing and optimizing CUDA applications. Understanding and applying them consistently enables high-performance outcomes while maintaining code robustness and efficiency.

Chapter 10

Case Studies and Real-World Applications

This chapter presents detailed case studies across various industries to illustrate real-world applications of CUDA programming. It includes examples from image processing, scientific computing, deep learning, real-time rendering, financial modeling, bioinformatics, autonomous vehicles, and big data analytics. Through these case studies, the chapter demonstrates the practical impact and effectiveness of CUDA in solving complex computational problems and highlights future trends and developments in CUDA programming.

10.1 Introduction to Real-World CUDA Applications

The Compute Unified Device Architecture (CUDA) framework, developed by NVIDIA, represents a paradigm shift in the way we approach parallel processing. By harnessing the computational power of Graphical Processing Units (GPUs), CUDA enables extensive parallelization of complex computational tasks, which traditionally relied on Central Processing Units (CPUs). Throughout this chapter, we explore an array of practical applications where CUDA programming has proven to be instrumental, addressing a variety of challenges across multiple disciplines.

Initially conceived for graphics rendering, the utility of GPUs has evolved significantly. Their massively parallel architecture, coupled with CUDA's programming capabilities, provides a robust platform for accelerating computations across various fields. We begin our expedition into these applications by examining image processing and computer vision.

Modern image processing tasks, ranging from simple filtering operations to sophisticated image recognition algorithms, benefit immensely from CUDA's parallel processing capabilities. CUDA's ability to handle large datasets, apply concurrent computations, and reduce processing time is critical in handling high-resolution images and real-time video streaming.

Scientific computing encompasses a broad spectrum of applications, from physics simulations to computational chemistry. These tasks are typically characterized by intensive numerical computations that demand high processing power. Leveraging CUDA, researchers can execute complex simulations significantly faster than with traditional CPU-based computations. For example, in fluid dynamics, the Navier-Stokes equations can be solved more efficiently using GPU-accelerated functions.

Deep learning and neural networks have seen a remarkable surge in popularity, driven by advancements in computational hardware and algorithms. The training of deep learning models, particularly convolutional neural networks (CNNs), is computationally expensive. CUDA accelerates this process by parallelizing operations such as matrix multiplications and convolutions. This parallelization is crucial in handling the vast amounts of data and high-dimensional computations involved in training large neural networks.

In graphics and real-time rendering, CUDA-based rendering techniques such as ray tracing can produce highly realistic images by simulating the physical behavior of light. These methods require immense computational resources due to the complexity of the calculations involved. CUDA's parallel processing capability reduces the time required to generate high-fidelity images.

Financial modeling and risk analysis involve running numerous simulations to predict market behaviors and assess risks. Monte Carlo simulations, a staple in this field, are particularly well-suited for parallel execution. By utilizing CUDA, financial institutions can perform risk assessments and scenario analyses more rapidly and accurately.

Bioinformatics and genomics have gained a new dimension with the advent of CUDA. The analysis of genetic data, often comprising terabytes of information, can be expedited using parallel computing techniques. Programs like sequence alignment and protein structure prediction have been significantly optimized through CUDA.

In the domain of autonomous vehicles and robotics, real-time processing capabilities are paramount. Autonomous systems require the rapid processing of sensory data and execution of complex algorithms for navigation, object recognition, and decision making. CUDA provides the necessary computational speed and efficiency to meet these stringent requirements.

Big data analytics, which deals with the processing and analysis of extremely large datasets, benefits greatly from CUDA's ability to parallelize data processing tasks. Techniques such as MapReduce, k-means clustering, and various machine learning algorithms have all been enhanced through GPU acceleration.

Each of these applications underscores the transformative potential of CUDA programming in solving real-world problems more efficiently and effectively. As we delve into the specific case studies, we will highlight practical implementations and performance gains achieved through CUDA. This exploration will illuminate the profound impact of GPU-accelerated computing across diverse fields, paving the way for future innovations.

10.2 Case Study: Image Processing and Computer Vision

Image processing and computer vision are fields extensively leveraging CUDA to accelerate complex computations. CUDA provides the necessary parallelism to handle large-scale data and intricate algorithms efficiently. This section explores specific applications within image processing and computer vision where CUDA's capabilities are beneficial.

A common operation in image processing is convolution, utilized in numerous tasks, such as edge detection, blurring, sharpening, and feature extraction. Convolution operations are inherently parallelizable as each output pixel can be computed independently. The following CUDA code demonstrates a simple convolution kernel.

```
__global__ void convolutionKernel(float *input, float *output, float *filter, int width,
    int height, int filterWidth) {
    int x = blockIdx.x * blockDim.x + threadIdx.x;
    int y = blockIdx.y * blockDim.y + threadIdx.y;
    int halfFilterWidth = filterWidth / 2;

    float sum = 0.0f;
    for (int ky = -halfFilterWidth; ky <= halfFilterWidth; ky++) {
        for (int kx = -halfFilterWidth; kx <= halfFilterWidth; kx++) {
            int pixelX = min(max(x + kx, 0), width - 1);
            int pixelY = min(max(y + ky, 0), height - 1);
            sum += input[pixelY * width + pixelX] * filter[(ky + halfFilterWidth) *
                filterWidth + (kx + halfFilterWidth)];
        }
    }
    output[y * width + x] = sum;
}
```

This kernel function computes the convolution of an image with a given filter. The input image is a 2D array represented in a 1D format for compatibility with CUDA devices. Each thread computes the sum for one pixel in the output image by multiplying the corresponding filter coefficients with the input pixels and accumulating the result.

Consider edge detection using the Sobel operator, a common technique in computer vision. The Sobel operator applies two convolutional filters to compute gradient magnitude in the x and y directions. Below is the code showing the Sobel filter application using CUDA.

```
// Sobel filter kernels in x and y directions
__constant__ float Sobel_X[3][3] = {{-1, 0, 1}, {-2, 0, 2}, {-1, 0, 1}};
__constant__ float Sobel_Y[3][3] = {{ 1, 2, 1}, { 0, 0, 0}, {-1, -2, -1}};

__global__ void sobelFilterKernel(float *input, float *output, int width, int height) {
    int x = blockIdx.x * blockDim.x + threadIdx.x;
    int y = blockIdx.y * blockDim.y + threadIdx.y;

    if (x >= width || y >= height) return;

    float Gx = 0.0f;
    float Gy = 0.0f;

    for (int ky = -1; ky <= 1; ky++) {
        for (int kx = -1; kx <= 1; kx++) {
            int pixelX = min(max(x + kx, 0), width - 1);
            int pixelY = min(max(y + ky, 0), height - 1);
            float pixelValue = input[pixelY * width + pixelX];
            Gx += pixelValue * Sobel_X[ky + 1][kx + 1];
            Gy += pixelValue * Sobel_Y[ky + 1][kx + 1];
        }
    }
    float G = sqrt(Gx * Gx + Gy * Gy);
    output[y * width + x] = G;
}
```

The sobelFilterKernel function utilizes two constant memory arrays, Sobel_X and Sobel_Y, to store the Sobel filters. Each pixel in the output image is computed by the combined gradient magnitude $\sqrt{G_x^2 + G_y^2}$, where G_x and G_y represent gradients in the x and y directions, respectively.

Another significant application is image segmentation, where the goal is to partition an image into meaningful segments. One effective approach is using graph cuts, solvable through CUDA's parallel processing. Consider an energy minimization process via graph cuts, where CUDA can efficiently handle the large-scale computations required.

```
// Placeholder for a graph cut energy function example
__global__ void graphCutKernel(float *nodes, float *edges, int numNodes, int
    numEdges) {
    int idx = blockIdx.x * blockDim.x + threadIdx.x;
    if (idx >= numNodes) return;

    // Graph cut algorithm implementation iterating over nodes and edges
    for (int i = 0; i < numEdges; i++) {
        int node_a = edges[i * 2];
        int node_b = edges[i * 2 + 1];
        if (nodes[node_a] < nodes[node_b]) {
            nodes[node_b] = nodes[node_a] + 1; // Example of updating edges
        }
    }
}
```

In this simplified example, the kernel iterates over nodes and edges to perform an update operation typically involved in graph cut algorithms. The algorithm's specific operations depend on the energy minimization technique chosen.

Another widespread usage in computer vision is object detection, often facilitated through deep learning models like Convolutional Neural Networks (CNNs). CUDA is essential for training and deploying such models due to its ability to parallelize matrix multiplications, convolutions, and other operations.

The forward pass of a CNN layer can be effectively executed using CUDA as follows:

```
__global__ void convLayerForward(float *input, float *output, float *weights, float *
    bias, int width, int height, int channels, int filterWidth, int filterHeight, int
    numFilters) {
    int x = blockIdx.x * blockDim.x + threadIdx.x;
    int y = blockIdx.y * blockDim.y + threadIdx.y;
    int filterIdx = blockIdx.z * blockDim.z + threadIdx.z;

    if (x >= width || y >= height || filterIdx >= numFilters) return;

    float sum = 0.0f;
    for (int c = 0; c < channels; c++) {
        for (int ky = 0; ky < filterHeight; ky++) {
```

```
            for (int kx = 0; kx < filterWidth; kx++) {
                int pixelX = x + kx - filterWidth / 2;
                int pixelY = y + ky - filterHeight / 2;
                if (pixelX >= 0 && pixelX < width && pixelY >= 0 && pixelY <
                    height) {
                    sum += input[(c * height + pixelY) * width + pixelX] * weights[((
                        filterIdx * channels + c) * filterHeight + ky) * filterWidth + kx
                        ];
                }
            }
        }
    }
    output[(filterIdx * height + y) * width + x] = sum + bias[filterIdx];
}
```

In this code, the convLayerForward kernel convolves an input tensor with multiple filters, applying biases to produce feature maps. Each thread computes the output for a specific location and filter independently, leveraging CUDA's parallel processing capabilities.

Effective usage of CUDA in image processing and computer vision also includes: - Optimizing memory access patterns. - Minimizing data transfer between host and device. - Ensuring maximum utilization of GPU resources.

These examples illustrate the power and flexibility of CUDA in handling diverse, computationally intensive tasks within these domains.

10.3 Case Study: Scientific Computing and Simulations

Scientific computing and simulations represent crucial aspects of research in a diverse array of scientific disciplines, including physics, chemistry, biology, and engineering. In this section, we will elucidate the practical use of CUDA programming in performing large-scale simulations, focusing on a real-world case study: climate modeling.

Climate models involve complex mathematical formulations that represent physical processes within the climate system, including atmospheric dynamics, ocean circulation, and interactions between the biosphere and geosphere. Due to the complexity and the need for high resolution, these simulations are computationally intensive, making them ideal candidates for acceleration using CUDA on NVIDIA GPUs.

To demonstrate the power of CUDA in enhancing the performance of climate simulations, we will explore a simplified two-dimensional advection-diffusion equation commonly used in atmospheric transport and dispersion modeling. The advection-diffusion equation can be expressed as follows:

$$\frac{\partial C}{\partial t} + u\frac{\partial C}{\partial x} + v\frac{\partial C}{\partial y} = D\left(\frac{\partial^2 C}{\partial x^2} + \frac{\partial^2 C}{\partial y^2}\right)$$

where C is the concentration of the pollutant, u and v are the wind velocities in the x and y directions respectively, and D is the diffusion coefficient.

To solve the advection-diffusion equation using CUDA, we first discretize the partial differential equation (PDE) using a finite difference method. The time derivative is approximated using a forward difference, and spatial derivatives using centered differences:

$$\frac{C_{i,j}^{n+1} - C_{i,j}^{n}}{\Delta t} + u\frac{C_{i+1,j}^{n} - C_{i-1,j}^{n}}{2\Delta x} + v\frac{C_{i,j+1}^{n} - C_{i,j-1}^{n}}{2\Delta y}$$
$$= D\left(\frac{C_{i+1,j}^{n} - 2C_{i,j}^{n} + C_{i-1,j}^{n}}{\Delta x^2} + \frac{C_{i,j+1}^{n} - 2C_{i,j}^{n} + C_{i,j-1}^{n}}{\Delta y^2}\right)$$

Rearranging the terms to solve for the concentration at the next time step $C_{i,j}^{n+1}$ yields:

$$C_{i,j}^{n+1} = C_{i,j}^{n} + \Delta t\left(-u\frac{C_{i+1,j}^{n} - C_{i-1,j}^{n}}{2\Delta x} - v\frac{C_{i,j+1}^{n} - C_{i,j-1}^{n}}{2\Delta y}\right.$$
$$\left.+D\left(\frac{C_{i+1,j}^{n} - 2C_{i,j}^{n} + C_{i-1,j}^{n}}{\Delta x^2} + \frac{C_{i,j+1}^{n} - 2C_{i,j}^{n} + C_{i,j-1}^{n}}{\Delta y^2}\right)\right)$$

This computation can be parallelized effectively using CUDA. Each thread will be responsible for computing the concentration at a specific grid point (i, j) for the next time step.

Here is an implementation of the advection-diffusion equation in CUDA:

```
__global__ void advectionDiffusionKernel(float *C, float *C_new, float u, float v,
    float D, float dt, float dx, float dy, int Nx, int Ny) {
  int i = blockIdx.x * blockDim.x + threadIdx.x;
  int j = blockIdx.y * blockDim.y + threadIdx.y;

  if (i > 0 && i < Nx-1 && j > 0 && j < Ny-1) {
    float advection_x = -u * (C[(i+1)*Ny+j] - C[(i-1)*Ny+j]) / (2.0f * dx);
    float advection_y = -v * (C[i*Ny+(j+1)] - C[i*Ny+(j-1)]) / (2.0f * dy);
    float diffusion_x = D * (C[(i+1)*Ny+j] - 2*C[i*Ny+j] + C[(i-1)*Ny+j]) / (dx *
         dx);
    float diffusion_y = D * (C[i*Ny+(j+1)] - 2*C[i*Ny+j] + C[i*Ny+(j-1)]) / (dy *
         dy);

    C_new[i*Ny+j] = C[i*Ny+j] + dt * (advection_x + advection_y + diffusion_x
         + diffusion_y);
```

```
    }
}

int main() {
    int Nx = 512, Ny = 512;
    float u = 1.0f, v = 1.0f, D = 0.1f, dt = 0.01f, dx = 1.0f, dy = 1.0f;
    float *C, *C_new;
    float *d_C, *d_C_new;

    // Allocate host memory
    C = (float*)malloc(Nx * Ny * sizeof(float));
    C_new = (float*)malloc(Nx * Ny * sizeof(float));

    // Initialize with some initial conditions
    for (int i = 0; i < Nx; ++i) {
        for (int j = 0; j < Ny; ++j) {
            C[i*Ny+j] = expf(-0.1f * ((i-Nx/2)*(i-Nx/2) + (j-Ny/2)*(j-Ny/2)));
        }
    }

    // Allocate device memory
    cudaMalloc((void**)&d_C, Nx * Ny * sizeof(float));
    cudaMalloc((void**)&d_C_new, Nx * Ny * sizeof(float));

    // Copy initial conditions to device
    cudaMemcpy(d_C, C, Nx * Ny * sizeof(float), cudaMemcpyHostToDevice);

    // Define thread block and grid dimensions
    dim3 dimBlock(16, 16);
    dim3 dimGrid((Nx + dimBlock.x - 1) / dimBlock.x, (Ny + dimBlock.y - 1) /
        dimBlock.y);

    // Time-stepping loop
    for (int n = 0; n < 1000; ++n) {
        advectionDiffusionKernel<<<dimGrid, dimBlock>>>(d_C, d_C_new, u, v, D,
            dt, dx, dy, Nx, Ny);
        cudaDeviceSynchronize();
        std::swap(d_C, d_C_new);
    }

    // Copy result back to host
    cudaMemcpy(C, d_C, Nx * Ny * sizeof(float), cudaMemcpyDeviceToHost);

    // Free memory
    cudaFree(d_C);
    cudaFree(d_C_new);
    free(C);
    free(C_new);

    return 0;
}
```

Executing the preceding CUDA kernel on a modern NVIDIA GPU ameliorates the computational load significantly, thereby accelerating the simulation. The kernel leverages numerous GPU cores to perform the spatial discretization calculations concurrently for each grid point. Efficient memory access patterns are crucial to achieving high performance; in this kernel, each thread accesses contiguous memory locations, which is optimal for the CUDA memory architecture.

The result from one time step of this simulation can be visualized as follows:

```
Time step 1000:
 C[256][256] = 1.2345
 ...
 (Other grid points' values)
```

This simple advection-diffusion equation example can be extended to more complex climate models, incorporating multi-layer atmospheric structures, variable wind fields, and additional physical processes such as convection and chemical reactions. By utilizing CUDA, researchers can perform higher resolution simulations, achieving greater accuracy and insight into climate phenomena.

The case study demonstrates the invaluable role of CUDA in scientific computing, providing researchers with the computational power necessary to conduct large-scale simulations efficiently. This capability enhances our understanding of complex systems, leading to more accurate predictions and better decision-making in addressing global challenges like climate change.

10.4 Case Study: Deep Learning and Neural Networks

Deep learning has revolutionized the field of artificial intelligence, achieving remarkable success in various domains such as image classification, natural language processing, and game playing. Neural networks, particularly deep neural networks, are at the heart of these advancements. With the advent of CUDA (Compute Unified Device Architecture) programming, the training and inference of these deep neural networks have become significantly more efficient, leveraging the parallel processing capabilities of GPUs.

Deep neural networks consist of multiple layers of neurons, each transforming its input into a more abstract representation. Training these networks involves adjusting the weights of connections between neurons to minimize the error in predictions. This process, called backpropagation, requires substantial computational power, especially for large datasets and complex network architectures.

To illustrate the practical application of CUDA in deep learning, consider the training of a Convolutional Neural Network (CNN) for image classification. A CNN consists of multiple convolutional layers, pooling layers, and fully connected layers. The convolutional layers apply filters to the input image, detecting features such as edges and textures. Pooling layers reduce the spatial dimensions of the feature maps, while fully connected layers perform the final classification based on the extracted features.

The following code snippet demonstrates the initialization and forward pass of a simple CNN using CUDA.

```
#include <cuda_runtime.h>
#include <device_launch_parameters.h>
#include <iostream>

// CUDA kernel for convolution operation
__global__ void conv2D(float* input, float* output, float* kernel, int width, int
    height, int kernelSize) {
    int x = blockIdx.x * blockDim.x + threadIdx.x;
    int y = blockIdx.y * blockDim.y + threadIdx.y;

    if (x < width && y < height) {
        float sum = 0.0f;
        for (int i = -kernelSize / 2; i <= kernelSize / 2; ++i) {
            for (int j = -kernelSize / 2; j <= kernelSize / 2; ++j) {
                int ix = x + i;
                int iy = y + j;
                if (ix >= 0 && ix < width && iy >= 0 && iy < height) {
                    sum += input[iy * width + ix] * kernel[(i + kernelSize / 2) *
                        kernelSize + (j + kernelSize / 2)];
                }
            }
        }
        output[y * width + x] = sum;
    }
}

int main() {
    int width = 5, height = 5;
    int kernelSize = 3;

    float input[25] = { /* input image data */ };
    float kernel[9] = { /* kernel data */ };
    float output[25];

    float* d_input, *d_output, *d_kernel;
    cudaMalloc(&d_input, width * height * sizeof(float));
    cudaMalloc(&d_output, width * height * sizeof(float));
    cudaMalloc(&d_kernel, kernelSize * kernelSize * sizeof(float));

    cudaMemcpy(d_input, input, width * height * sizeof(float),
        cudaMemcpyHostToDevice);
    cudaMemcpy(d_kernel, kernel, kernelSize * kernelSize * sizeof(float),
        cudaMemcpyHostToDevice);

    dim3 blockSize(16, 16);
    dim3 gridSize((width + blockSize.x - 1) / blockSize.x, (height + blockSize.y - 1) /
        blockSize.y);
    conv2D<<<gridSize, blockSize>>>(d_input, d_output, d_kernel, width, height,
        kernelSize);
```

```
    cudaMemcpy(output, d_output, width * height * sizeof(float),
        cudaMemcpyDeviceToHost);

    cudaFree(d_input);
    cudaFree(d_output);
    cudaFree(d_kernel);

    for (int i = 0; i < height; ++i) {
        for (int j = 0; j < width; ++j) {
            std::cout << output[i * width + j] << " ";
        }
        std::cout << std::endl;
    }
    return 0;
}
```

In this code, the conv2D kernel computes the convolution of the input image with a given filter. The main function allocates memory on the GPU, copies the input data and kernel to the GPU, executes the kernel, and retrieves the output from the GPU. This parallel execution of the convolution operation significantly accelerates the computational process.

Once the forward pass is computed, the backpropagation algorithm updates the weights. The gradient computation for each weight involves the derivative of the loss function with respect to the weights. CUDA plays a vital role in efficiently computing these gradients across all neurons and connections.

Consider a simple neural network layer defined as follows:

```
__global__ void backpropagation(float* d_weights, float* d_outputs, float* d_error,
    float learningRate, int numWeights, int numNeurons) {
    int idx = blockIdx.x * blockDim.x + threadIdx.x;

    if (idx < numWeights) {
        int neuronId = idx / numNeurons;
        float oldWeight = d_weights[idx];
        float gradient = d_outputs[neuronId] * d_error[neuronId];
        d_weights[idx] = oldWeight - learningRate * gradient;
    }
}
```

The backpropagation kernel updates the weights based on the computed gradients and learning rate. This kernel is executed in parallel across all neurons and their corresponding weights, significantly reducing the time required for training deep neural networks.

The execution of these kernels and the overall parallelization of the training process are what make CUDA a fundamental component in contemporary deep learning implementations. The ability to leverage thousands of GPU cores to perform matrix operations, convolutions, and gradient computations concurrently has drastically improved the efficiency and feasibility of training deep neural networks, enabling breakthroughs in accuracy and speed.

When deploying the trained models for inference, CUDA also optimizes the real-time execution, ensuring quick and reliable predictions. This efficiency is crucial for applications such as autonomous vehicles, where real-time image recognition and decision-making are essential for safety.

Overall, CUDA's influence on deep learning and neural network training is profound. It facilitates the scalability and performance necessary to handle large-scale datasets and complex models, driving progress in AI research and its real-world applications.

10.5 Case Study: Real-Time Rendering and Graphics

Real-time rendering and graphics are quintessential in numerous domains including gaming, virtual reality, architectural visualization, and more. The core objective is to generate and display images in rapid succession, typically at 60 frames per second (FPS) or higher, to create the illusion of motion and interactivity. CUDA programming plays a pivotal role in achieving the high performance required for these applications by leveraging the parallel processing capabilities of modern GPUs. This section details a case study focused on the implementation of a real-time rendering engine using CUDA. Key topics such as ray tracing, shading models, texture mapping, and performance optimization are covered.

Ray Tracing: Ray tracing is a rendering technique that simulates the way light interacts with objects to produce realistic images. The fundamental process involves tracing the path of light rays as they travel through the scene, interact with surfaces, and reach the camera. CUDA allows for efficient parallelization of this computationally intensive task. Each thread can be assigned to handle the computation for an individual pixel or ray, enabling the concurrent processing of millions of rays.

Consider the following CUDA kernel for a basic ray tracing algorithm where each pixel's color is determined by the interaction of rays with a single sphere:

```
__device__ bool hit_sphere(const float3& center, float radius, const float3&
```

```
        ray_origin, const float3& ray_dir) {
    float3 oc = ray_origin - center;
    float a = dot(ray_dir, ray_dir);
    float b = 2.0f * dot(oc, ray_dir);
    float c = dot(oc, oc) - radius * radius;
    float discriminant = b*b - 4*a*c;
    return (discriminant > 0);
}

__global__ void ray_trace_kernel(float3* output, int width, int height, float3
        sphere_center, float sphere_radius) {
    int x = blockIdx.x * blockDim.x + threadIdx.x;
    int y = blockIdx.y * blockDim.y + threadIdx.y;
    if (x >= width || y >= height) return;

    float u = float(x) / float(width);
    float v = float(y) / float(height);

    float3 ray_origin = {0.0f, 0.0f, 0.0f};
    float3 ray_dir = normalize(make_float3(u - 0.5f, v - 0.5f, -1.0f));

    float3 pixel_color = {0.0f, 0.0f, 0.0f};
    if (hit_sphere(sphere_center, sphere_radius, ray_origin, ray_dir)) {
        pixel_color = make_float3(1.0f, 0.0f, 0.0f); // Red color for the sphere hit
    }

    int pixel_index = y * width + x;
    output[pixel_index] = pixel_color;
}
```

Shading Models: To enhance realism, ray tracing engines often implement various shading models. One of the simplest and most widely used models is the Phong shading model, composed of ambient, diffuse, and specular components. Each of these components can be computed in parallel using CUDA, where the contributions to the final pixel color are determined based on the material properties and lighting conditions.

Texture Mapping: Texture mapping involves applying a 2D image (texture) onto a 3D surface to provide detailed surface characteristics. CUDA can be employed for efficient texture fetching and interpolation. For instance, bilinear interpolation can be performed in parallel for each pixel to achieve smooth and high-quality textures.

```
__device__ float3 bilinear_interpolate(const float3* texture, int tex_width, int
        tex_height, float u, float v) {
    u = u * tex_width - 0.5f;
    v = v * tex_height - 0.5f;
    int x = floor(u);
    int y = floor(v);
    float u_ratio = u - x;
    float v_ratio = v - y;
    int x_next = min(x + 1, tex_width - 1);
    int y_next = min(y + 1, tex_height - 1);

    float3 c00 = texture[y * tex_width + x];
```

```
    float3 c01 = texture[y * tex_width + x_next];
    float3 c10 = texture[y_next * tex_width + x];
    float3 c11 = texture[y_next * tex_width + x_next];

    float3 c0 = lerp(c00, c01, u_ratio);
    float3 c1 = lerp(c10, c11, u_ratio);
    return lerp(c0, c1, v_ratio);
}
```

Performance Optimization: Achieving real-time performance necessitates meticulous optimization. Key strategies include efficient memory usage, minimizing divergent branches, and exploiting the inherent parallelism of GPU architectures. Techniques such as grid and block size tuning, memory coalescing, and shared memory usage are instrumental in enhancing performance.

The overall performance impact of these optimizations can be evaluated by profiling tools like NVIDIA Visual Profiler (nvprof) or NVIDIA Nsight Systems. These tools provide detailed insights into the bottlenecks and performance characteristics of the CUDA kernels, allowing for targeted optimizations.

```
Time(%) Total Time Kernel                 Block  Grid
------- ----------- ---------------------- ----- -----
  12.34   0.001234 ray_trace_kernel       (16,8) (50,50)
  87.66   0.008766 shading_model_kernel   (32,16)(25,25)
------- ----------- ---------------------- ----- -----
```

The integration of these components—ray tracing, shading models, texture mapping, and performance optimization—constitutes a potent real-time rendering engine capable of producing high-quality images at interactive frame rates. Each aspect of this case study underscores the necessity and effectiveness of CUDA programming in the realm of real-time graphics and rendering, pushing the boundaries of visual realism and computational efficiency.

10.6 Case Study: Financial Modeling and Risk Analysis

Financial modeling and risk analysis are critical components in the realm of finance, where speed and accuracy can influence significant decision-making processes. CUDA programming offers a substantial advantage in performing complex calculations required for financial modeling, providing significant performance improvements over traditional CPU-based approaches. This case study delves into how CUDA can be employed to optimize algorithms such as Monte Carlo simulations, options pricing models, and Value at Risk (VaR) calculations, which are pivotal in financial risk assessment.

The Monte Carlo simulation is a mathematical technique that allows for the estimation of the probable outcomes of an uncertain event. It is extensively used in financial modeling to simulate the behavior of asset prices, interest rate paths, and other stochastic processes. The primary advantage of leveraging CUDA for Monte Carlo simulations lies in its ability to parallelize the computation of multiple simulation paths, leading to a drastic reduction in computational time.

Consider the following example demonstrating a CUDA-based Monte Carlo simulation for evaluating European option pricing:

```
#include <cuda_runtime.h>
#include <curand_kernel.h>
#include <iostream>

__global__ void initCurand(curandState *state, unsigned long seed) {
    int id = threadIdx.x + blockIdx.x * blockDim.x;
    curand_init(seed, id, 0, &state[id]);
}

__global__ void monteCarloKernel(curandState *state, float *d_results, float S, float
    K, float T, float r, float sigma, int N) {
    int id = threadIdx.x + blockIdx.x * blockDim.x;
    curandState localState = state[id];
    float payoff_sum = 0.0;
    float dt = T / N;
    for (int i = 0; i < N; ++i) {
        float gauss_bm = curand_normal(&localState);
        S += r * S * dt + sigma * S * sqrtf(dt) * gauss_bm;
    }
    float payoff = max(S - K, 0.0f);
    d_results[id] = expf(-r * T) * payoff;
}

int main() {
    int num_paths = 1000000;
    int threads_per_block = 256;
    int blocks = (num_paths + threads_per_block - 1) / threads_per_block;

    float *d_results;
    curandState *d_state;
    cudaMalloc((void**)&d_results, num_paths * sizeof(float));
    cudaMalloc((void**)&d_state, num_paths * sizeof(curandState));

    initCurand<<<blocks, threads_per_block>>>(d_state, time(NULL));
    monteCarloKernel<<<blocks, threads_per_block>>>(d_state, d_results, S_init,
        K, T, r, sigma, N);

    float *h_results = (float*)malloc(num_paths * sizeof(float));
    cudaMemcpy(h_results, d_results, num_paths * sizeof(float),
        cudaMemcpyDeviceToHost);

    float option_price = 0.0;
    for (int i = 0; i < num_paths; ++i) {
        option_price += h_results[i];
```

```
    }
    option_price /= num_paths;

    std::cout << "Option Price: " << option_price << std::endl;

    cudaFree(d_results);
    cudaFree(d_state);
    free(h_results);

    return 0;
}
```

In the provided CUDA program, the Monte Carlo simulation for European option pricing considers a significant number of paths, thus illustrating the parallel computation capabilities. The curandState is utilized for random number generation, which is essential for simulating asset price paths under the risk-neutral measure. Each thread uniquely initializes the random number generator state and computes the payoff based on the simulated path, culminating in an averaged result that estimates the option price.

Another crucial aspect of financial modeling and risk analysis is the computation of Value at Risk (VaR). VaR quantifies the risk level of a portfolio and estimates the potential loss in value with a given confidence interval over a specified time horizon. The histogram-based method is one frequently employed technique to calculate VaR, which can be massively parallelized using CUDA.

To exemplify, consider the implementation of the histogram method for VaR estimation on CUDA:

```
#include <cuda_runtime.h>
#include <curand_kernel.h>
#include <algorithm>
#include <iostream>

__global__ void simulateLossesKernel(curandState *state, float *d_losses, int
      num_trades, float mean, float stddev) {
    int id = threadIdx.x + blockIdx.x * blockDim.x;
    curandState localState = state[id];
    float loss = 0.0;
    for (int i = 0; i < num_trades; ++i) {
        float trade_loss = curand_normal(&localState) * stddev + mean;
        loss += trade_loss;
    }
    d_losses[id] = loss;
}

__global__ void initCurand(curandState *state, unsigned long seed) {
    int id = threadIdx.x + blockIdx.x * blockDim.x;
    curand_init(seed, id, 0, &state[id]);
}

int main() {
    int num_simulations = 1000000;
```

```
    int threads_per_block = 256;
    int blocks = (num_simulations + threads_per_block - 1) / threads_per_block;
    int num_trades = 100;
    float mean = 0.0f;
    float stddev = 1.0f;

    float *d_losses;
    curandState *d_state;
    cudaMalloc((void**)&d_losses, num_simulations * sizeof(float));
    cudaMalloc((void**)&d_state, num_simulations * sizeof(curandState));

    initCurand<<<blocks, threads_per_block>>>(d_state, time(NULL));
    simulateLossesKernel<<<blocks, threads_per_block>>>(d_state, d_losses,
        num_trades, mean, stddev);

    float *h_losses = (float*)malloc(num_simulations * sizeof(float));
    cudaMemcpy(h_losses, d_losses, num_simulations * sizeof(float),
        cudaMemcpyDeviceToHost);

    std::sort(h_losses, h_losses + num_simulations);
    float var_95 = h_losses[(int)(0.05 * num_simulations)];

    std::cout << "Value at Risk (95%): " << var_95 << std::endl;

    cudaFree(d_losses);
    cudaFree(d_state);
    free(h_losses);

    return 0;
}
```

In this example, the kernel simulateLossesKernel is responsible for simulating portfolio losses based on a normal distribution for each trade. The results are later transferred back to the host, where the losses are sorted to determine the 95th percentile, representing the Value at Risk.

Beyond Monte Carlo simulations and VaR, CUDA's high computational capabilities can also be harnessed for numerous other financial models and risk-analysis approaches, such as the Black-Scholes model for options pricing, interest rate models, and credit risk assessments. These applications demonstrate the profound impact of CUDA programming on enhancing the efficiency and precision of complex financial computations.

10.7 Case Study: Bioinformatics and Genomics

Bioinformatics and genomics represent a significant field where CUDA programming has a transformative impact. The need for high-throughput data processing and analysis in bioinformatics aligns perfectly with CUDA's ability to harness the parallel processing power of GPUs. This section delves into leveraging CUDA to accelerate genomic tasks such as sequence alignment, genome assembly, and variant discovery.

In bioinformatics, sequence alignment involves arranging sequences of DNA, RNA, or protein to identify regions of similarity. Traditional sequence alignment algorithms like the Needleman-Wunsch and Smith-Waterman are computationally intensive. To illustrate the application of CUDA in this domain, consider the Smith-Waterman algorithm, which is used for local sequence alignment. The algorithm's dynamic programming nature makes it ideal for parallelization.

Below is a CUDA implementation example of the Smith-Waterman algorithm:

```
#include <cuda_runtime.h>
#include <iostream>
#include <vector>
#include <algorithm>

#define GAP_PENALTY -1
#define MATCH 2
#define MISMATCH -2

__global__ void smithWatermanKernel(const char *seq1, const char *seq2, int *H, int
      len1, int len2) {
   int idx = blockIdx.x * blockDim.x + threadIdx.x;
   int idy = blockIdx.y * blockDim.y + threadIdx.y;

   if (idx > 0 && idx <= len1 && idy > 0 && idy <= len2) {
      int up = H[(idx-1) * (len2+1) + idy] + GAP_PENALTY;
      int left = H[idx * (len2+1) + (idy-1)] + GAP_PENALTY;
      int diag = H[(idx-1) * (len2+1) + (idy-1)] + (seq1[idx-1] == seq2[idy-1] ?
            MATCH : MISMATCH);
      H[idx * (len2+1) + idy] = max(0, max(diag, max(up, left)));
   }
}

void smithWatermanCUDA(const std::string& seq1, const std::string& seq2) {
   int len1 = seq1.length();
   int len2 = seq2.length();

   int *H = new int[(len1+1) * (len2+1)]();
   char *d_seq1, *d_seq2;
   int *d_H;

   cudaMalloc((void**)&d_seq1, len1 * sizeof(char));
   cudaMalloc((void**)&d_seq2, len2 * sizeof(char));
   cudaMalloc((void**)&d_H, (len1+1) * (len2+1) * sizeof(int));

   cudaMemcpy(d_seq1, seq1.c_str(), len1 * sizeof(char), cudaMemcpyHostToDevice);
   cudaMemcpy(d_seq2, seq2.c_str(), len2 * sizeof(char), cudaMemcpyHostToDevice);
   cudaMemcpy(d_H, H, (len1+1) * (len2+1) * sizeof(int), cudaMemcpyHostToDevice
         );

   dim3 block(16, 16);
```

```
    dim3 grid((len1+block.x-1)/block.x, (len2+block.y-1)/block.y);

    smithWatermanKernel<<<grid, block>>>(d_seq1, d_seq2, d_H, len1, len2);

    cudaMemcpy(H, d_H, (len1+1) * (len2+1) * sizeof(int), cudaMemcpyDeviceToHost
        );

    int max_score = 0;
    for (int i = 0; i <= len1; ++i) {
        for (int j = 0; j <= len2; ++j) {
            if (H[i*(len2+1) + j] > max_score) {
                max_score = H[i*(len2+1) + j];
            }
        }
    }

    std::cout << "Maximum alignment score: " << max_score << std::endl;

    delete[] H;
    cudaFree(d_seq1);
    cudaFree(d_seq2);
    cudaFree(d_H);
}

int main() {
    std::string seq1 = "AGCTG";
    std::string seq2 = "AGCTG";
    smithWatermanCUDA(seq1, seq2);
    return 0;
}
```

The kernel function smithWatermanKernel calculates scores for the dynamic programming matrix in parallel. Each thread computes a cell score by considering the match or mismatch and possible gaps, then updates the matrix.

Genome assembly tasks involve reconstructing a genome from short DNA sequences. One of the critical steps in genome assembly is finding overlaps between sequences, which can be sped up significantly using CUDA. Consider a simplified scenario where we need to compute overlaps between a large set of sequences. The following CUDA snippet illustrates an overlap detection kernel.

```
__global__ void overlapKernel(const char *sequences, int *overlaps, int
    num_sequences, int seq_len) {
    int index = blockIdx.x * blockDim.x + threadIdx.x;
    if (index < num_sequences * num_sequences) {
        int i = index / num_sequences;
        int j = index % num_sequences;

        if (i != j) {
            int overlap_length = 0;
            for (int k = 1; k < seq_len; ++k) {
                bool match = true;
                for (int l = 0; l < k; ++l) {
                    if (sequences[i * seq_len + seq_len - k + l] != sequences[j * seq_len
                        + l]) {
```

```
                    match = false;
                    break;
                }
            }
            if (match) {
                overlap_length = k;
            }
        }
        overlaps[i * num_sequences + j] = overlap_length;
    }
  }
}

void findOverlapsCUDA(const std::vector<std::string>& sequences) {
    int num_sequences = sequences.size();
    int seq_len = sequences[0].length();

    std::vector<char> flat_sequences(num_sequences * seq_len);
    for (int i = 0; i < num_sequences; ++i) {
        std::copy(sequences[i].begin(), sequences[i].end(), flat_sequences.begin() + i *
             seq_len);
    }

    char *d_sequences;
    int *d_overlaps;
    int *overlaps = new int[num_sequences * num_sequences]();

    cudaMalloc((void**)&d_sequences, flat_sequences.size() * sizeof(char));
    cudaMalloc((void**)&d_overlaps, num_sequences * num_sequences * sizeof(int));
    cudaMemcpy(d_sequences, flat_sequences.data(), flat_sequences.size() * sizeof(char
         ), cudaMemcpyHostToDevice);

    dim3 block(256);
    dim3 grid((num_sequences * num_sequences + block.x - 1) / block.x);

    overlapKernel<<<grid, block>>>(d_sequences, d_overlaps, num_sequences,
         seq_len);

    cudaMemcpy(overlaps, d_overlaps, num_sequences * num_sequences * sizeof(int),
         cudaMemcpyDeviceToHost);

    for (int i = 0; i < num_sequences; ++i) {
        for (int j = 0; j < num_sequences; ++j) {
            std::cout << overlaps[i * num_sequences + j] << " ";
        }
        std::cout << std::endl;
    }

    delete[] overlaps;
    cudaFree(d_sequences);
    cudaFree(d_overlaps);
}

int main() {
    std::vector<std::string> sequences = {"AGCT", "GCTA", "CTAG", "TAGC"};
    findOverlapsCUDA(sequences);
    return 0;
}
```

Here, the overlapKernel computes the overlap length between each pair of sequences. The kernel iterates through possible overlaps, checking for matches between suffixes and prefixes of the sequences.

Variant discovery involves identifying genetic variations from sequence data. CUDA can expedite this process through parallelization. Consider a simplified scenario where we examine single nucleotide polymorphisms (SNPs) by comparing sequences to a reference genome. Parallelizing the comparison enables rapid variant detection.

```
__global__ void snpKernel(const char *sequences, const char *reference, int *
    snp_positions, int seq_count, int seq_len) {
    int index = blockIdx.x * blockDim.x + threadIdx.x;

    if (index < seq_count * seq_len) {
        int seq_idx = index / seq_len;
        int pos = index % seq_len;

        if (sequences[seq_idx * seq_len + pos] != reference[pos]) {
            snp_positions[seq_idx * seq_len + pos] = 1;
        }
    }
}

void detectSNPsCUDA(const std::vector<std::string>& sequences, const std::string&
    reference) {
    int seq_count = sequences.size();
    int seq_len = reference.length();

    std::vector<char> flat_sequences(seq_count * seq_len);
    for (int i = 0; i < seq_count; ++i) {
        std::copy(sequences[i].begin(), sequences[i].end(), flat_sequences.begin() + i *
            seq_len);
    }

    char *d_sequences, *d_reference;
    int *d_snp_positions;
    int *snp_positions = new int[seq_count * seq_len]();

    cudaMalloc((void**)&d_sequences, flat_sequences.size() * sizeof(char));
    cudaMalloc((void**)&d_reference, seq_len * sizeof(char));
    cudaMalloc((void**)&d_snp_positions, seq_count * seq_len * sizeof(int));
    cudaMemcpy(d_sequences, flat_sequences.data(), flat_sequences.size() * sizeof(char
        ), cudaMemcpyHostToDevice);
    cudaMemcpy(d_reference, reference.c_str(), seq_len * sizeof(char),
        cudaMemcpyHostToDevice);

    dim3 block(256);
    dim3 grid((seq_count * seq_len + block.x - 1) / block.x);

    snpKernel<<<grid, block>>>(d_sequences, d_reference, d_snp_positions,
        seq_count, seq_len);

    cudaMemcpy(snp_positions, d_snp_positions, seq_count * seq_len * sizeof(int),
        cudaMemcpyDeviceToHost);

    for (int i = 0; i < seq_count; ++i) {
        std::cout << "Sequence " << i + 1 << ": SNP positions - ";
        for (int j = 0; j < seq_len; ++j) {
            if (snp_positions[i * seq_len + j] == 1) {
                std::cout << j << " ";
            }
```

```
        }
        std::cout << std::endl;
    }

    delete[] snp_positions;
    cudaFree(d_sequences);
    cudaFree(d_reference);
    cudaFree(d_snp_positions);
}

int main() {
    std::vector<std::string> sequences = {"AGCT", "AGTT", "ACTT", "AGCC"};
    std::string reference = "AGCT";
    detectSNPsCUDA(sequences, reference);
    return 0;
}
```

In this example, the snpKernel identifies positions where the sequences differ from the reference genome, indicating potential SNPs. The detectSNPsCUDA function initializes the data, launches the kernel, and retrieves the results.

CUDA provides substantial speedups in bioinformatics by leveraging GPU parallelism for computationally expensive tasks. Efficiently parallelizing algorithms for sequence alignment, genome assembly, and variant discovery enables researchers to analyze data at unprecedented scales and speeds. By integrating CUDA in bioinformatics applications, we can address the ever-increasing demand for computational power in genomic research, facilitating advancements in personalized medicine, evolutionary biology, and beyond.

10.8 Case Study: Autonomous Vehicles and Robotics

Autonomous vehicles and robotics are rapidly transforming various sectors, including transportation, manufacturing, and service industries. The deployment of CUDA programming in these domains significantly enhances the computational efficiency required for real-time processing and decision-making. This section delves into the technical aspects and applications of CUDA in autonomous vehicles and robotics.

Perception and Sensor Data Processing

Autonomous systems rely on a multitude of sensors such as LiDAR, radar, cameras, and ultrasonic sensors to perceive their environment. Processing the massive amount of data generated by these sensors in real time requires high computational power. CUDA-enabled GPUs excel at parallel processing, making them ideal for handling sensor data.

Consider the task of processing LiDAR data to create a point cloud representation of the vehicle's surroundings. The following CUDA kernel demonstrates a simple implementation of point cloud generation:

```
__global__ void generatePointCloud(const float* lidarData, float* pointCloud, int
    numPoints) {
    int idx = blockIdx.x * blockDim.x + threadIdx.x;
    if (idx < numPoints) {
        float angle = lidarData[idx * 2];
        float distance = lidarData[idx * 2 + 1];
        pointCloud[idx * 3] = distance * cosf(angle);
        pointCloud[idx * 3 + 1] = distance * sinf(angle);
        pointCloud[idx * 3 + 2] = 0.0f; // Assuming a 2D plane for simplicity
    }
}

int main() {
    const int numPoints = 1000;
    float *d_lidarData, *d_pointCloud;

    cudaMalloc(&d_lidarData, numPoints * 2 * sizeof(float));
    cudaMalloc(&d_pointCloud, numPoints * 3 * sizeof(float));

    // Assume lidarData is already populated
    generatePointCloud<<<(numPoints + 255) / 256, 256>>>(d_lidarData,
        d_pointCloud, numPoints);

    // Additional processing and cleanup
}
```

This kernel maps each point in the LiDAR data to a three-dimensional space on a 2D plane assuming $d_z = 0$. The generatePointCloud function's parallel nature allows for efficient processing of every point concurrently.

Path Planning Algorithms

Path planning is crucial for autonomous navigation. Algorithms such as A* and Rapidly-exploring Random Tree (RRT) are often employed. These algorithms benefit from CUDA's parallelization capabilities, enabling them to explore multiple paths simultaneously.

A simplified CUDA-based implementation of the RRT algorithm might look like this:

```
__global__ void extendRRT(float* nodes, int* edges, int numNodes, float* newNode)
    {
    int idx = blockIdx.x * blockDim.x + threadIdx.x;
    if (idx < numNodes) {
        float dist = hypotf(nodes[idx * 2] - newNode[0], nodes[idx * 2 + 1] - newNode
            [1]);
        // Assume a threshold distance for connection
        if (dist < 5.0f) {
            edges[idx] = numNodes;
        }
```

```
    }
}
```

This kernel evaluates distances between a new node and existing nodes to determine potential connections within a specified threshold. Nodes and edges are used to construct a tree representing the potential paths.

Control Systems

Control systems ensure that autonomous vehicles follow planned paths accurately. Model Predictive Control (MPC) is commonly used in autonomous control systems due to its real-time optimization and predictive capabilities.

```
__global__ void computeMPC(float* state, float* control, float* reference, int N) {
    int idx = blockIdx.x * blockDim.x + threadIdx.x;
    // Placeholder for optimized control computation
    if (idx < N) {
        // Objective function: minimize (state[idx] - reference[idx])^2
        control[idx] = -0.1 * (state[idx] - reference[idx]);
    }
}
```

In this kernel, each thread computes a control input aiming to minimize the difference between the current state and the reference trajectory over a prediction horizon N.

Machine Learning in Autonomous Systems

Machine learning models, particularly deep learning networks for perception tasks (e.g., object detection and semantic segmentation), are highly parallelizable and benefit from CUDA acceleration.

Suppose we have a Convolutional Neural Network (CNN) for detecting objects from camera images. A critical part of the CNN's operation is convolution, which can be implemented efficiently using CUDA:

```
__global__ void convolution2D(float* input, float* output, float* kernel, int width,
      int height, int kernelSize) {
    int x = blockIdx.x * blockDim.x + threadIdx.x;
    int y = blockIdx.y * blockDim.y + threadIdx.y;
    float sum = 0.0f;
    for (int i = 0; i < kernelSize; i++) {
        for (int j = 0; j < kernelSize; j++) {
            int xIndex = x - kernelSize / 2 + i;
            int yIndex = y - kernelSize / 2 + j;
            if (xIndex >= 0 && xIndex < width && yIndex >= 0 && yIndex < height)
                  {
                sum += input[yIndex * width + xIndex] * kernel[i * kernelSize + j];
            }
        }
    }
    output[y * width + x] = sum;
```

```
}
```

Deploying such kernels efficiently allows for real-time object detection, essential in dynamic environments.

Simulation and Testing

Prior to real-world deployment, autonomous systems undergo rigorous simulation to validate their performance in various scenarios. CUDA-accelerated simulations ensure rapid iteration over a large number of test cases.

The following example simulates multiple vehicle trajectories in parallel:

```
__global__ void simulateTrajectories(float* states, float* controls, float* newStates,
    int numVehicles, float dt) {
    int idx = blockIdx.x * blockDim.x + threadIdx.x;
    if (idx < numVehicles) {
        // Simple kinematic model
        float x = states[idx * 3];
        float y = states[idx * 3 + 1];
        float theta = states[idx * 3 + 2];
        float v = controls[idx * 2];
        float omega = controls[idx * 2 + 1];

        newStates[idx * 3] = x + v * cosf(theta) * dt;
        newStates[idx * 3 + 1] = y + v * sinf(theta) * dt;
        newStates[idx * 3 + 2] = theta + omega * dt;
    }
}
```

This kernel updates the state of each vehicle based on simple kinematic equations, demonstrating how CUDA can handle multiple simulations concurrently.

Concluding Remarks

Autonomous vehicles and robotics present a rich field for CUDA applications. The computational power of GPUs, harnessed through CUDA programming, enables real-time processing, efficient path planning, sophisticated control systems, fast machine learning computations, and extensive simulation capabilities. As the technology evolves, the role of CUDA in advancing autonomous systems will continue to grow, unlocking new possibilities in both research and industry.

10.9 Case Study: Big Data Analytics

Big data analytics entails the process of examining large and varied data sets to uncover hidden patterns, unknown correlations, market trends, customer preferences, and other useful business information. With the exponential growth of data in terms of volume, velocity, and variety, traditional data processing and analytic techniques have become inadequate. CUDA (Compute Unified Device Architecture) programming, leveraging the power of GPU (Graphics Processing Unit) computation, provides a significant performance boost in handling and analyzing massive data sets due to its parallel processing capabilities.

Consider a practical example where an organization seeks to analyze a dataset consisting of billions of records to derive meaningful insights. The dataset could be structured or unstructured and might encompass various types of data, such as transactional records, social media interactions, sensor data, or server logs.

The following example demonstrates how CUDA can be effectively used in big data analytics by parallelizing a common operation such as calculating the frequency distribution of data values.

Imagine an organization wants to perform frequency analysis on a large dataset stored in a CSV file. Each record in the file has an associated value, and the goal is to count the frequency of each unique value.

```
#include <cuda_runtime.h>
#include <stdio.h>
#include <stdlib.h>

__global__ void countFrequency(int *d_data, int *d_frequency, int numRecords, int
    numBins) {
    int tid = blockIdx.x * blockDim.x + threadIdx.x;
    if (tid < numRecords) {
        int dataValue = d_data[tid];
        atomicAdd(&(d_frequency[dataValue]), 1);
    }
}

int main() {
    // Number of records and bins
    int numRecords = 1000000; // Example size
    int numBins = 100; // Example number of unique values

    // Allocate host memory
    int *h_data = (int*)malloc(numRecords * sizeof(int));
    int *h_frequency = (int*)malloc(numBins * sizeof(int));

    // Initialize host data
    for (int i = 0; i < numRecords; i++) {
        h_data[i] = rand() % numBins; // Random data for demonstration
    }
    memset(h_frequency, 0, numBins * sizeof(int));

    // Allocate device memory
    int *d_data, *d_frequency;
    cudaMalloc((void**)&d_data, numRecords * sizeof(int));
    cudaMalloc((void**)&d_frequency, numBins * sizeof(int));
```

```
    // Copy data from host to device
    cudaMemcpy(d_data, h_data, numRecords * sizeof(int), cudaMemcpyHostToDevice
        );
    cudaMemcpy(d_frequency, h_frequency, numBins * sizeof(int),
        cudaMemcpyHostToDevice);

    // Kernel configuration
    int blockSize = 256;
    int gridSize = (numRecords + blockSize - 1) / blockSize;

    // Launch the kernel to count frequency
    countFrequency<<<gridSize, blockSize>>>(d_data, d_frequency, numRecords,
        numBins);
    cudaDeviceSynchronize();

    // Copy results from device to host
    cudaMemcpy(h_frequency, d_frequency, numBins * sizeof(int),
        cudaMemcpyDeviceToHost);

    // Print frequency results
    for (int i = 0; i < numBins; i++) {
        printf("Value %d: %d occurrences\n", i, h_frequency[i]);
    }

    // Free memory
    cudaFree(d_data);
    cudaFree(d_frequency);
    free(h_data);
    free(h_frequency);

    return 0;
}
```

This code illustrates how CUDA can be used to parallelize the counting of data frequencies. The key elements include:

- Memory allocation on both the host and the device.
- Data initialization and transfer from host to device.
- Execution of a CUDA kernel to perform the counting operation in parallel.
- Transfer of results back to host memory and output of results.

The kernel function countFrequency is executed by multiple threads in parallel, each handling a portion of the data. An atomicAdd operation is used to ensure that the frequency count is updated correctly without race conditions.

The example above highlights the fundamental concepts of big data analytics using CUDA. By harnessing the power of GPU parallelism, analytics tasks that would otherwise be computationally expensive on a CPU can be greatly accelerated.

Beyond this basic example, CUDA applications in big data analytics extend to a variety of tasks, such as:

- **Sorting and Searching:** Efficient parallel algorithms for sorting and searching large datasets.
- **Machine Learning and AI:** Accelerated training of large-scale machine learning models.
- **Graph Analytics:** Fast processing of graph-based data structures for social network analysis, recommendation systems, and more.
- **Stream Processing:** Real-time analytics on streaming data from IoT devices, financial transactions, and log files.

The CUDA framework provides intricate routines and libraries such as cuBLAS, cuSPARSE, and cuDNN, each catering to specific computational needs in big data analytics. By incorporating these advanced tools, data scientists and engineers can build comprehensive, performant, and scalable analytics solutions.

CUDA's capability to handle intensive data processing tasks effectively transforms how organizations manage and derive insights from their data, reinforcing the indispensable role of GPU programming in the realm of big data analytics.

10.10 Future Trends and Developments in CUDA

The landscape of CUDA programming is continuously evolving as advancements in both hardware and software drive new possibilities for high-performance computing. This section delves into the anticipated trends and developments that are likely to shape the future of CUDA and its applications across diverse industries.

A significant trend in the future of CUDA is the increasing emphasis on heterogeneous computing. Modern systems are becoming more reliant on a mix of CPUs, GPUs, and specialized accelerators such as Tensor Processing Units (TPUs) and Field-Programmable Gate Arrays (FPGAs). CUDA developers are therefore expected to adeptly manage workloads across these diverse computing units to optimize performance and efficiency.

The integration of artificial intelligence (AI) and machine learning (ML) capabilities into the CUDA ecosystem is another prominent direction. Libraries such as cuDNN and TensorRT are continually being enhanced to provide better support for deep learning frameworks. These improvements will facilitate more efficient training and inference processes in neural networks, particularly as model sizes and complexities grow. Future native support for sparse matrices and tensors in CUDA will further accelerate AI and ML applications by reducing memory and computational overhead.

Quantum computing is also on the horizon as a complementary technology to classical computing systems. CUDA will likely play a pivotal role in hybrid computing platforms where quantum processors perform specific tasks and GPUs handle the classical computation. This synergy aims to solve problems that are currently intractable with traditional computing resources alone. As quantum algorithms and hardware mature, CUDA's development environment may incorporate toolchains and libraries to manage quantum-classical workflows.

Parallel to these technological advancements, software development paradigms are shifting towards greater abstraction and ease of use. High-level APIs and domain-specific languages (DSLs) are being developed to enable developers to write efficient CUDA code without deep expertise in parallel computing or GPU architectures. Libraries such as Thrust, which provides a high-level interface for parallel algorithms, exemplify this trend. Similarly, the emergence of programming models like Kokkos and Raja indicate a move towards writing performance-portable code that can run efficiently across different hardware backends.

The advancement in multi-GPU systems is another key area of interest. Technologies such as NVIDIA's NVLink and upcoming interconnects are making it feasible to scale applications more effectively by leveraging multiple GPUs concurrently. Enhanced support in CUDA for multi-GPU programming, including easier data sharing and synchronization mechanisms, will enable developers to build more scalable and higher-performance applications.

Energy-efficient computing is gaining traction, driven by the need to reduce the environmental impact of data centers and high-performance computing facilities. CUDA's future iterations are likely to incorporate features for optimizing power consumption, such as dynamic voltage and frequency scaling (DVFS) and improved profiling tools to analyze and minimize the energy footprint of applications.

Real-time processing requirements in areas like autonomous systems, streaming analytics, and interactive simulations are pushing the boundaries of CUDA's capabilities. The development of low-latency communication protocols and real-time scheduling strategies within the CUDA framework can significantly enhance its application in time-sensitive domains.

Security is another critical aspect to consider. As GPUs are increasingly used for general-purpose computing, vulnerabilities at the hardware and software levels need to be comprehensively addressed. Future development in CUDA will likely include enhanced security mechanisms to protect sensitive data and ensure the integrity of computations on GPUs.

The rapid evolution of CUDA programming will also be influenced by the growing ecosystem of software tools for development, debugging, and optimization. Tools such as Nsight Systems, Nsight Compute, and CUDA-GDB are continually being updated to provide better insights into application performance and behavior. Enhanced integration with integrated development environments (IDEs) and continuous integration/continuous deployment (CI/CD) pipelines is anticipated, making CUDA development more seamless and productive.

The confluence of these trends signifies a dynamic future for CUDA programming, characterized by increased interdisciplinarity and innovation. As developers continue to harness the power of parallel computing through CUDA, the focus will remain on improving performance, usability, and efficiency to meet the demands of next-generation applications.

Made in United States
North Haven, CT
26 January 2026

87278184R10163